Chasing Music

My crazy campervan adventures in America

Jan Dale

First published by Busybird Publishing 2021

Copyright © 2021 Jan Dale

ISBN
978-1-922465-55-9 (paperback)
978-1-922465-56-6 (ebook)

This work is copyright. Apart from any use permitted under the *Copyright Act 1968*, no part of this publication may be reproduced, stored in a retrieval system or transmitted in any form or by any means, electronic, mechanical, photocopying, recording or otherwise, without the prior written permission of Jan Dale.

Cover Image: Jan Dale
Cover Design: Busybird Publishing
Layout and typesetting: Busybird Publishing
Images: Jan Dale
Author photo: Susan Gordon-Brown

Busybird Publishing
2/118 Para Road
Montmorency, Victoria
Australia 3094
www.busybird.com.au

In memory of
my much loved brother,
John.

Contents

About the Author	1
Foreword	3
Introduction	5
Planning	9
Taking the Plunge	11
The 'Right' Vehicle	13
Open Road at Last	17
National Parks and Bears	26
Heading South	33
Back to California	45
Into the Desert	52
Roswell and Bud's Bar!	63
Dancing & Romancing across Texas	69
Fort Worth	80
Oklahoma	97
Memphis: Elvis and The Blues	106
Blues in the Mississippi Delta	113
Deeper South	124
New Orleans and All That Jazz	133
Rural Louisiana and More Cajun Music	148
Alabama to Nashville	152
Falling in love with Bluegrass Music	161
Back to Texas	175
On The Way North	178
Buffalo Bill	180
Trading Post in the Pioneer Country	182
Repairs in Rapid City	186
Off Again Through South Dakota	189

Wisconsin and The House on the Rock	194
Upper Mississippi River	196
The Tennessee Fall Homecoming Festival	201
Back to Nashville	207
Detroit and a Visit Back Home	213
On the Road with Sand Mountain	217
Travelling in the North-east	225
Loons and Lobsters	232
South Through Virginia	241
Western Music in Western Setting	247
The Final Dash	253
Acknowledgements	259
MAP - Outline of My Journey	260

About the Author

Jan Dale is an internationally recognised Australian radio producer/presenter and guest speaker. Her show, Southern Style, can be heard on Melbourne's PBS FM.

Jan Dale - Southern Style
Tuesdays 1-3 pm
PBS FM 106.7
https://www.pbsfm.org.au/program/southern-style

She was nominated in 2019 for the International Bluegrass Music Association's Broadcaster of the Year award, becoming the first ever non-US based nominee. This followed her selection for the 2018 Mick Geyer Award, recognising her outstanding contribution to community radio and the general music community in Australia.

She has been MC at various Bluegrass events in the United States and Australia and has interviewed hundreds of musicians, both in the studio and in the field.

Jan has written many articles for the American magazine Bluegrass Unlimited, and has also been published in a variety of other magazines.

She is an adventurous traveller and has been to over 70 countries, often backpacking alone.

Foreword

This adventure traces my extended solo travels in the USA during the 1990s in a small campervan – from making the decision to get on the road and rent out my house in Australia, to buying the van in California and driving 160,000 miles over a period of nearly six years.

It's a tale of the many exciting adventures I had on the road – living on a shoestring budget, often 'camping' in supermarket carparks to save money.

You'll get a glimpse up close of American culture and the people I met, with all their eccentricities, against the sights of America and the many strange and funny things that happened to me. I also share the story of my background which has made me the person I am and sheds some light on why I chose to do this trip.

By 1996 I was helping to put together radio programmes with music I picked up in the U.S. and co-presenting them on radio when I happened to be in Australia. I was also working on consultancy projects in the film industry whenever I was home.

I flew home again in January 1997 and was offered a six month job as Acting Marketing Manager of Open Channel, which conducted film courses. This is when I did my certificated radio course and started my own show *Southern Style* at Melton FM as a volunteer.

I took time off to return to the U.S. in September for several months, collecting the van from Nashville and heading out to see more festivals, where I was then interviewing some very important Bluegrass musicians.

Then the final trip in 1998 – heading out on the road with Sand Mountain band, collecting the van from Detroit, then to Niagara, Cape Cod and right down to Tucson in Arizona. Along the way I returned to Poppy Mountain Festival, Kentucky, in my role as radio presenter. Finally, a last dash from Tucson to Denver and the flight home again.

This is my story …

Introduction

Being struck by lightning at the Grand Canyon was bad enough, but having my van break down yet again was downright depressing. I didn't know it at the time, but I was still only part way through my road trip. I had hoped to get off the beaten track, immerse myself in American roots music and see some spectacular scenery – but couldn't have imagined that I'd end up driving over 160,000 miles in 48 states; happily sleeping alone in my van in rather strange places, attending exotic events like The Southern New Mexico Roadeo and The National Conference of Bankruptcy Judges, discovering Bluegrass and Cajun music, and having a romance or two.

My sense of adventure was fuelled by my visits to the library as a young child. They were always the highlight of my week. One day I found a book about the explorer Lieutenant Colonel Percy Fawcett, who disappeared in 1925 with his eldest son when searching for the 'lost city of Z' in the Amazonian rainforests of Brazil. I was particularly excited by the description of him battling a 160 foot anaconda! Although his story might have been a bit exaggerated, my plan to drive myself around the United States seemed incredibly insignificant in comparison, but still a big adventure for me.

I fell in love with American music when I first heard Elvis Presley's 'Heartbreak Hotel'. I'd never heard anything like it before. It was so full of emotion, so exciting. I also loved it because my parents *hated* it! Until then the only music in our strict Methodist home was a hymn or two on Sunday, or classical, which my mother played on the piano. I didn't do well at school and started work as a shorthand typist for a shipping company when I was 15, spending most of my first pay on records to play (quietly) on my secondhand Chrysler bakelite roll top radiogram. I still have many of those 45s – Elvis, Fats Domino, Jerry Lee Lewis – but sadly not that wonderful radiogram.

Elvis was heavily influenced by the African American blues musicians of the Mississippi Delta not far from where he was born, so in my teens I started to explore their music, too. I especially loved the country blues musicians like Big Bill Broonzy and the blues-folk music of Huddie Leadbetter (Leadbelly). Dancing wasn't allowed in my family but sometimes I snuck out at night to go to a rock 'n roll or jazz dance. I climbed out of my bedroom window then onto the roof of our garage, dropped down over the fence and through the grounds of the unoccupied Baby Health Centre next-door so I couldn't be seen from my parents' bedroom. My dream even then was to be able to visit the places which inspired so much wonderful music. Although I travelled a great deal – to the U.S. and even to places like Yemen and the Amazon – this particular dream didn't happen until 1992.

In the meantime, I took a job as a personal assistant to the owner of a small film production and distribution company. In 1973 I opened an office for them in London. I jumped at the chance as I had lived there before with my British ex-husband and I'd loved it. This job involved driving myself all over the U.K. in a red VW Beetle to visit prospective purchasers. I enjoyed the challenge and freedom. I bought a flat for the company in Ealing, and would show films to clients on an old 16mm projector in the living room.

After six years I returned to the Australian office as the company's National Marketing Manager. We represented many overseas filmmakers and I travelled extensively to the U.S., Europe and even Japan. One of the larger distributors was in Chicago. I visited them regularly and went to see some legendary Chicago blues musicians – Son Seals, BB King, Buddy Guy, Zora Young and others. Once I was surprised to come across Ray Charles playing in my hotel bar. I had only been to the large cities but now I wanted to see more of the small towns and countryside.

1992 was a time to seriously consider my future. Both my parents were now gone, I had recently separated from my partner and had

Introduction

no dependants. I loved my job as General Manager of the Australian Film Institute's Distribution Company, but it felt time to move on and I handed in my resignation. I had just turned fifty, so thought I'd better start fulfilling some more of my dreams.

Planning

While saving up enough money for this trip, I spent a lot of time thinking about the best way to get around America. I wanted to go for a whole year and considered flying or taking buses, but that would mean I wouldn't be able to get off the beaten track. I also hated the idea of carting luggage around. Buying my own vehicle seemed the best option. I could be independent and flexible and, if it was big enough for me to sleep in, I would save heaps of money on accommodation and be able to camp out in wilderness areas. So that's what I decided.

Camping and driving a van wasn't new to me. I'd spent a lot of time exploring Europe in one with my ex-husband, and in Australia with a partner. Camping alone was also something I felt comfortable with, and had many holidays roughing it in the Australian bush – no toilets (just a spade), and cooking on an open fire. My upbringing helped. Camping was an affordable way for our family to have summer holidays. My three older siblings and I always loved these trips.

In the end, that first year of travelling in America in 1992 extended until 1998 with a number of visits home. The U.S. government at that time issued tourist visas for a maximum of six months so I had to leave the country every time mine was due to expire. After the first six months I went to England to visit my brother John and his family and got another six months when I returned. At the end of the year I went back home to Australia to earn a bit of money as a consultant and spend time with family there before starting out again. When I was away from America I stored my van in a number of different places – once at a commercial storage facility, and several times on friends' properties. This usually meant it wasn't driven for months at a time and a new battery had to be installed whenever I returned. It was a small price to pay for the convenience of a suitable vehicle waiting for me, which also served as a storage 'shed' for my belongings.

My travels became a real journey of discovery, not only about America, its music, its geography and its people, but also about *me*. I was surprised at how self-reliant I could be and how quickly I bounced back when things went wrong. This book is a kind of compilation of those multiple trips I made to America.

Taking the Plunge

After resigning from my job in 1992, I put all my belongings into storage, rented out my little cottage and arranged to have my mail redirected to my sister. By mid-July I was on a plane to San Francisco with what I hoped would be enough money to buy a small camper van and travel for a year, provided I stuck to a really stringent budget. I had my savings and weekly rent from my tenant.

Packing for all possible weather conditions and occasions was challenging. I tried hard to keep it to a minimum. I could always buy things along the way. I was a bit worried about feeling the cold so my prized possession was a quality lightweight sleeping bag my friends had given me for my birthday just before I left. My sister, a great packer, managed to stuff mum's old mohair rug into my already overflowing rucksack. I have photos of myself at the airport waving goodbye and looking rather odd. I wore my best black trousers but, to save weight in my suitcase, on my feet were my heavy hiking boots. As I couldn't risk my elegant black Italian hat getting squashed, I wore that, too. On my back was my bulging old rucksack.

I wondered whether I'd done the right thing. It was a bit scary. I'd left behind all my security – a wonderful job (*would I ever find another?*), my family, my friends and my home. I'd travelled independently and alone in India, the Philippines and other countries, but I wondered if I would be happy alone for such a long time. Would being a woman make it more difficult? How easily would I adapt to driving on the other side of the road, coping with those huge freeways? And what about the drive-by shootings and car jackings we always seemed to be hearing of? I remembered that on an earlier visit, when I was alone on a walking trail in Muir Forest just outside San Francisco, I'd came across a sign: *'Beware! A number of hikers have been murdered on these trails!'*

But it was so exciting to have at least a whole year's travelling ahead of me, with all the freedom and adventure that meant, and the challenge of doing it alone. Maybe this was because I wanted to test myself, or perhaps because having nobody else to consider meant I could do exactly as I wished. Probably the latter.

That United Airlines flight was a good introduction to American culture. The language was certainly different. The flight attendant, collecting dinner trays – *'Are you all done, kid?'*

For the first time I saw credit card phones behind each seat. Imagine being able to phone from a plane mid-flight! I could even listen to flight control operators and pilots communicating – unthinkable, these days. The in-flight magazine duty-free section advertised odd things such as electric nose hair trimmers. There was a full page ad: '8 Ways to Protect your Security.' It included a bomb sniffer *'developed for use by non-professionals'*, as well as a portable protection device which looked like a flashlight but could immobilise an attacker with a burst of bright light, and a lightweight vest which could *'stop up to a .357 magnum!'*

Golly, I thought – if people feel they need these things to keep safe in America, how was *I* going to manage?

The 'Right' Vehicle

Over the 20 years I worked in the film industry, I made many friends amongst the overseas distributors and filmmakers. One of these was Paul, who lived in San Francisco. He'd offered a place to stay and help to look for the right vehicle. It was exciting to be back in this wonderful city with its steep hills and little cable cars. Paul lived in an especially beautiful area not far from the Golden Gate Bridge, which was partly shrouded by mist when we arrived back from the airport. I was so exhausted that I went straight to bed and slept for 16 hours, causing his young daughter Julia some concern. I think she may have thought I'd expired!

When we visited used car yards, Paul often brought a friend along. This was great for me because the pushy salesmen assumed the men were the buyers and I was left to wander around in peace. The 'right' van turned out to be an eleven year old Volkswagen 'Vanagan' with a pop-top roof. This was the fifth Volkswagen van I'd owned so I was quite used to them and liked the fact that they were not a large vehicle and easy to drive. The interior was a German Westfalia conversion, extremely well designed to make maximum use of the space. I loved it and thought it was just like a kid's cubby house. There was a small fridge, two-burner stove, fresh water tank, sink, wardrobe, lots of cupboards and little storage niches, a fold out table and a bed in the roof as well as one 'downstairs'. This would be where any visiting friends could sleep. The front passenger and driver's seats swiveled around so that the comfortable seating could face the interior. It even came with a portable toilet, but I decided I didn't want to sleep and eat with this right next to me, so I got rid of it. There were times when I regretted that, but I always managed somehow. One important feature was that it was possible to walk from the rear living section into the driving cabin without having to go outside. I needed this for security. If I was camped or parked somewhere and felt unsafe for any reason, I could quickly slip from the back to the front and drive away without showing myself or exposing myself to outside danger.

I bought the van privately after having it checked by a local garage and then had to make a number of lengthy visits to government departments – first to obtain a temporary permit so I could park in the street near Paul's house, then to pay the sales tax and have the registration transferred to my name. There was also the obligatory 'smog' test, plus insurance. Despite a letter of recommendation from my Australian insurance company, my biggest headache at this stage was finding a company who would insure a vehicle owned by an *alien*. (Americans use the term 'alien' a lot and it always made me feel as though they thought I was from outer space.) I was never certain why this was so, but assumed it was due to difficulties of checking up on driving records. Having an American driving licence would have made all the difference but this was impossible without a Green Card or some other permission to reside in the U.S., plus a Social Security number. Finally I located a company which specialised in insuring overseas visitors, but at $800 for twelve months it was much more expensive than I expected, especially as it did not even cover damage to my *own* vehicle.

Paul's daughter Julia and I spent lots of time mucking around in my van figuring out how everything worked, including how to extend the roof. It was by releasing a catch and pushing forward on an iron bar, which took a bit of brute force. I often didn't bother later in the trip. I just slept in the downstairs bed. When I did use that bed in the roof I had a little window to peep out of, which also opened on to the luggage rack so I could lean out to access my rooftop storage boxes. I had to climb on bits of the built-in furniture to get to the top. A handy discovery was an empty compartment under the passenger seat, which was meant to house a spare battery. It was difficult to access and most people would have no idea it was there, so I used it to hide valuables. It was a quirky vehicle with a great deal of character and apparently a strong mind of its own, which I would discover later was not necessarily to my advantage.

The 'Right' Vehicle

As music and radio are so important to me, one of the first things I did was have a decent sound system installed – a radio/cassette player at that time. I'd bought a few cassettes with me, including some of my old favourites – Elvis, Fats Domino, Delbert McClinton, bluesman Little Milton and country musicians Alan Jackson and George Strait. I also found plenty of country music radio stations to listen to.

Before I bought the van, Paul had insisted that I drive his car around to get used to driving on the right. He had to insist because I could hardly bear the thought of damaging someone else's vehicle. I'd rather mess up my own. It took a while before I stopped reaching for the gear lever on the left instead of the right. I also found it difficult to know exactly where the vehicle was on the road, and often narrowly missed swiping parked cars. Apparently this is a common problem for drivers used to sitting on the other side of the vehicle.

On my first evening out alone in my van, I went to hear some blues music at Eli's Mile High Bar in Oakland on the other side of the bay. It was in a fairly seedy part of town. Fortunately there was a parking area right next door, so I didn't have to walk down any of the dark streets by myself. It was my first time alone in a black blues bar. There was only one other white face. I felt a bit apprehensive but everyone was friendly and the music was wonderful. At the end of the evening their security man escorted me to my van. I later discovered that in 1979 the owner, Eli Thornton, had been gunned down behind the bar by an ex-girlfriend! However the only bad part of *my* night was getting back to San Francisco.

I had to cross back over the Bay Bridge – surprisingly busy for that time of night. Seventeen lanes condensed to about six – frightening for me because nobody seemed to slow down much. I managed to negotiate it without incident (American drivers are generally quite courteous), but then took a wrong turn and found myself driving up one of those almost vertical San Francisco hills with a stop sign on every crossroad. The van's gears were manual and I nearly burnt out the clutch doing some terrifying hand-brake starts. I was glad it was in the early morning hours so nobody could witness this appalling lack of driving skills. Strangely, the clutch was just about the only part of the vehicle that didn't have to be replaced during my travels! I arrived back at Paul's, shaking.

I ventured out to another blues club the next night – within walking distance, thank goodness. An attractive young Irish tourist invited me out on a date. I resisted because I could see he was much younger than me. I was convinced that when he saw me in the sobering light of day he'd be disappointed. He was very persuasive and in the end I agreed to meet him for lunch next day. It was my first date in years. I was excited, flattered and a bit nervous. Paul and Julia took great interest in helping me to select the right clothes and makeup for maximum effect, i.e. to knock off a few years! I arrived at the restaurant on time but he wasn't there, and after 45 minutes I left. I'd been stood up. How disappointing and humiliating to have to slink back home again.

I decided to concentrate on getting everything ready for my travels. It was fun shopping for kitchen utensils, crockery, cutlery, wine glasses, folding camping chairs and other bits and pieces.

Linen and saucepans were supplied by my very generous relatives Sally and her husband John. My sister was married to Sally's brother and I had met them a number of times before. I drove down to see them in Los Gatos, just south of San Francisco. Sally had described in great detail how to cope with driving on the American freeway systems: *'Broken lines on the left-hand side of your lane means something's going to happen soon! Exits often come up quickly and can be either on the right or left, so sitting in the middle lane is the safest bet. Roads marked with the letter 'I' before the number are the large interstate freeways. Odd numbers went roughly in a north-south direction; even numbers east-west.'* Interstate 80/ I-80 goes from Chicago all the way west to San Francisco; I-35 from Laredo on the Mexican border north to Duluth on Lake Superior not far from Canada. Other advice was to *'keep the doors locked at all times, and if the vehicle breaks down, stay in it with the hazard lights flashing until the highway police arrive.'* Mobile phones weren't in general use then.

My membership of the Australian Automobile Association gave me reciprocal rights to services offered by the American equivalent, so I visited them and loaded up with free maps and wonderfully detailed travel books covering every state. These membership rights were especially valuable on later occasions when the van had to be towed.

Open Road at Last

I left San Francisco in the very early morning to avoid the traffic. I'd lost my driving confidence on those steep hills and was anxious to get out of the city. As I was already on the west coast, my idea for the first few weeks was to visit a number of national parks right through northern California, Oregon, Washington, across Idaho to Montana and on to the Canadian border; then south following the Rocky Mountains through Wyoming, eventually to the Grand Canyon and Albuquerque in New Mexico. After that I wanted to hunt music in Texas, Louisiana and the Mississippi Delta, but I didn't want to make too many plans in advance. I'd just take things as they came.

I set off north driving along the Californian coast, slightly apprehensive but excited that the real adventure had finally begun. I kept reminding myself to stay on the right, and there were one or two scary lapses when I came face to face with an oncoming vehicle and had to scoot back. It wasn't that I just drifted over to the left but that I'd driven off on the wrong side after parking somewhere. This was easy to do if there was no traffic around for guidance. Disappointingly the fog rolled in from the sea, hiding most of the spectacular rugged coastline. The first night I slept in my van I stayed in a deserted private campground on the edge of a cliff. Occasionally the fog cleared offering glimpses of the sea, but it was too windy and damp to sit outside. By the time I left next morning nobody had appeared to collect fees. An excellent start economically!

Next day I was on the famous Redwood Highway. I just loved those majestic redwood trees, many well over 300 feet high and some more than 1,500 years old, with the oldest over 2,500 years! The scenic

Avenue of the Giants passes right through the middle of one. I camped amongst them at Albee Creek Campground in Humboldt Redwoods State Park. Of Humboldt's 53,000 acres, 17,000 are old growth coastal redwoods. There are lots of beautiful hiking trails and the remains of an interesting old fort, but best of all for me was the cool creek in which I lazily wallowed to escape the summer heat.

The next state was Oregon and I stayed at the spectacular Crater Lake, which at 1,932 feet is the deepest in the U.S. It's 6,000 feet above sea level, several miles across and with rims up to 1,000 feet high. No way of dipping into this to cool off. The sky was clear and the lake a beautiful dark blue.

Then I spent a couple of days visiting Steve, another business contact, who lived in a large house on a couple of acres just outside the small city of Eugene. The first thing he did was drive me to see the four and a half acres of old growth forest he'd recently bought. It was beautiful with a little cottage perched on the edge of a deep gully with a gurgling stream. Conservation was his main reason for buying it. He wanted to make sure it stayed in its pristine condition. Then we drove to a recreation area in the Cascade Mountains and Steve managed to lock his keys in the car! He had a spare set at home but we were miles from there. Eventually a young man in a VW Kombi came along and offered to give us a lift. He had driven all the way from North Carolina on the other side of the country to attend a Grateful Dead concert with his dog called Legbone. He was pleasant enough but his van was in such an incredible mess, we couldn't imagine how he could possibly live in it or even find space to lie down and sleep. I put my water bottle on the floor and was never able to find it again. It had simply disappeared into the rubble.

Next morning after driving Steve back to collect his car, I continued on north to the city of Portland, travelling most of the way on a large interstate highway which was busy with enormous, rowdy, polluting trucks. It was very hot and with no air conditioning I had to keep the windows open and suffer the noise or suffocate in the stifling August heat. It was horrible and I vowed to get off those busy highways whenever I could.

In San Francisco Paul had introduced me to a friend of his from Portland, Goody Cable. We found we had a lot in common – music, literature, travel etc. – and got on really well. She was fascinated with my plans to drive all over the country alone, thought I was gutsy, and invited me to visit her. In 1980 she had opened the Rimsky-Korsakoffee House in Portland and also had a partnership in the historic Sylvia Beach Hotel on the coast at the town of Newport. Named by the Oregonian newspaper as *'Portland's most interesting woman of the year'*, she was intelligent, fun and spontaneous, and had the habit of suddenly leaving for another state on a whim with barely half an hour's notice. We became friends and I visited her on a number of occasions. Her life was so frenetic that I never knew where I might be sleeping each night.

I was there on the fourth of July and Goody decided to rush downtown to see if we could book into the Marriott Hotel on the Willamette River to watch the Independence Day fireworks. We were lucky to find a room with a wonderful view and checked in with only a small battered cardboard box and a vase of flowers, which she didn't want to leave wilting at home! Nobody commented on our strange 'luggage'. I guess hotel staff are used to just about anything. Goody then invited lots of friends over. We squashed 30 into the tiny room, scouring all the hotel corridors for chairs.

While waiting for the fireworks I hung out of the window listening to the Waterfront Blues Festival, which was in full swing below. We were amused to see a group of teenagers pour cold water onto a couple smoking on a balcony below them, shouting out, *'cigarettes are bad for your health!'*

Outside the hotel I noticed a car with a sign: *'Grand Exalted Ruler Vincent Collura and Donna. Benevolent & Protective Order of Elks. Share Elkdom with America.'* A national Elks Convention was in progress. I'd never heard of this organisation, so I asked some of its members to explain what it was. They gave me a conference brochure with a program of the 'One Hundred and Twenty Ninth Session of the Grand Lodge of the Benevolent and Protective Order of Elks of the United States of America.'

Here are some extracts from their first business meeting agenda:

> 8.55 am Delegates Called by Grand Esquire
>
> 9.00 am Call to Order - Invocation - Opening Ceremony
>
> 9.15 am Presentation of Colors
>
> 9.25 am Introductions: Past Grand Exalted Rulers, Grand Lodge Officers, Board of Grand Trustees, Grand Forum, Committee on Judiciary and Agency Heads.

Other events included 'Ritualistic Finals at the Governor Hotel', 'District Deputy-Designate pictures taken with the Grand Exalted Ruler-Elect', and 'Exalted Rulers Ball.' A comment – *'ladies invited and admitted to Business Session'* – led me to realise this must be a Men's Only club. It all sounded so serious, but I noticed that evening entertainment included Las Vegas Show Girls, wine tastings and *'free roses for the first 500 ladies!'*

Apparently this organisation was founded in the 1860s as a private drinking club called Jolly Corks, and soon evolved into a fraternal and charitable society open only to white males with U.S. citizenship. There are now over a million members and in 1973 membership was extended to *all* U.S. males. Finally, as recently as 1995 (after my encounter with them) women were admitted. It's quite difficult to join. You must believe in God and although you don't have to be a Christian you *do* have to swear on the Bible. You have to be sponsored by a member, then co-sponsored by two other members. After that, the Investigating Committee interviews you and reports back to the Lodge where a vote is taken. Then you undergo secret initiation rites. (I'd love to know what these are!) The organisation does do many good things, such as giving donations to charities like the Salvation Army and the Red Cross, helping veterans and the handicapped and running a college scholarship program. But I couldn't help being intrigued by all the ritualistic procedures and grand names, not to mention the Las Vegas Show Girls.

But back to Goody and The Rismky-Korsakoffee House. Named after the 19th century composer Nikolai Rimsky-Korsakov, it sold only desserts and non-alcoholic drinks and was in a charming old two-storey house. Goody said, *'I opened it so I wouldn't have to clean my house for music parties.'* There was an old piano in the main dining room and people often dropped in to give impromptu performances – sometimes with other musicians. The place was quirky. In one room there was a large round coffee table with assorted armchairs. I sat here on my first evening and chatted to some interesting people – writers, artists, scientists and an 86 year old man, who had recently taken up cycling after a 70 year interval and felt he had found a new lease of life. I reached out for my cup only to discover that it had somehow made its way around to the other side. I hadn't noticed that the table was slowly revolving.

Equally disconcerting was another table, which imperceptibly rose until people leaning on it suddenly realised that they were sitting with their elbows almost up to their *ears*. When they reached underneath to check out the mechanism, they made contact with a revolting collection of grizzly rubber objects. Another table might suddenly disappear as it could be pulled through the wall from the kitchen. Points were awarded for the speed at which the occupants grabbed the sugar bowl. Yet another shook when a button was pressed in the kitchen. Occasionally staff played a loud recording of breaking crockery followed by some shouting. This usually resulted in an embarrassed silence in the restaurant, but when it happened a second time, in the space of a few minutes, everyone realised it must be a joke. All of this fun was designed to help break down barriers and create an atmosphere where people freely talked to each other, and it really worked. People are always more friendly when they are having fun!

For environmental reasons, only reusable serviettes were used. They were made by various friends and family out of fabric remnants, and I often undertook the job of putting them through the washing machine and folding them all up, sometimes hundreds at a time. I also occasionally served in the restaurant which was always busy, so it was really hard work. Their desserts were absolutely delicious and high on chocolate, which I happen to be allergic to. I had to employ some pretty heavy willpower not to sneak a slice from time to time.

Goody also whisked me off to Sylvia Beach hotel for a night. She and Sally Ford had opened this hotel in an historic wooden building overlooking a beautiful stretch of sandy beach at Newport. It has a literary theme and is named after Sylvia Beach who opened the famous bookshop, 'Shakespeare and Company', in Paris. Each of the rooms is decorated after a particular author. I had a bed in the dorm but snooped around a bit and found an Edgar Allan Poe room which included a wooden bed with a canopy, stuffed raven and a pile of his books on the bedside table. Among the many other authors represented are Agatha Christie, Mark Twain and Ernest Hemingway.

As at the Rimsky-Korsakoffee House, the atmosphere was designed to encourage guests to mingle. At the dinner table I shared we played "Two Truths and One Lie" in which each person has to tell two truths about themselves and one lie. The others have to guess which is the lie. This was enormous fun and we learnt a lot about each other. What a diverse group we were. There was a young man studying Suni Muslims, somebody else was writing a book about inter-racial marriage, another was studying the ethics of ecology, and Jon Newton was Music Director for Portland Civic Theater. He was a friend of Goody's and had brought with him Harry Crossfield, a singer and actor flown over from New York to star in the Frank Loesser musical play, 'The Most Happy Fella,' about to open in Portland. Around midnight Harry gave an impromptu performance and next morning invited Goody and me to the opening night.

I finally left Portland and began to settle into life on the road, gradually getting to learn about the 'American way'. Shopping in the huge supermarkets felt like an endurance exercise. I didn't know any of the brands of course, and the range of choices was almost overwhelming – long aisles of just bread, for example. I have some food allergies so the ingredients in everything had to be carefully checked, and my limited budget meant I had to watch the cost, too. Calculators attached to the handles of some of the trolleys helped, but doing the most basic shop seemed to take hours, and I sometimes hated it for taking me away from the scenery. But it was also an interesting cultural experience to see what was available and how different it was from Australia. Some items that were easily bought at home simply couldn't be found in the average supermarket in America. One of these was good quality loose tea, and on future trips I brought my own supply with me. It was also hard ensuring variety in my diet because I only had two gas burners – no grill or oven – and no desire to spend hours preparing anything. But I did try to eat healthily, and by the end of my travels I'd become quite lean. If I had been able to afford to eat out often, I'm sure this wouldn't have happened.

I had worked out a way of managing my finances and drew US $400 cash fortnightly from my account. This had to cover all living expenses including petrol, camping, food etc. If I had some left over I'd save it up for unexpected expenses or treats. My close friend Barb worked as manager of card services in an Australian bank and looked after my debit card balance. As a customer I could occasionally phone her reverse charge to check my financial state and have a lovely chat. She was always *very* encouraging.

One thing I often saw in supermarkets (usually near the check-outs) was a newspaper – *Weekly World News* – with the most incredible stories. I bought one which was liberally sprinkled with photos of partially clad women and articles such as: 'Wax Dummy Found in JFK's Coffin! Final proof he wasn't assassinated.' As well as a picture of the dummy, it included one purporting to be an elderly JFK as he looked in 1993. Others were: 'UFO chases Jetliner for 22 Minutes!', 'Amazing Proof of Reincarnation! Children recall vivid details of past lives!', 'Prince Charles: I'm Giving Up Sex', 'Cars of the future will be grown – from living bugs!' The centrefold had startling photos of women with the headline, 'These gals' breasts are the world's weirdest.' One was supposedly three breasted. I wondered if people really believed these stories or whether, like me, they bought the paper to see what bizarre tales it could come up with next.

I drove further north through Oregon and Washington, camping in a series of beautiful forests. After buying a little portable barbecue for $3.50, I decided to try it out with hamburgers. Somehow I didn't have the knack. The charcoal wasn't hot enough, the hamburgers fell to bits and I had to resort to the frying pan and gas stove. A few nights later I had a proper barbecue over a wood fire and had even managed to buy some lamb chops – common enough in Australia at that time, but not always easy to find in America where they were expensive and considered a specialty food, often imported from New Zealand. Beef and chicken were always readily available.

Jan Dale in her newly aquired Camper Van 1992

At Crater Lake, Oregon

With Goody Cable & Harry Crossfield.
Taken by Jon Newton

With Goody Cable

National Parks and Bears

Olympic National Park is in the northwest of the state of Washington, just below the Canadian border. From Hurricane Ridge in the park, I was excited to see my first glaciers and some beautiful mountains, including the 8,000ft Mt. Olympus. Also glimpses of local wildlife – a beautifully patterned rusty coloured garter snake, jumping mouse, black-tailed deer and tiny grey shrews scooting around like clockwork mice. The forest here is lowland with spruce, hemlock and huckleberry. My van and I took the ferry from Bremerton across the Puget Sound to Seattle. From the deck I could see the spectacular active volcano Mt. Rainier. At 14,410 feet and covered with snow, it reminded me of Mt. Fuji. I loved these huge mountains. They looked so impressive to me, as Australia is a fairly flat country, with the highest peak the 7,310 foot Mt. Kosciusko.

Seasons sometimes change rapidly in North America. A cold snap can arrive suddenly after quite hot weather. One of these heralded autumn when I was starting to travel east across Washington. I drove past wheat and corn growing areas, through the city of Spokane with its beautiful river, and into the panhandle of northern Idaho.

The squirrels were busy getting their winter supplies. Amongst some tall conifers in the delightfully named Bumblebee State Forest, I was forced to move because one particularly industrious creature was pelting me with small pine cones, which it had apparently bitten off the treetop. Its aim was accurate, and the strange thing was that after a while it came down and started taking them back up again – maybe to its nest, or perhaps to take aim at me again. Squirrels are great little conservationists because they usually bury the cones and nuts, but forget where many of them are and so, by default, do an excellent job planting new trees. Another species which does an even better job is the Clark's Nutcracker, a bird which can hide up to 90,000 whitebark pine seeds in a single year – many of which germinate and grow into new trees. As it was beginning to cool down at night I enjoyed sitting by an open fire, using wood some nearby campers had given me before they left.

At the small town of White Fish in Montana, I discovered that last time I bought fuel I hadn't replaced the petrol cap. It was too far to go back, but only a cap made specially for a Volkswagen van would fit. Fortunately there was a VW dealer here, but parts for old vehicles like mine were not easy to come by. If I'd realised this before I bought the van I may have reconsidered.

A cap had to be ordered from Los Angeles – first shipped by air to Alberta in Canada then flown somewhere south and finally sent by road to White Fish. The total cost would be $70. Freight alone was $28! (Remember, this was 1992.) It would take a few days, and as there was nothing much to hold my attention at White Fish – not even any music – and as I was not far from a spectacular scenic area, I decided to drive on and come back for it later.

Eventually I arrived at one of the trip's many highlights: Waterton-Glacier International Peace Park. Glacier is the southern section in north western Montana, USA, and Waterton over the border in Alberta, Canada. Named to commemorate the long history of peace between the two nations, it contains about one and a half million acres of mountains and forest, 50 glaciers, 200 lakes and a great variety of wildlife. It's a refuge for almost every species of mammal found in the U.S. It was now September and the weather was clear and perfect. I was so lucky, as just a week earlier many of the higher roads had been closed due to heavy snowfalls.

Coming from a sparsely populated country like Australia, I was continually surprised to see so many people in these parks. For example, The Great Smoky Mountains now have over nine million visitors annually, The Grand Canyon four million and Yellowstone and Yosemite over three million each. I was often told that it would finally be possible at Glacier to 'get away from it all'. So it was a bit off-putting to discover when I arrived at 10 am that there was a long queue to get in, and that I needed to go straight to the campground to secure a site as it was expected to be full by *eleven*. Oh well, I thought, *once I get out on the trails I'll leave the crowds behind*. No such luck.

My first walk was a short one to Avalanche Lake, and in less than an hour I passed 182 people coming out! I could understand why that trail is so popular, as the lake is in a kind of amphitheatre with waterfalls plunging down two hundred foot walls. Later I did find some less frequented trails, and because the park is so large, there are even a number of remote areas.

This is in the heart of bear country and I was absolutely fascinated by them. Glacier had approximately 300 grizzly (brown) bears (a large one can weight up to 1,400 lbs.) and several hundred of the smaller black bears (average weight 140-220 lbs). All kinds of precautions had to be taken. There was an average of about two bear attacks a week, but only ten people had been killed since 1910. Just three weeks earlier a ranger was attacked when she inadvertently came between a mother and cub. She was badly mauled, but survived.

Bears don't like surprises, so if possible it's best to keep upwind so it knows you are there. While on the trails, the advice was to continually yell in order to alert any animals that might be lurking around the next bend. Some hikers had bells attached to their boots or walking sticks so it could be pretty noisy out there, but apparently the sound of the bells simply doesn't carry far enough to be of any real use. Yelling was definitely considered more effective, but I decided to save my energy and risk a bear confrontation.

I learnt the correct way to behave should I meet a grizzly close up. At that time the advice was to stay calm (though how could you?), avert your eyes, make yourself appear very small so as not to look threatening, and slowly back away hoping it doesn't follow. A brochure advised to *'never run from a bear. If you do you may look like food.'* Bears are very fast – up to 40 mph in short bursts – making it impossible to outrun them. If they charge you should stand firm, as often these are 'false' charges. (But what if they're not?) The other option is lie still on the ground curled in a ball, protecting your head with your arms. I imagined this part would be fairly easy for me because if a bear came too close, I'd probably pass out with fright. On the other hand, a ranger told me, *'If one starts licking you, fight back!'*

There is a story about two hikers who saw a grizzly coming towards them. One started removing his large boots and when the other asked what he was doing, he said, *'I'm going to make a run for it.'* His friend replied, *'You know you can't outrun grizzlies.' 'Yes, but I only have to outrun you!'* Native Americans and other people who live in close contact with bears tend to take a different approach, and seem to be able to calm the animals by talking gently to them.

At the campground everyone had to be very careful not to attract bears. Leaflets advised to *'avoid cooking smelly or greasy foods.'* All food and utensils were to be locked away in a hard top vehicle and no 'grey' water (wash up water etc.) tipped on the ground. It all had to be carried to a special gully trap. Rubbish bins were located in secure metal enclosures. For tent campers there were special bear proof containers – for the food, not the campers – and sometimes a very high pole suspended between trees on which you had to hang your bag of food, but not too close to the trees as grizzlies can climb. It occurred to me that this also means you can't hope to escape a pursuing bear by shinning up the nearest tree. One of the park brochures described these food storage procedures and added, somewhat superfluously, *'These restrictions do not apply to food that is being transported, consumed or prepared for consumption.'* I also found the animal's Latin name amusingly descriptive – *Ursus arctos horribilis*.

Surprisingly, grizzly bears are dexterous enough to be able to remove lids from jars. They have poor eyesight but excellent hearing and a tremendous sense of smell. They can locate a mole a foot or two underground and scoop it up with their huge paws. Most ominously, a bear leaflet also warned: *'Sleep some distance uphill from your cooking area. Keep sleeping bags and personal gear clean and free of food odour. Don't sleep in the clothes you wore whilst cooking, and don't wear perfume or deodorant.'* Women were advised to consider staying out of bear country during their menstrual period. All this potential drama was exciting, but I was glad to be sleeping in a hard-topped vehicle and not a tent, and kept peeping out during the night in case I saw a bear passing by. I never did.

Next day I met a very agitated woman. She had been walking behind her husband when he swore loudly and stopped suddenly. Looking beyond him she saw an enormous grizzly on the trail in front. They did all the right things and fortunately the bear didn't follow, but of course they were rather shaken. I half wanted to see one on a trail myself just for the thrill of it but didn't have any close encounters, which was probably just as well.

If confronted with a black bear, a person's behaviour should be different than when encountering a brown bear (grizzly). On first encounter, if a black bear is showing signs of recognising your presence; e.g. stops feeding or changes its travel direction, you should slowly back away, keeping your eyes on it. If it persistently follows you change direction, and if it *still* follows, stand your ground and don't look away. If it gets closer, the advice is to look as big and threatening as possible, stand on a log or rock and shout waving your arms around or preferably a stick. If it attacks you, fight back. So I realised that if I saw a bear, I'd better be sure which species it was.

In Glacier Park I also saw elk, antelope, deer, fluffy white mountain goats, bighorn sheep with their huge curved horns (which I thought looked more like goats than the goats), and many smaller creatures such as squirrels, chipmunks and marmots. In 1984, the first documented den of wolf pups in over sixty years was discovered in the park. There were approximately fifty wolves when I visited, plus mountain lions – also known as cougars, pumas or panthers. I found a pile of entrails on the track, which the ranger said would probably be the remains of a squirrel eaten by a mountain lion. Tourists still feed these wild animals, despite warnings and education programs. Recently a moose that often aggressively begged for food in the park suddenly died. An autopsy revealed its stomach was full of plastic wrappers, rope and a tablecloth! It had died of starvation. Other animals have to be destroyed if they become dangerously aggressive searching for human food. I often saw the phrase *'A fed bear is a dead bear.'* It's hard to believe that only a few years ago, in some of these parks the rangers took tourists to the rubbish dumps to watch bears foraging.

American national parks are very well organised with excellent information centres. In the high season there are usually ranger-led walks during the day and informative campfire talks at night. At Glacier I went to one about wolves, and was interested to learn that they do not really live up to their fierce reputation. It is extremely rare for them to attack humans.

I was surprised by the many Americans I met who said they would be scared of coming to Australia because of our dangerous creatures. We have nothing as big or as scary as a bear or a mountain lion. However, we do have plenty of dangerous snakes, spiders, sharks, crocodiles, dingoes, stingrays, jelly fish, stone fish etc. Only saltwater crocodiles, sharks and dingoes could consider humans to be food, and are fairly easily avoided. As far as I know, dingoes have only attacked babies and small children, in areas where they have become used to tourists. Snakes and spiders don't attack unless you disturb them and even then they prefer to get away. So when I thought about it, I realised our list is actually quite ominous but, although I would be nervous camping alone in the middle of the forests of the northern U.S. or Canada, I hardly give it a second thought in Australia. I suppose it's largely about what you know and the size and habitat of the animals.

One of the park's highlights is the spectacular 'Going-to-the-Sun Road.' Completed in 1932, it's still considered a great engineering feat. It is fifty miles long and crosses the park from east to west via Logan Pass at an elevation of 6,680 feet. My luck was continuing as the weather was just perfect, while the previous weekend the road had been closed with two feet of snow. It was absolutely stunning. I was *oohing* and *ahhing* out loud every few minutes, and wished I didn't have to concentrate so much on driving. Logan Pass, being the highest point of the road, is a major attraction, but its large parking area was overflowing when I arrived. I had to admire the views while driving around in slow circles.

A five mile walking trail along the side of a mountain took me to Iceberg Lake, which was a brilliant blue-green with small white icebergs floating around. Then I spent a lazy afternoon writing letters and indulged myself with a rare dinner out at the Glacier Park Lodge. Built in 1914, it's an amazing building – all wooden, with an enormous atrium lobby constructed from sixty Douglas fir tree trunks, forty feet high and estimated to have been between five and eight hundred years old when cut. There are also *huge* stone fireplaces. I wandered through the accommodation area, which is reminiscent of an old passenger ship with narrow wooden corridors and slightly sloping floors. Oddly, despite happily travelling alone, I still felt self-conscious when *'table for one for Dale'* was announced.

Before moving on from Glacier National Park, I was able to have my first shower for ten days. It felt wonderful. Life on the road certainly makes one appreciate the simple things which are normally taken for granted.

Mountain Goats

Heading South

Montana is referred to as 'big sky country,' which sounds silly until you are there and see what they mean. The air is clean and clear, and the high altitudes make you feel as though you can see forever. There are wonderful open prairies, covered with velvety grasses in delicate shades of gold, mauve and soft moss greens waving in patterns in the wind. The men really do wear cowboy hats, and drive pickups with rifles mounted on racks in the rear window. I heard there was some good local music, but I didn't take the time to check it out. I knew there'd be plenty of opportunities for music later on in the trip.

At the town of Augusta I ventured into the Senior Citizen Center to ask if I could use their toilet. They were very surprised to have an Australian wander in and showed me around the building, offered me a cup of tea and insisted I sign their visitors' book. Several asked if they could have their photographs taken with me, making me feel like a visiting dignitary.

Next was a brief visit to Yellowstone National Park, a bit further south in Wyoming. It was also busy with tourists. Wild animals such as herds of buffalo (bison) beside the roads led to traffic jams. These creatures are unpredictable, weigh up to 2,000 pounds and sprint at 30 mph, so it's wise to be respectful. A park brochure has a graphic drawing of a tourist, his camera askew, being flung into the air by a very angry charging buffalo, with the words *'Many visitors have been gorged by buffalo.'* I was so excited to see some up ahead that I didn't notice a large one standing right next to me. I leapt out of the van, almost hitting the creature with the door! Fortunately it was too busy eating to bother about me.

I also saw beautiful and delicate looking pronghorn antelope with their beige, white and dark brown markings. They are actually the fastest hoofed mammals on earth. I also saw some snow-footed rabbits (their feet are larger than normal so act as a kind of snow shoe), elk, moose, marmots, mule deer (which are short and solid), and rabbit-sized furry creatures called pikas, which live amongst the rocks and have a high-pitched call that sounds just like those stuffed toys that squeak when you squeeze them. There were also the usual chipmunks and squirrels as well as the Old Faithful geyser, which conveniently erupted soon after I arrived.

I left Yellowstone in heavy rain, which turned to sleet and then snow. My run of good weather was coming to an end, and a little further south the spectacular Teton Mountains were capped with cloud. This impressive range has 12 peaks reaching above 12,000 feet, and looks like paper cutouts when seen against a blue sky. I camped there and it eventually stopped snowing, but the temperature went down to 16 degrees Fahrenheit. When the engine was turned off I had no heating, and ice formed on the outside and *inside* of the van windows. I managed reasonably well in my thermal underwear and sleeping bag.

Early next morning walking at 8,500 feet in lightly falling snow, I passed an enormous male elk sitting in the long grass beside the trail. His antlers were bloody and I was worried he'd been injured, but later discovered this bleeding is normal when antlers are being shed each year.

When I got back to the campground it was still well below freezing, and I was astonished to see a young woman sitting on the ground washing her hair under a cold water tap! There were no showers, and she was apparently desperate. I'd most certainly rather put up with greasy hair, but was usually able to at least have warm water washes in the van every day. All the passes I had just driven over from Glacier National Park were now closed. It was time to head further south.

The next day everything seemed to go wrong. First, I forgot to put the pop-up roof down and drove on the highway for some miles before realising that the noise I was hearing was its canvas sides flapping in the wind. Fortunately no damage was done, but I felt foolish and incompetent.

I could have lost the whole roof and caused a nasty accident. Then the van developed a hot oily smell and a mechanic near the town of Jackson, Wyoming, diagnosed oil leaking on to a very hot part of the motor, which he said could easily catch fire. I left it there for repairs, and hitched a lift into town with another of their customers. I thought Jackson was a touristy place pretending to be a western town, but maybe I was just annoyed to be held up by something as boring as mechanical problems. My trip to the post office was disappointing, too – no mail and I hated not hearing from home. Contact with my friends and relatives was especially important because I was planning to be away for such a long time and was already missing them. Sally and John in California had agreed for all my mail to be sent care of them. Whenever I was able to give her an address – usually a post office – Sally would package it up and send it on to me.

Towards the end of the day I collected the repaired van and stocked up on groceries, only to discover somebody had backed into it in the supermarket car park, leaving a sizeable dent. I was so upset because I'd really been trying to look after this vehicle – partly because I hoped to sell it at a good price at the end of my journey and already had a couple of interested buyers in San Francisco – and partly because I loved it. While I was fussing around about that, I also discovered I'd lost my good sunglasses.

Later on, forgetting this was a different vehicle from the older, more rugged Volkswagen I had in Australia which seemed to be happy to go wherever I wanted it to, I foolishly drove down a very steep gravel road looking for a camping place beside a river. There was nowhere suitable and I had terrible trouble getting back up to the main road, and nearly burnt the clutch out trying. In the end the irascible creature allowed itself to be reversed out. A very strange smell under the front had me worried, but it seemed to drive OK back on the level road. It was now starting to get dark, so it was a relief to finally find a pleasant free camping spot in the forest by another river. I was exhausted and needed a couple of stiff vodkas to recover from the stress of it all.

It's interesting how seemingly small things matter such a lot when you are living on the road as I was. Still in Wyoming, I spent the next night at a town campsite in Pinedale, and was absolutely delighted to discover wash troughs as well as the usual automated laundry. Not wanting to spend my precious money on machines, I did all my washing by hand, expecting to hang it out in the fresh air and sunshine as I would at home. However it was forbidden to hang out washing in this campground, so I had to resort to the electric drier after all.

That night I had the luxury of eating out at a little family restaurant called Wranglers. They made the best raspberry pie I've ever tasted. After dinner I wandered into a couple of local bars looking for music. I didn't find any, but did discover the power of an Australian accent in this part of the world. Perhaps being a woman with long, red curly hair may have helped, too! As soon as I opened my mouth, people (mostly men) wanted to buy me drinks, invite me out etc. *'You're not from 'round here, are you?'* Hmmm! What fun, and how healthy for the budget. Early on in my trip I decided that, with one or two exceptions, never to say no if somebody offered to buy me a drink, and to sort out any possible consequences later! Nothing bad ever happened to me. Most people were simply being friendly to a visitor. Of course my response to occasionally being invited home was somewhat different.

I continued on south, heading for Bryce Canyon through the sagebrush country of Wyoming, and into the much lower and drier Utah. I had been driving up and down mountains at altitudes of around 6,000 ft. for over two weeks, and now the poor old van groaned over a pass of 8,400 ft. It really felt as though it needed to be encouraged and coaxed. Being underpowered for this kind of terrain, it was often struggling along in first gear while the fast American-made vehicles roared past.

The colours of the country were changing from delicate mauves, lemons and greys to brilliant red rocks and deep jagged canyons with splashes of autumn shades. The aspens with their white trunks and yellow leaves were particularly spectacular against the dark mountains. One of the tapes I played in my van was by John Denver, who sang a beautiful song written by Kent Lewis called 'Song of Wyoming'.

I passed Big Rock Candy Mountain. Yes, it really *does* exist and it's well named, as it's a startling yellow with some red and mauve and absolutely no vegetation cover at all. As well as changes in the scenery, the weather was changing. As I moved further south it was much warmer at night, which was a relief. I could sit outside for dinner, instead of being cooped up in the van.

I'd never imagined anything as geologically exotic as Bryce Canyon in Utah. Named after Mormon pioneer Ebenezer Bryce, who tried to settle on land here and described it as *'a hell of a place to lose a cow,'* it's a vast amphitheatre filled with thousands and thousands of quite extraordinary tall sandstone columns called hoodoos. They are weathered into fantastic shapes and colours, which vary with the changing light. The Paiute Indians' name for it translates as *'red rocks standing like men in a bowl-shaped canyon.'* There are walking trails over, around and through them via tunnels and narrow passages. This was the most spectacular walking I'd ever done. The highest point in the national park is 9,200 feet and from there I could see Mt. Navajo about eighty miles away. I stayed overnight in the campground, watched the sunset from Bryce Point, and despite being very tired from all the driving of the last few days, dragged myself out of bed to see the sun rise over the canyon, before taking off for that other canyon, the Grand, just over the border in Arizona.

My idea of camping in Australia is to be out in the wilderness away from the noise of other people and their dogs, kids and machinery, so I was keen to find somewhere like that in America, rather than being restricted to organised campgrounds. I finally achieved this near the northern rim of The Grand Canyon in a national forest area of wildflowers and trees. I even had a little campfire, but had trouble keeping it alight long enough to cook dinner because a great storm came over, with lots of thunder and lightning and plenty of rain. I stood outside with my umbrella over the fire. Despite this and the fact that my bedding became damp from condensation on the ceiling, it was *great* just to be there in the elements all alone. I was suffering slightly from the altitude – just a shortness of breath, which made walking a bit difficult – and as I huddled up in my warm clothing in the cold little van, I laughed to read the following in the 'High Altitude - Health' section of the *AAA Tourbook*: *'Finally, after you lounge in the sauna or whirlpool bath at your lodgings, remember to stand up carefully, for the heat has relaxed your blood vessels and lowered your blood pressure.'* I reminded myself that people often miss out on so many of the joys of life by worrying too much about the comforts.

At the other extreme, I learnt that people actually run from one rim of the Grand Canyon to the other – a distance of ten miles with a descent and ascent of several thousand feet, and they can do it in fourteen hours! Why anyone would actually *want* to was beyond me. I guess it's the challenge, but I was happy to amble along the ridge path with a short trip down one of the trails, which was a bit spoilt because of all the mess and smell the tourist-carrying donkeys leave behind.

The violent storm continued next day, but I didn't want to spend more time here than necessary, so did my best to ignore the weather and set out to explore the fantastic north rim of the canyon. At around 9,000 feet it's the highest rim. Lightning and thunder raged all around. A sign beside the trail warned of the danger and frequency of lightning strikes: '*If there is a smell of ozone or a person's hair stands on end you are in danger and must immediately leave for a safer spot, preferably your vehicle*'.

The lookout was an exposed rocky ledge, and from the railing I could catch a glimpse of the Colorado River about 6,000 ft. below. There were two other people braving the elements and we chatted for a while. Suddenly I felt a strange sensation and heard a buzzing sound, which the others said they *couldn't* hear. I touched the metal guard rail and received a nasty shock. I removed my hood. They exclaimed, '*Gosh, your hair is completely standing on end!*' This must have been an arresting sight, because I have a lot of hair. There was another *enormous* clap of thunder and bolt of lightning which appeared to be practically at our feet. I turned and ran without a second thought about what was happening to them, but we all made it safely back to our vehicles.

Later I learnt that a woman had recently been killed by lightning at that same spot. Fortunately, the only obvious after-effect of my dramatic encounter was a black mark extending two inches from the corner of my mouth. It took about ten days to fade and for several years it occasionally reappeared in a smaller form. There was also a lot of electricity in my body, which was activated whenever I touched metal or unrolled my synthetic covered sleeping bag. Every night when I was getting ready for bed, I involuntarily put on a kind of light and sound show. Someone later told me there may also have been black marks on the bottom of my feet, where the electricity had left my body.

On and on I drove through more of northern Arizona's spectacular scenery, overnighting at Monument Valley, owned and managed by the Navajo Nation. It wasn't the best campground I'd stayed in, and it was *so* busy I felt as though I was in a parking lot, but the picturesque setting more than made up for that. The evening was warm and I was able to sit outside with my drink, watching the sunset reflecting on the exotically weathered shapes of the ancient mountains so familiar as backdrops to many old western movies. Dinner that night was special too – salmon and a glass of wine. I normally didn't have any problems filling in the evenings, as I was usually so tired after hectic days of driving and exploring that I simply fell into bed soon after dinner. My meals, by necessity, continued to be simple fare, generally lots of pasta and vegetable dishes.

I was amazed at the size of the enormous American travel vans or recreation vehicles (RVs). They normally carried only two people – usually a retired couple – and could be as large as a Greyhound bus, often with a fold-out satellite dish, two air conditioners and pulling a 'run-around' vehicle the size of my van. I even saw one towing a small helicopter!

At Mesa Verde National Park campground in south western Colorado, 44 of these vehicles arrived one afternoon in a large convoy. I was bemused to see that, despite camping in a stunning setting, the occupants appeared to pay little attention to their surroundings, ate inside their individual vans and spent the evening watching *television*. There was no electricity provided, so a cacophony of generators drowned out any natural sounds. Thank goodness I was some distance away, in a peaceful spot with families of wild turkeys and deer wandering past. I had a lovely rest day reading and writing letters at the picnic table, before attempting to explore this large park.

Mesa Verde is famous for its ancient cliff dwellings and they are truly astonishing. There are 600 as well as over 3,000 other archaeological sites. Many artefacts found in the ruins are displayed in a museum. These included some beautiful belts woven from human or dog hair, and blankets made from turkey feathers. The dwellings date from around 1200 AD and were usually built in a hollow or alcove under a sheer cliff overhang, with another sheer drop of up to a *thousand feet* below. Nobody really knows why they were placed in such positions, but presumably as a protection from invaders. They grew their crops on the mesas (flat tops of the weathered mountains), so had to climb in and out of their houses almost daily. Sometimes you could see the weathered remains of steps, but the occupants, known as the Anasazi people, often used a series of finger and toe holds carved into the cliff face. They often left a code at the beginning of this perilous ascent or descent to ensure the climber started with the correct foot to avoid the unthinkable dilemma of having to cross legs halfway.

It is possible to visit some of these houses, and it's best to have a good head for heights and not suffer from claustrophobia or altitude sickness as they vary from 6,000 to 8,500 feet above sea level. To reach Balcony House, I had to climb up a couple of almost vertical ladders with a big drop below and crawl through a two and a half foot high tunnel. I also saw about 40 cliff dwellings from various lookout points along a six mile loop road, and on one of the short trails came across a handsome rattlesnake – the only one I saw in the wild on my whole trip – but sadly somebody had recently killed it.

When I finally arrived in Albuquerque it was raining heavily. I decided on a rare splurge and booked into a cheap motel, appreciating every facility that it offered. I soaked in the bath then washed all my clothes (in the bath), hung them around the room and turned up the heating to dry them. I brought in my wash-up bowl and used more hot water to properly clean my cooking utensils. Having to live so frugally meant I rarely visited a laundromat or used the camper van stove to heat water. Finally I filled my cooler with ice from the free machine. The historic Route 66 passes through Albuquerque, so of course my theme song here was '(Get Your Kicks on) Route 66.' Written in 1946 by Bobby Troup, the lyrics follow the path of Route 66, which traversed the western two-thirds of the U.S. from Chicago, Illinois, to Los Angeles, California.

Somebody told me about a nearby night club, which turned out to be a large western dance venue with a live band. Although they were currently all the rage in America, it was the first honky-tonk I had been to. Most of the men wore cowboy hats, and after a while somebody asked *me* to dance. I didn't know how to but said yes, hoping he wouldn't mind teaching me. He was patient but I felt awkward and decided to sit out the rest, then try practicing on my own when nobody else was around. Several more men did approach me and one asked quite seriously if I had refused him because he wasn't wearing a hat! I laughed about this, but must admit that I found the hats gave an exotic and attractive appearance to men, who in reality were probably quite ordinary. I discovered later that most hats leave a kind of dent in the hair of the wearer, referred to as 'hat hair.' This is to be avoided at all costs, so hats are never removed in company, except when the national anthem is played or when doffed as a mark of respect. When removed at night, they are always placed crown down so the shape of the brim is not spoilt. Sometimes both male and female dancers wore large cowboy hats, which made dancing close together difficult if not impossible – a plus in certain situations, I supposed.

The New Mexico State Fair was on, and I had an interesting day watching the 65 years and over section of a fiddlers' competition. The oldest participant was 87, and so frail that he had to be physically supported while he played. Fiddlers' competitions are really popular in the U.S. and apparently date right back to 1736. I tasted Indian fry bread (good but rather indigestible); paid fifty cents to admire the 1,200 pound winner of the Midwest Giant Hog Round-up; looked at other agricultural exhibits in the livestock halls; saw cakes and quilts; watched some bungee jumping and generally enjoyed the crowds. In the program I noticed some unusual events like 'Pigmy Goat Judging' and 'Rooster Crowing Contest' which unfortunately I'd missed. I wondered how they made them crow on demand, but supposed it only needed one to start and the rest would follow. There was also a nightly professional rodeo contest, but I decided to leave the city and camp at Coronado State Park, the site of an old Pueblo village right on the Rio Grande River between Albuquerque and Santa Fe.

Albuquerque is at an altitude of 5,000 feet, so the air is crisp and clear, colours seem brighter and cleaner, and the starry sky on a cloudless night is wonderful. I was woken just before dawn by the eerie hooting of a great horned owl. Looking out the window, I could just see it silhouetted on the top of an escarpment. Each of the sites at this lovely campground had a little three sided adobe shelter, with a picnic table from which you could see the beautiful Sandia Mountains. The only disturbing element was the sound of a busy freeway. All over the country, even in seemingly remote national parks, I found it quite difficult to get away from traffic sounds – freeways, aeroplanes etc.

Lots of mail from home was waiting for me at the Santa Fe post office. Such a cheery treat. The city is really interesting, especially the historic area where I saw the Palace of Governors, an adobe construction which dates back to 1610. It is the oldest government building in the U.S. Santa Fe's strict building regulations meant that even the newer areas were built in an adobe style so they fitted well into the semi-desert environment. There was a wonderful exhibition at the Museum of International Folk Art – 200,000 dolls and toys from around the world, arranged in tableaus or whole village scenes. They were all originally part of a private collection. I discovered in my travels that philanthropy is very strong in America, and lots of museum exhibits were items collected and then donated by wealthy citizens.

After a night at Canyon Campground in the Santa Fe National Forest just a few minutes' drive from the city, I couldn't get the van started. A friendly woman drove me to a public telephone and then kindly invited me to stay at her home. This was tempting, but I declined because I really wanted to sort out my vehicle problems. The American Automobile Association eventually sent a tow truck. The driver knew absolutely nothing about Volkswagens or air cooled engines, but did manage to get it started. It appeared to be some kind of petrol blockage, so I thought I'd better look for a suitable garage to have it checked out and serviced. I wanted to avoid being stranded somewhere really remote.

Mechanics specialising in the older air cooled Volkswagens are a rare breed in America, especially in the south, so I decided to drive back to the larger city of Albuquerque. On the outskirts I took the first city exit off the freeway, and asked at a car parts supplier if they could recommend a VW mechanic. Amazingly one just happened to be standing right next to me so I followed him back to his workshop – a friendly family business run by his wife and himself. They really looked after me, charged a fraction of the price of any other place I'd been to, fed me pizza for lunch and let me sleep overnight in my van in their parking area, while waiting for parts to arrive.

Around the corner was another large western club called Cowboys, where I spent a dreamy evening dancing with a tall handsome blue-eyed cowboy. (I'd been practicing my steps!) He was a horse breeder just passing through town, and a great dancer. Although he barely talked all night he practically swept me off my feet, giving me little kisses from time to time – and then, like Cinderella, disappeared at midnight. I never saw him again.

Cliff palace, Mesa Verde, Colorado

Grand Hog Exhibition, New Mexico

Pre Dinner drinks

At Mesa Verde Campground

WARNING

MANY VISITORS HAVE BEEN GORED BY BUFFALO

BUFFALO CAN WEIGH 2000 POUNDS AND CAN SPRINT AT 30 MPH, THREE TIMES FASTER THAN YOU CAN RUN

THESE ANIMALS MAY APPEAR TAME BUT ARE WILD, UNPREDICTABLE, AND DANGEROUS

DO NOT APPROACH BUFFALO

Back to California

I was really enjoying the challenge of travelling alone and the different adventures I was having. I suppose my early upbringing had something to do with this. I had lived in small Australian country towns until I was about eleven. Dad was a Methodist minister and they had to move every three or four years. The church owned the houses and contents, including crockery. I remember excitedly rushing around each new house, exploring and checking in case something was accidentally left behind. Under the cushions of the couch often yielded interesting results in the way of pens, coins and once a pound note.

So moving around was part of my normal life and I had learnt to enjoy it. Of course, it meant losing friends and making new ones wasn't always easy – especially when you were the minister's daughter. People were often uncomfortable visiting our home, and felt they should be on their best behaviour. By the time I was about eight, my much older siblings had left home and so I became used to being alone.

Now instead of concentrating mainly on the natural environment, I decided to explore more of the culture, particularly the music – but first I wanted to make a trip back to California to see my relatives Sally and John, and to visit a couple of national parks along the way.

Arches National Park back in Utah looks a bit like an imagined lunar desert landscape, with stunning rock formations which include large balanced rocks, spires, pinnacles and more than 2,000 sandstone arches. There is some controversy about how big an opening should be before it can be classified as an arch. The National Parks people here decided that an arch is an opening that extends at least three feet in any one direction. Landscape Arch, with a span of 306 feet and a height of 105 feet, is one of the world's longest natural stone arches.

Although the weather was uncomfortably hot, there were lots of people around. The campground was full, but I was lucky to find a place alone out in the desert – alone that is, except for the little creatures which seemed to be running over the roof of the van all night. I didn't catch sight of them, but assumed they were ground squirrels or pack rats or something similar. Fortunately they didn't get inside. The nights here were cool and clear, and I enjoyed sitting outside under a gorgeous ceiling of stars. Being alone in an environment like this has many advantages. Having nobody to talk to meant that I sat quietly and was able to hear more of the night sounds, and I discovered I really liked that slightly scary feeling of knowing there was almost certainly nobody else around for miles. It was a comfort that there were no bears in this area, and that any snakes were not likely to be as dangerous as those I was used to seeing in Australia.

Canyonlands National Park in south eastern Utah is also impressive. It's a huge maze of deeply eroded canyons where the Green and Colorado Rivers meet, and is a great place for hiking which, when I was there, had to be done in the cool of the early morning or evening. It is rugged with an area called The Maze Country, ranking as one of the most remote and inaccessible parts of the United States. Most of the roads are only suitable for four wheel drive vehicles with high road clearance so I was a bit restricted, but was able to get to some wonderful lookout points, including Island in the Sky, a huge level mesa with stunning views over the canyons. I was really beginning to appreciate what an incredible country the United States is, with extraordinarily diverse geographic regions on such a grand scale, and generally much more accessible than many of Australia's scenic areas. The only drawback for me continued to be the number of people visiting these parks. I'm not too keen on crowds (probably another effect of my childhood days) unless they're in a dance hall, and even there a couple of good available dancers are enough.

I finally dragged myself away from these wonderful parks and drove some distance on Interstate Highway 70, a freeway which also passes through striking scenery – dry and stony with high mesas, steep cliffs, deep gorges and lots of hills. This provided a real challenge for the VW, which seemed to be getting slower and slower. I was hoping it was just because the hills were steeper, but perhaps it was getting tired! I was still in Utah, but soon joined highway 50 which would take me right across to California. It was a much smaller road with almost no traffic.

As usual, I found myself singing something appropriate to keep myself awake on the long drive. This time it was Al Jolson's 'California Here I Come,' written by Buddy DeSylva and Joseph Meyer. The road crossed a flat plain past a huge salt lake – Sevier Lake – glistening white against desert mountains. There were no trees at all, just saltbush or sagebrush. Then I coaxed the ever more reluctant van up over the 6,000 ft. Skull Rock Pass and into Nevada. The very hot weather I'd been experiencing meant a very hot engine, and my biggest fear was breaking down, especially somewhere inhospitable with no help readily available. Fortunately, although it was now sunny and windy, it was much cooler, which was a relief. I camped that night at Cave Lake State Park in eastern Nevada, at an elevation of around 7,000 feet. The lake was a lovely bright blue, surrounded by low stunted pines and stony ground with flowering cacti. Being near water was a welcome contrast to the dry areas of Utah and Arizona, and I took my chair down to its edge to watch wading birds and a beautiful sunset.

Next morning I was on the road at 6:30, which actually turned out to be 5:30 as I'd just crossed into another time zone without realising. By 9 am I'd driven 100 miles over more high passes, followed by the large flat plains of the Nevada deserts with the occasional glimpse of cattle and plenty of salt lakes, but very little sign of human habitation and almost no other traffic. Arriving at the small town of Eureka I passed a sign: *'You are entering the loneliest town on the loneliest road in America.'* I stopped to post a letter, and couldn't get the van started again. Fortunately I was on a slope, and there was a garage a few blocks further down the hill, so I was able to roll down. They immediately took it in for inspection.

I was hoping I wouldn't be stuck in this remote place for very long, but I had a call to make and there was a phone box nearby. Afterwards I referred to this as the 'magic phone box' because it connected me with the number I dialed and then immediately *returned* my coins. After one interstate call, I decided to try another and the same thing happened.

Then I phoned my sister in Australia, and talked for half an hour. Then my brother who also lives in Australia, followed by my brother in England, and a few friends around the world. Every few minutes a recording would tell me to put in more money so I just returned the same coins. Due to the high cost of international phone calls from public phones, I hadn't spoken with my family or friends for ages, and I thought I may as well make the most of it. I was in that phone box for three hours, and my fingers were black from the continual handling of the coins! In the end I ran out of steam, but it was great that something good had come out of my vehicle problems. This kind of luck was to happen many times during the rest of my American travels, although I never found a phone like that again.

Back at the garage, they told me the problem was simply dirty battery terminals which they'd cleaned, and the van now started immediately. Much relieved, I drove off into the desert, passing another sign which said, *'You are now leaving the loneliest town on the loneliest road in America!'*

There was 100 miles between towns here. After about 50 miles I noticed some unusual aircraft flying over, stopped to look at them and foolishly turned off the motor. Once again, it wouldn't restart! I couldn't believe my bad luck. Here I was in one of the situations I'd dreaded – stuck in a remote area with no towns within 50 miles, no houses in sight and virtually no traffic. I tried a number of times to get the thing going. Unfortunately I was parked in a very flat spot, so there was no chance of trying a rolling jump start.

After about an hour, which I whiled away by making a sandwich and a cup of tea, I spotted a vehicle in the distance and, against all advice to lone women travellers, rushed to the edge of the road and flagged it down. Out jumped a large rough-looking character wearing a dirty singlet and shorts and covered with tattoos! This was a bit unnerving, but he seemed OK and, although not exactly enthusiastic, was willing to help. I explained the problem and suggested that a push start would probably work. He agreed and I got into the van to turn on the ignition and put it into gear, expecting him to push it using his own strength. To my surprise he started his own vehicle, and simply rammed it into the back of mine. But it *did* work, and at that stage I was beyond caring about any possible vehicle damage. It was just a relief to be on my way.

I was too scared to stop again in case the engine stalled and I'd be stuck once more, so I drove and drove until I came to a reasonable sized town.

All this had taken lots of time. It was now after dark and I looked for a camping place – preferably on a hill or with people around to help so I could get started next day and find another garage. I was thinking the problem might be the starter motor when the inevitable happened and, probably through nerves and tiredness, I managed to stall the motor at traffic lights in the middle of town. This time I just sat there with the hazard lights flashing and the doors locked until someone offered to help. What a traumatic day and what a relief when I finally got to a friendly campground.

Next morning the van started immediately, but a local garage *did* confirm starter motor problems. They didn't have spare parts for Volkswagens and said that provided I did not try to start the engine while it was hot, I should be OK to get to California. So off I set again, feeling a bit more vulnerable. I drove all day until I got to Los Gatos where Sally and John lived. I *did* turn the motor off for a couple of hours in the middle of the day to rest and have lunch, and had no trouble restarting it – but on the edge of Los Gatos, I stopped to phone Sally to check directions to their house. I waited until I thought the engine had cooled enough, but in the end they had to come and get me. We left the van in the supermarket car park overnight.

I was so happy to feel safe and looked after, and although I always loved sleeping in my van, it did feel good to be in a nice, big, comfy bed, and to have my own lovely indoor bathroom. I could shower whenever I wanted, without having to wear thongs or watch for creepy crawlies on the floor.

It was a relief next morning to find the van still where I'd left it. Fortunately there are lots of Volkswagens in California, so I had no trouble locating a good garage and getting the starter motor replaced within a day or two, but at U.S. $300 it took a big chunk out of my budget. In the meantime, I'd encouraged Sally and John to come to a large honky-tonk, which had a live band and a big dance floor. It was *great* to be listening to music again. Sally and I danced while John sat quietly smiling at us – possibly working on complicated equations. He was a physicist and his mind was often elsewhere!

After a few days of pampering and good company, I was ready to go on the road again. This time I drove south towards Fresno in the heart of California's food growing region. Sally and John's son Jonathan and his wife Nancy were on a walnut and cotton plantation, and I had arranged to spend a few days there. On the way I noticed water leaking from somewhere under the sink, and presumed it was from the fresh water tank, which would have been virtually impossible to replace. But Jonathan diagnosed it as a problem with the water pump, which he was able to fix. He was concerned that I was travelling with virtually no tools at all and few comforts, so he insisted on giving me a good screwdriver, a power cord so I could hook up to electricity in campgrounds that provided it, and a tiny electric heater which came in handy later on when I again encountered sub-zero temperatures. The screwdriver also proved useful a few days later, when one of the cupboards in the van started to fall down. I found I had to go over all the built-in furniture every month or so checking and tightening the screws, which tended to become loose after a lot of shaking about on the roads.

Arches N.P., Utah

Sally and John - on the hill behind their house, Los gatos, California

Into the Desert

It was time to move on again. I was eager to get to Death Valley National Park on the California-Nevada border about which I had, rightly or wrongly, some rather romantic images. On the way south through the Mojave Desert I passed by a strange sight – a kind of aeroplane graveyard. There were rows and rows of them discarded and rusty, parked side by side. An almost surrealistic scene. Apparently airlines rent space for craft they no longer use, and often access them later for spare parts or even to fly again. The dry and relatively smog-free desert environment helps to preserve these relics. Then I drove through Trona, with its huge chemical works processing borate for use in a variety of products such as Borax soap, textiles, pesticides, paper, paint, fertiliser, metal alloys, antifreeze, adhesives, plastics etc.

The van, which I was now convinced definitely had a mind of its own, managed to get over the 4,956 ft. Towne Pass and into Death Valley. At more than three million acres, this national park was much larger than I imagined. The road from one end to the other is over 100 miles. It's surrounded by high mountains often covered with snow. I inspected the campground at Stovepipe Wells Village. It wasn't much more than a gravel parking area, so I moved on to Furnace Creek. It was much nicer, but because there was no electricity provided, the noise and fumes of the generators of recreation vehicles dominated. During the day coyotes were 'begging' along the roads, but at night, when everyone else had gone to bed and the generators were turned off, I heard them howling. There seemed to be a family group, with little ones still practising their call and not quite getting it right. Lots of yelping. One night this was mysteriously accompanied by somebody playing 'The Last Post' on a trumpet!

At 280 feet below sea level in one area and with temperatures up to 133°F, Death Valley is the lowest point in the western hemisphere and the hottest place in the United States. Despite the heat the air is usually extraordinarily clear, and the sky blue with only an occasional cloud. I didn't experience any of this because I was there on the only two days it rained all year, and it was unusually cool, almost chilly. Without sunshine, the beautiful colours in the sand and mountains were not as vibrant as the photos I'd seen, but I could still enjoy them. Artists Drive wound through hills resembling an artist's palette with colours of pale milky turquoise, chocolate, lemon, salmon, rust and cream. One large area of the park is called the Devil's Golf Course. It's covered with crystallised salt pillars, which are so sharp and jagged I could barely walk over them without severe damage to my shoes or ankles. I was surprised to discover that despite the harsh environment, over 50 species of mammals, hundreds of birds and reptiles and over 1,000 plants exist there. Some stunted plants on the valley floor have roots which grow down ten times the height of an average person. They are desperately searching for water.

In 1849 a group of pioneers heading for the California goldfields arrived at Salt Lake City. It was far too late in the year for them to attempt to cross the usual route over the Sierra Mountains, so they decided to take a less direct route around the southern end of the Sierras. Some tried to take short cuts and became lost, eventually abandoning their wagons near present day Death Valley and continuing on foot. One person – an elderly man – died there, and as the group left the area one of the women turned and said, *'Goodbye, death valley,'* and apparently that's how it got its name.

Borax was discovered here in the 1880s and mined on and off until the early 1970s. At one stage, it was transported to the railroad using 20-mule teams. They carted enormous loads and the back wheels of the wagons were huge – higher than a person. You can still see the remains of mines and in one area there are abandoned charcoal kilns built by Chinese labourers.

A friendly couple in the campground invited me to go to a square dance held in one of the National Park halls. It was a local club meet and naturally I was just an onlooker, as square dancing is complicated and takes ages to learn. What really surprised me was the way they dressed. They all appeared to be well over 60, many much older, and some very overweight. The women wore fancy ruffled blouses and short full skirts with lots of petticoats and frilly knickers, plus flowers, bows and ribbons in their hair, like overgrown little girls. The men had checked shirts, dark trousers, brightly coloured braces and bow ties. I wished I'd taken my camera. It was lots of fun and they were all excellent dancers. What a great way to keep fit.

Driving further south to Joshua Tree National Park (still in California), I saw lots of large birds racing along the edges of the road. They were road runners and they reminded me of those old cartoons I'd watched as a kid. There are also black-tailed jackrabbits which are a species of hares, named after their especially big ears which reminded people of an ass's ears. Amazingly they can run at speeds of up to 45 mph, with leaps of more than 10 feet. The park itself is marvellous, with desert vegetation unlike anything I'd ever seen before and lots of rocky outcrops with huge boulders. I camped right among them at the appropriately named Jumbo Rocks campground. It was a wonderful setting, but very windy and cold enough to force me inside to eat dinner. I left my wash-up water outside, and next morning it was covered with two inches of ice.

There are two desert regions within the park – the Colorado and the higher and cooler Mojave where the Joshua trees grow. They were named by the Mormons, who thought their limbs resembled the spreading arms of Joshua leading them to the Promised Land. They're mostly found at altitudes of between 2,000 and 6,000 feet and look a bit like big cacti or palms, but are actually a yucca, part of the lily family. They never branch until they bloom and they don't bloom every year. Conditions have to be just right. Some have *never* bloomed and are just straight stalks. Native Americans used their tough leaves to make baskets and sandals, and roasted the seeds to eat. Their age is hard to work out, as they don't have growth rings. One tree in the park is estimated to be around 300 years old.

I also loved the species of cholla cacti, commonly known as 'jumping teddy bears' because they look furry, have little arms and seem to jump at you as you walk past. In fact they are not furry at all, and are covered with terrible spines which at the slightest touch penetrate the flesh and can only be extracted with great difficulty and extreme pain. I kept well clear of them.

Even though it was still windy and cold at the campground, I decided to spend the next couple of days there. It was so beautiful and I needed a rest. I enjoyed sorting out the van, vaguely planning the next part of my trip, writing my diary, reading and sleeping. I didn't move the van all day and snuggled up in bed early with a hot water bottle.

At 4 am I was woken by scratching and gnawing noises coming from behind the dashboard. A little animal appeared to be eating the wiring. I spent ages trying to chase it out with no success at all. I just hoped that it would be gone by morning, as most of these desert creatures are nocturnal and spend the daylight hours in their nests. All was quiet when I got up next day, so I assumed it had left. However the noise – which now sounded as though it was actually *sawing* – started again as soon as I got into bed the next night. It drove me mad. I couldn't sleep, and felt terribly frustrated and worried that it would cause an electrical short or, even worse, a fire behind the dashboard.

I checked at the ranger's office. They told me it would almost certainly be a pack rat (desert wood rat) which were notorious for chewing through wiring and starting fires. Great! What could I do? The answer was very little, except to make as much noise as possible, remove the dashboard cover and shine a torch in, hoping it would be disrupted enough to leave. None of that worked.

I continued my trip, but after three more sleepless nights I felt desperate. A fellow camper, who'd had a similar experience, suggested I buy a trap and glue a peanut to it, *'because,'* he said, *'they absolutely love peanuts'*. The National Parks people couldn't suggest this as all their wildlife is protected. In America it's virtually impossible to buy a small packet of anything, so I ended up shelling and eating my way through a pound of nuts. I carefully glued one to the trap, set it in place and retired to bed. By now the creature was obviously pretty hungry and was getting into the food cupboards. I could hear it rustling around about a foot from my head, but it evidently didn't like peanuts. At 2 am I decided to resort to a more traditional method and got out the cheese. The poor thing really must have been starving because its little head popped up while I was still cutting a slice and, within one minute of resetting the trap and turning out the light, it was caught. What a relief. I leapt up with delight, forgetting where I was and hitting my head on the roof. Actually I *hated* having to kill this pack rat. It was a gorgeous little animal and I felt guilty as I dumped it into the rubbish bin, but I really had little choice. I learnt later that they scramble all over the cholla cactus and often get stuck on those terrible spines. Rather than struggle, they calmly pull out the spines with their sharp little teeth.

I was starting to travel east and crossed the California border into Arizona – still in desert, of course. I decided to bypass Phoenix – 'Valley of the Sun' and a popular retirement destination – and instead spend time in the smaller and reputedly more beautiful Tucson. On the way I found a lovely place to camp in a national forest near a lake, and built a driftwood fire to sit by in the cold evening. I even lit it again in the morning, and had the luxury of (slightly burnt) campfire toast for breakfast. I moved on, intending to stay in Coronado State Park near Tucson, and was really disappointed to discover that their campground was full. While I was standing at the gate trying to decide what to do, somebody left and I got in after all. This was great because I was able to have a hot shower. Although almost on the edge of Tucson, it is a beautiful and fairly wild park and the sites are well separated amongst the trees, so it didn't feel overcrowded. Once again I could hear coyotes howling at night, and next morning there was frost on the ground and ice on the van.

One of the star attractions in the Tucson area is the Arizona-Sonora Desert Museum. It's a zoo, a natural history museum, aquarium and botanical garden. Exhibits recreate the natural environment with lots of desert creatures including mountain lions, bob cats, kit foxes, black bears (plentiful in the mountains around here), prairie dogs, coyotes and a lizard exotically called the Gila Monster. It has 1,300 species of plants indigenous to this area and a marvellous geological exhibit. This includes caves which, I only realised after very close inspection, are actually fabricated. Best of all for me was the fabulous walk-through hummingbird enclosure. It was just buzzing with these tiny birds. Some had bright iridescent feathers in red, blue or green and I really enjoyed watching them hovering at the nectar feeding stations, squabbling together, and zipping past my head.

I had now left behind the Joshua trees and entered the desert of the huge saguaro cactus (*cereus giganteus*). It is the well-known 'picture postcard' cactus with the fluted stem and 'arms,' a real symbol of the American southwest. Unique to the Sonoran Desert, it's the state flower of Arizona. Unlike the Joshua tree, the saguaro flowers every year. When it rains, its outer pulp can expand like an accordion to store water and this can increase its weight by up to a ton. I just loved them and took lots of photos. Sometimes the arms looked more like noses, ears or even more interesting appendages!

That night I went to a nightclub called Wild Wild West. It was huge and advertised as *'one acre of dancin' and romancin'.'* As I wasn't yet confident about my dancing and wasn't particularly interested in romancin', the main attraction for me was the $4 all you can eat buffet dinner and the band, but I did get a few dances. I also discovered some wonderful Mexican food and especially enjoyed enchiladas – soft corn tortillas wrapped around a delicious spicy filling with beans, plenty of cheese, sometimes chicken or beef and covered with sauce – and chimichangas, which are similar but deep fried. Terribly fattening, of course.

The O'odham Tash Indian Pow Wow was held at the small nearby town of Case Grande. First there was a street parade with various Native American groups taking part, some Arizona fiddlers, war veterans, cowboys and plenty of school kids.

The Shriners were also there. I'd never seen them before. Dressed in their burgundy fez style hats with long black tassels, they first rode by in a reasonably dignified manner in a series of vintage cars, then on ordinary motorbikes, then in a succession of really hilarious vehicles. Enormous men were squashed into miniature kid-sized cars. Large bicycles carried five or six large men. The fezzes looked oddly out of place here in Arizona. Each vehicle or contraption was to me funnier than the last. I nearly collapsed with laughter, which I tried desperately to control because I wasn't quite sure if they were *meant* to be funny and whether I might be frowned upon for insulting them. A recent check of their website revealed that The Shrine, previously known as the Ancient Arabic Order of the Nobles of the Mystic Shrine (you can see why they shortened their name), is another of those fraternal and charitable organisations like the Elks which I'd encountered in Oregon earlier in the trip. Shriners specialise in colourful parades, circuses and clowns, and had built twenty-two hospitals which provide free orthopaedic and burn care for children. Like the Elks, they were originally founded in the 19th century, with the aim simply to provide fun and friendship. All members must be Masons and believe in a 'supreme being.' Women related to a Shriner are eligible to join a separate women's group. Headquartered in Florida, they extend to many parts of the world, including Canada, Brazil, Mexico, Europe and even Australia, although I'd never heard of them there.

This Pow Wow was the first I'd seen. The audience was a mix of Native Americans, African Americans, Anglo Americans and Mexican Americans. There were lots of food vendors selling local delicacies such as red beans and chilli. Drummers and singing groups were from as far away as Canada. The performers' costumes were wonderfully intricate with feathers, wool strands (like mops), lots of beading – even on their boots – and some odd touches like a Mickey Mouse decoration or an embroidery of a car. Some men topped these exotic costumes with rather ordinary baseball caps. The Zuni women from New Mexico danced with large earthenware pots balanced on their heads, and the Comanche war dancers looked suitably ferocious with huge feathered head dresses and painted faces and bodies.

After all this activity, my thoughts again turned to the possibility of a nice quiet campground to catch up on some rest, and to have another go at sorting out the van, which took only a few days of neglect to become very messy. Then I noticed Tombstone on the map, and decided I really couldn't miss this famous old silver and gold mining town. It had been a violent and lawless place described as *'too tough to die.'* Apparently it got its name in 1877 when a soldier from nearby Camp Huachuca decided to go prospecting. His companions told him he would probably find his own tombstone rather than silver so he named his first claim Tombstone.

It's a lovely old town – somewhat commercialised of course (this is America after all) – but not nearly as spoilt as I'd imagined, although there were lots of other tourists around. I think most people would have received their impressions of the history of Tombstone from Hollywood movies, and I was no exception. There was still the actual OK Corral where the infamous Wyatt Earp/Ike Clanton gun battle was fought. It only lasted thirty seconds! A re-enactment is held every afternoon. In its heyday in the 1880s, Tombstone had 110 saloons and 14 gambling halls – more than any other town in the country. The gorgeous Bird Cage Theatre remains virtually unchanged since being built in 1881. All the original fixtures and furnishings are still in place. It was known as the bawdiest night spot between Basin Street and the Barbary Coast. What I took to be private boxes for viewing the shows were where the prostitutes had worked. They simply closed the curtains when they had a client. These 'boxes' were suspended from the ceiling and referred to as The Bird Cages.

The local newspaper *The Tombstone Epitaph* was still going strong, continuously published since 1880. Boothill Cemetery, dating from 1879, contains lots of outlaws who had been shot, lynched, knifed, hung, or killed by Indians. It got its name because, in the lawless years when the west was settled, many people died unexpectedly and were often buried in a hurry with their boots on. Some of the epitaphs were intriguing. One said: *'Johnny Blair. Died of smallpox. Cowboy threw rope over feet and dragged him to his grave.'* Another: *'Charley Storms, shot by Luke Short 1881.'* Apparently Storms was rated by Wyatt Earp as one of the deadliest guns in the west, but Short was referred to as the undertaker's friend! I laughed on discovering that one of the main streets is called Toughnut.

A day immersed in Wild West history was enough for me, so after admiring the 'world's largest rosebush,' which covers 8,600 feet, I spent the night at Chiracahua National Monument not far from the Arizona/New Mexico border. It is in the Chiracahua Mountains at elevations of between 5,100 and 7,800 feet and extremely rocky. The campground was particularly attractive and very peaceful with no noisy generators. I saw lots of native animals, including a beautiful ringtailed cat, which is not actually a cat but part of the racoon family – also a fox squirrel, which was a lovely rusty colour like dried pine needles. Two skunks came right up to the open door of my van and there were lots and lots of birds to watch through my binoculars. The whole area is full of canyons and unusual shaped rocks of varying sizes.

Next day I took a hikers' shuttle bus, which dropped me at the 7,000 ft. Masai Point. From there I walked down a scenic trail past a formation called the Totem Pole, which is 137 feet high but only three feet thick at its narrowest point, and Big Balanced Rock, weighing 1,000 tons and resting on a base about four feet thick.

I'd noticed some liquid leaking on to the floor of the van on the passenger side and thought I'd better have it checked out as soon as possible. Also the heater wasn't working, and it was getting chilly. $260 later, the brake master cylinder had been replaced and the mechanic had been able to make some adjustments to the heating system. I continued driving, only to discover after a couple of days that there was *still* a leakage – so took it to another garage in another town, where I was told it was just a screw which had become loose. Maybe the mechanic had a screw loose, because the problem continued. I wasn't too far from Albuquerque, so decided to go back to the mechanic I had discovered there. He diagnosed the leakage as clutch fluid, and suggested it had been a mistake to replace the brake master cylinder. It would not have needed it. So now the clutch master cylinder had to be replaced!

I left Albuquerque another $200 poorer, but feeling more confident to continue driving further east towards Texas. Of course, it often occurred to me on this trip that some mechanics were probably taking advantage of the fact that I was a woman who didn't know a lot about vehicles, but also the fact I was a foreigner just passing through. There wasn't much I could do about that. When mechanical problems arose I simply *had* to have them fixed or end the trip. Being continually on the road meant I could rarely go back to the same garage.

I stayed that night on the edge of a little town called Moriarty. The campground was windswept and completely devoid of trees, and I was the only person there. I felt very exposed and very much alone, until a hungry and skinny half-wild kitten joined me after dinner and wolfed down everything I gave her, including an entire carton of strawberry yoghurt. Then she mooched around looking for affection, meowing pitifully when I locked her outside. Poor thing. I felt really mean and was tempted to take her with me, but she would have been too much of a hindrance on the road – and what on earth would I do with her every six months when I had to leave the country? Anyway, I'm allergic to cat hair. If I were to have any animal with me, I thought it probably ought to be a dog that could at least earn its keep by offering some protection.

20 Mule Wagon, Harmony Borax Works, Death Valley

A Joshua Tree

Camping at Moriaty, New Mexico

Native American dancer

Roswell and Bud's Bar!

The next evening I was still in New Mexico, and decided to spend the night at the small town of Roswell – a typical southern American desert town with a population of around 45,000. I'd heard about it in relation to UFOs as there was a purported crash of one in the desert near here in 1947. I really enjoyed a sampling of everyday American life here.

It's also where I discovered Bud's Bar, which changed my life forever. I'd noticed the neon sign while looking for a place to camp. Even though I was very tired, I couldn't resist checking it out immediately because it advertised live music. It was a small friendly place with a band from Texas. There was a marvellous wooden dance floor, full of couples strutting the Texas two-step or waltzing. Both are partner dances similar to ballroom dancing. The two-step is rather like the fox-trot with two quick steps and two slow, often with the addition of a few twirls and fancy manoeuvres. The dancers looked wonderful, and eventually somebody asked me – a tall, handsome man from Georgia, who was an excellent dancer. Sadly he had to leave for home the very next day. Although I had enjoyed dancing with the cowboy in Albuquerque, I was now definitely on my way to becoming a serious *addict*. I stayed on and on in Roswell, and danced at Bud's Bar every night until I literally had blisters on my blisters, and had to doctor my feet before each evening out.

Apparently they had never had an Australian woman in the bar before, so I was a great novelty. People really went out of their way to please me. By the time I'd walked from the door to the bar, my chosen drink was waiting for me on the counter and one of my newfound dance partners was hovering near the dance floor. The band remembered my favourite songs and launched into them soon after they spotted me. One was 'Lone Star Beer and Bob Wills Music,' written by Glenn Sutton and Red Steagall. I eventually added Steagall's original recording to my van's play-list. I was being spoilt, and loving it.

Most of the men dancing were tall and wore cowboy hats and boots, and many were *real* cowboys from ranches out in the semi-desert areas. They were polite and courteous and always escorted me back to my seat, doffed their hat and thanked me for the dance. And what wonderful dancers – often learning when they were children. Lessons should be obligatory for every male! Line dancing was also all the rage, often danced to 'Boot Scootin' Boogie' by the country duo Brooks & Dunn and written by Ronnie Dunn, or Billy Ray Cyrus's 'Achy Breaky Heart,' written by Don Von Tress. (Both were also eventually added to my van's playlist.) I'd never seen line dancing before, and some of the women persuaded me to have a go. It was fun and had the advantage of not needing a partner, but I really preferred partner dancing – especially the waltz. It was explained to me that during a waltz I should slide my feet across the floor rather than lifting them, imagining that if I had a $100 bill under my foot it should still be there at the end of the dance. I was an enthusiastic and willing learner. My love of music and sense of rhythm helped, but it was to take many months or even years to get it right, and styles tended to differ slightly from town to town, often influenced by local dance teachers.

Dancing was wearing out my boots, so I had them repaired at Mr. Thompson's shop in the main street. He had been in business for 37 years, and it looked as though his shop hadn't changed in that time. Sadly his wife had died a few months earlier and he was selling some of her jewellery very cheaply. I bought a beautiful rhinestone brooch and he seemed happy that it had gone to someone who appreciated it. It brightened up my black outfit. Like most of the people I met here, Mr. Thompson had never seen an Australian before and he complimented me several times on how well I spoke English! Somebody else said, *'Where are you from? With an accent like that you should be reading the news.'* Two days after I arrived, the State Fair arrived too, along with a regular rodeo and the Southern New Mexico Equipment Roadeo, and Bud's Bar became even more exciting. This was when I saw some idiot wearing *spurs* on the dance floor!

In addition to being the only Australian, I was often the only unaccompanied female at Bud's Bar, so I really couldn't lose! Men would sometimes ask to join me at my table or invite me to theirs. I usually refused. This was partly because I didn't want to give anyone the wrong impression of my intentions, and partly because nobody else would ask me to dance if they thought I was already with a man.

I did sometimes accept invitations to eat breakfast at a nearby restaurant in the early hours of the morning after the bar had closed, before going back to the campground to sleep off all that dancing. These early morning breakfasts after a night out are quite a tradition in various parts of America. The most entertaining experience for me was at one of the Waffle House chain of restaurants. It was busy. Four women were serving tables and three chefs cooking in an open kitchen. No orders were written down, but simply yelled by the waitresses to the chefs. There were so many choices and variations. For example, hash browns could be regular, 'double' or 'triple', and served in the following ways – Golden Brown; Large; Scattered on the Grill; Smothered with Onions; Covered with Cheese; Chunked with Ham; Topped with Bert's Chilli; or Diced with fresh Tomatoes. I decided to try the lot, mainly to hear the waitresses yelling, *'One regular golden brown hash brown, large, scattered, smothered, covered, chunked, topped and diced!'*

The Equipment Roadeo is a competition run by the New Mexico Department of Transport between people working with various pieces of heavy equipment. The best equipment operators come to Roswell each year from six regions of New Mexico, to competitively drive garbage trucks, graders, backhoes etc. Many of them spent their evenings at Bud's Bar, and I became their chief dancing partner and a kind of mascot, supporting them by going along to see some of the competition. I quickly discovered that you can only spend so much time watching someone back a truck around cones or dump garbage into a particular spot. These men were mostly Mexican-Americans, decent fellows who had wives and children at home, but who also enjoyed getting away for a while. They took their part in the competition very seriously. Their first language was Spanish, so we sometimes had a hilarious time trying to communicate. Before they left, they presented me with a wonderful large (and heavy) commemorative metal belt buckle with a raised image of a backhoe and the words '*92 Equipment Roadeo.*' It's one of my most treasured souvenirs, made all the more special because it belonged to one of the competitors who generously gave it up for me. I hoped he wouldn't regret this later.

The State Fair in Roswell was heralded by one of those marvellous street parades which Americans are so good at – two hours of marching military cadets, school football cheer squads, bands, vintage cars, floats, beauty queens, fire engines, mounted police, ambulances, scouts, church groups and just about everybody important or not so important in the town. I was delighted and amused to again see the Shriners doing their bit – this time in the form of a bagpipe marching band and wearing fezzes, of course! Later I met a couple of firemen, who invited me to climb the Brigade's new 115 foot extension ladder as a media publicity stunt. Although I hate heights, I immediately agreed because it would be a great adventure, and imagine having the photos to send home! Sadly, they were called out on an emergency and the photo shoot never happened.

I also went to my first traditional rodeo, which was held in an outdoor arena at sunset. It was quite exciting, especially the bull riding, but I worried about the animals. They looked to be in such obvious discomfort when they shot out of the holding stall. I wondered if it was the tight strap they had around their flanks or the annoyance of somebody on their back. One of the riders told me a rodeo bull only works twelve minutes a year and spends most of its time being well looked after. That made me feel a bit better, although I did wonder how they coped with being carted from rodeo to rodeo. Each bull rider only has to last eight seconds and holds on with a flat-braided rope wrapped around one hand. He must keep the other hand in the air. It requires excellent balance, co-ordination and quick reflexes, and most don't seem to be able to stay on for nearly that long. That's where the colourfully dressed rodeo clowns come into their own, as their job is to distract the bull until the fallen rider gets to safety.

Most entertainment in America, including rodeos, starts with the playing of the national anthem, so I did finally see lots of men take off their cowboy hats. The Fair included tributes to Hispanic and Native American cultures, with music and dancing, arts and crafts and food. There was also horse racing and an Alpine Mountain Sports Thrill Show, as well as the usual livestock exhibits and sales, a rodeo queen, cake show and fiddlers contests. I thoroughly enjoyed it all.

Roswell Museum & Art Center, with its fine collection of western paintings, early Native American artefacts and cowboy paraphernalia, was celebrating its 55th birthday with an evening of cowboy folk music, poetry and free traditional western food. This sounded fun so I dressed up in my best outfit, wearing Mrs. Thompson's rhinestone brooch and my smart black Italian hat, and off I went. The hat's always a good conversation starter and when people discovered I was Australian, I was feted as though I had come all that way *especially* for this occasion. One of the town councillors even gave me an official welcome from the stage. The food was hot and spicy with lots of Mexican and Native American influences, and everyone made sure I tasted it all – mini burritos and tacos, guacamole dips, fried cactus etc. The cowboy music and poetry were evocative of the Old West, with references to riding on the range, sagebrush and coyotes. Of course I went off to Bud's Bar afterwards, where people were now telling me that I was turning into a good dancer. This was encouraging. It gave me some confidence, and made it easier to ignore the pain of the blisters.

It was terribly embarrassing when one of my dancing partners turned up at the caravan park early one morning, and sat outside my van serenading me on his guitar! He was a local and invited me to park my van in his driveway, use the facilities in his house and so save the camping fees. I wasn't quite sure exactly what he had in mind, and thought it best to decline. In any case I preferred my independence, and was enjoying the caravan park where I had made friends with neighbours George and Edie Mills. A few years previously, after their children had grown up and left home, they moved south from Ohio in their caravan to escape the harsh winters and had never returned to the north. In America, people who do this are called Snowbirds, and most do go back north for the summer. George and Edie both worked at a local company which manufactured buses. George had a large fancy Harley-Davidson motorcycle and invited me for a ride. Edie lent me her fringed leather jacket with matching gloves and headband, and George drove me out into the desert at great speed – no helmets, and the stereo blasting away. This was fun and I felt as though I was now *really* entering into the spirit of America.

George and Edie were so kind, inviting me to share their meals and generally taking an interest in my wellbeing. This meant a lot because despite all the fun I was having, I was often missing my real friends and family. In George and Edie's large and comfortable caravan, I could enjoy lovely meals, real conversation and homely activities, like watching films on television – a treat when living on the road. I kept in touch with them and was occasionally able to revisit Roswell. Sadly, George became ill with a hereditary disease, so they moved back to the small town they'd left in Ohio to be close to their family. I visited them there several years later just before George died, and again on a later occasion when Edie took me to see his grave. On the headstone was an engraving of him riding his Harley-Davidson, with a space left for an illustration of Edie riding pillion.

Tackling Mexican Food

Dancing & Romancing across Texas

Eventually the blisters and late nights at Bud's Bar wore me down, and I decided to move on before this dancing addiction left permanent damage. I had lost heaps of weight and berated myself for never learning to take things more slowly – but it was worth it. I'd had such fun.

I limped off to Carlsbad Caverns National Park to see about two million bats emerging at dusk on their nightly insect foraging expeditions. They are Brazilian free-tailed bats, and live there April to October before migrating south for the winter. Then I crossed the Texas border, camping in the picturesque Guadalupe Mountains National Park on the edge of the Chihuahuan Desert. The forest is a mix of small oak, conifers, mahogany and cactus, and at 8,751 feet Guadalupe Peak is the highest in Texas.

A throat infection meant spending most of the next two days in bed. I was paying for my Roswell excesses and felt miserable, but I'd made it to Texas. This had always been one of my main goals, although I really didn't have a specific plan or itinerary for any of the trip, except to take things as they came. I had been playing a George Strait cassette and really loved his version of 'Amarillo by Morning' (by Terry Stafford & Paul Fraser), so I did put that town on my visiting list.

One evening I was sitting quietly by my van, when a mother skunk wandered past leading her three babies. Skunks often come around campsites looking for food. It's important not to frighten them, as the powerful and awful effects of their spray can't be removed from clothes, however many times you wash them. I think you just have to throw them out. I don't know what people do when their dogs get sprayed, although some say tomato juice helps. I was once staying in a house in San Francisco when skunks sprayed in the basement. The pungent aroma was so overwhelming it was almost impossible to sleep three floors above, despite open windows. A dead skunk on the road can be smelt for a mile or so downwind. The way to deal with them in a campground is to either ignore them – they'll move on when they are ready – or gently shepherd them away, keeping your distance and using only the beam of a torch.

Apart from Alaska, Texas is the largest of the states, although certainly not bigger than Australia, as one local tried to insist. (Australia is eleven times larger.) After arguing with him, I discovered he'd *never* even been outside Texas, let alone to the southern hemisphere. Anyway, it *is* large – approximately 850 miles long, and a similar width. I drove miles across the desert plains. At times there was so little to see that the glimpse of a rusty windmill was notable, and I was almost *excited* when I spotted a train moving in the distance. There were also plenty of oil wells pumping away, and some almost deserted and very run-down dusty little settlements. As well as the state being big, there's a certain amount of bragging about everything else being big. Honky-tonks boast the largest dance floors and, at 100,000 square feet, Billy Bob's Texas in Fort Worth is said to be the largest saloon in the country, and probably the world. I made a mental note to visit it as soon as I got to Fort Worth.

People in Texas drive large pickup trucks. Even the men seemed taller than everywhere else – and what large hats and long boots! I stopped at a restaurant proudly boasting *'Texas-sized donuts: Best West of the Pecos.'* Disappointingly, they didn't seem any larger than normal. Greed is encouraged, so no wonder there is so much obesity in America. (Australia is fast catching up.) I spotted a restaurant billboard alongside a Texas freeway stating: *'Free 72 oz. steak if eaten within twenty minutes.'* In a fast food restaurant window, a sign read, *'Big Meal Deal! Big Bite Hot Dog! Big Grab of Chips!'* Big. Big. Big.

There really is a certain 'redneck' attitude in Texas, and I often found the drivers to be faster and more reckless than the states I had driven in so far. One day when I was travelling right on the speed limit of 70 mph,

I was surprised to be easily overtaken by a large, powerful motorcycle, with the driver casually leaning on his backrest, both arms folded across his chest! The legal age for drivers in the U.S. varies from state to state, and for a learners permit it ranges from 14 to 16. The minimum age for driving licenses can start at 16, for example, in Alaska, Arizona or Texas. Seems very young to me, but sometimes there are restrictions, such as daylight hours only. Many young people have cars, and drive to their secondary schools. Despite this – or maybe because of this – I thought the U.S. drivers were generally much better than in Australia and many other countries – more polite, too. For example, if I found I was in the wrong lane and needed to move over quickly to reach an exit, other drivers always slowed down or moved over to let me go. They also often politely stop for pedestrians on the smaller roads, even when there isn't a crossing.

The town of Pecos in West Texas reeks of Wild West tales. In the late 19th century, anything west of Pecos was considered the *real* Wild West. The very first rodeo was held here on 4th July, 1883, when cowboys from three of the largest ranches – Hashknife, W. Lazy Y and NA – competed to see who was best at saddle-bronc riding, calf roping and steer riding. One thousand people watched and it became an annual event, but wasn't called a rodeo until 40 years later. It's still held there at the same time every year.

The old Orient Hotel & Saloon is now the West of Pecos Museum. The Saloon lived up to my Hollywood-influenced expectations of the Wild West. There was a double killing there in 1896. Plaques on the floor mark the places where the victims fell and you can still see bullet holes in the walls. There's an elegant wooden staircase leading to the first floor, and I could imagine beautiful women, dressed in gaudy low cut 19th century gowns, sweeping down it to relieve the cowboys of some of their hard-earned cash, whilst somebody played honky-tonk music on a battered piano. I learnt later that despite the popular conception that these bars all had pianos, they were much more likely to have a fellow playing a banjo (guitars weren't popular in the U.S. then). Pianos cost a fortune to transport to these remote settlements, and if they *did* manage to get one there, it would be virtually impossible to find anyone to tune it.

I discovered public telephones and post boxes which could be used without getting out of your vehicle (very handy, especially in wet weather), plus drive-in banks, drive-in restaurants where you are served while sitting in your car, and even a drive-in church. I liked that idea. You could sleep through the sermon with nobody noticing! I also saw some amusing signs along the highways. One, on an approach to a small town, said, *'Slow down and see our dam. Speed up and see our damn Judge.'* Another – *'Enjoy showing off your scar'* – was advertising a local vasectomy centre; and a third, *'Play with your Food,'* was for a theatre restaurant. Another had a large red heart with the words *'Jesus Sets Captives Free.'* This was an advertisement by a company offering bail bonds.

My adventure was becoming great fun, and I *loved* the idea of never knowing where I was going to be staying from one night to the next. I still had months left of this trip, so could afford to take my time and indulge in unexpected diversions. People often asked how long I was staying in their town and were surprised when I said I didn't know. They were even more taken aback to discover I often didn't even know where I was going next.

I tried to avoid the town RV or caravan parks as they were often depressing, treeless gravel yards, sometimes with a few broken down trailers and semi-permanent occupants. Even though they were usually more expensive, I much preferred the campgrounds run by State or National Parks, National Forest or the U.S. Army Corps of Engineers (the Federal Government agency responsible, amongst other things, for the nation's water supply). These are usually in beautiful forested settings on the shores of a lake, or some other interesting geographical, geological or historic feature. I loved the fact that individual sites were generally well separated from each other, and out of season I was often the only person camping in the whole area. Security was mostly excellent with armed park police regularly patrolling, and sometimes a gate which is locked at dark, with registered campers given the combination number. This not only kept undesirables out, but meant that I could go out to a club and get safely back into the park in the early morning hours. There are sometimes camp hosts – usually retired couples – who are given a free site for the whole season in return for looking after the area and the visitors. The larger campgrounds with hundreds of sites often have several hosts located in different sections.

You see some strange things in campgrounds. Once a man checked into the site next to me, set up a huge tent, took a chair, table and TV from his car into the tent, plugged in the TV, put it on the table, sat in the chair and watched it for three hours. After this he packed everything up including the tent and left. Perhaps he wasn't allowed to watch his favourite programme at home. Maybe his electricity was disconnected. But why the tent? The weather was perfect, no rain expected. Lots of campers in America seem to consider a campfire necessary. They often light enormous ones even in very hot and humid weather, which means they have to sit so far away from it they can barely converse with each other – a waste of wood, too.

There were plenty of dance venues in Texas. In one, I met Eddy. We got on well and enjoyed dancing together. In fact, I really *loved* dancing with him, especially the waltz, and met him several nights in a row. One of our favourite songs to dance to was 'Waltz Across Texas.' I found a used cassette with the original Ernest Tubb version (written by his nephew Quanah Talmadge Tubb), and played it regularly while driving. I still love it – it's rather romantic.

I finally moved on to the next city and to another honky-tonk, only to find him there waiting for me! He had decided to follow me and calculated that I'd end up in this particular club. Although I was pleased to see him and spend the evening dancing, I realised that he had misinterpreted my enthusiasm. This was awkward, especially as he had presented me with a most beautiful red suede jacket. I hadn't meant to lead him on and had to explain that I valued him as a friend and dancing partner, but wanted nothing more. I felt rather ashamed and vowed to be more careful in future.

Hunting is a popular past time in America, and is often allowed in parks. In Texas I heard about the Big Game Awards, run by Texas Parks & Wildlife Department and Texas Wildlife Association. Its stated aims include *'a need for management of both habitat and associated wildlife populations'* and the *'importance of hunting as a population management tool, and to encourage participation by young and new hunters.'* Animals can only be legally hunted in specific areas and in hunting season. Once when quietly walking along a trail, I unexpectedly came face to face with a hunter, rifle aimed directly at me. This made me very aware of the importance of knowing when and where hunting was allowed, so I could be sure to avoid these areas. I also didn't much enjoy seeing hunters bringing in their kill, sometimes hanging and skinning it in the campground.

I zigzagged right across Texas from the west, heading towards San Antonio. I was nervous about sleeping in highway rest areas, but near Abilene (of which I saw absolutely nothing, except the inside of the Cactus Moon honky-tonk), I found one which was so packed with people sleeping in their cars, trucks or campers that I decided it would be OK for me to stay, too. Nasty incidents do sometimes occur in deserted or semi-deserted rest areas, which are often not staffed over the 24 hour period. I was once diverted from stopping at one because there had been a shooting earlier that day, and the whole area was cordoned off by the police. I didn't experience any difficulties myself, but would only stop – even for a brief time during the day – if plenty of other people were there. I was always wary.

Near Abilene I was surprised to see a sign for the Annual Texas Rattlesnake Roundup, which is held at the town of Sweetwater every March. Apparently it is usual to catch at least *six tons* of snakes. This shocked me as I imagined these beautiful creatures would be protected. I didn't go, but learnt a little about the event which is operated by the Sweetwater Junior Chamber of Commerce. It draws thousands of people and brings in lots of money. The poor snakes are put into a large pit for people to see. Then some milking takes place, followed by measuring, and finally they are all killed and skinned and the meat prepared for cooking or sale. The event includes a downtown parade, 'Miss Snake-charmer Pageant', 'Rattlesnake Dance Artistes' and a rattlesnake meat eating contest! In Albuquerque I had gone to the American International Rattlesnake Museum and afterwards received their Certificate of Bravery *'for showing little or no hesitation and willfully entering into the previously frightening and now truly fascinating world of the rattlesnake ...'* I have the T-shirt as well!

Although it was mid-October when I finally arrived in San Antonio, it was still oppressively hot and humid, and the slightest exertion left me drenched with perspiration. I found it exhausting and nerve-wracking negotiating the city freeway system, and was relieved to *finally* find a good private campground in a central position, with the luxury of a pool and lots of trees and grass. A bus from the gate went straight into town. I spent the cooler mornings exploring the beautiful old Spanish missions (four built in the 18th century) and the Alamo (site of the famous battle for Texas independence, fought by James Bowie and Davy Crockett and others). I then spent my afternoons in the pool or writing my diary, and evenings in town listening to live music.

I tried in vain to find a good place to go dancing. The honky-tonks seemed to cater to elderly couples or young people on the prowl. I didn't fit into either of these categories. I just wanted to dance. I wasn't at all fussy about partners, as long as they were reasonably sober, relatively clean and could dance!

I wasted half a tank of precious fuel in this pursuit, and eventually gave up and went instead to hear some excellent traditional jazz at a club called The Landing. It was on the Riverwalk, a landscaped walk in downtown San Antonio with lush vegetation and little arched stone bridges, which reminded me of Venice. There was a variety of restaurants, night clubs, galleries and shops. The Jim Cullum Jazz Band had a nightly residency at The Landing. They'd been to Australia a year or two earlier and loved it, so welcomed me as a special guest and played two Australian songs in my honour. Being celebrated *simply* because I was Australian was still a fascinating experience for me. I was asked to stand and was clapped by everyone in the crowded bar. Various people wanted to buy me drinks. As I could still usually afford only one proper meal a day – home cooked, not bought – and one drink when I went out, these kind offers were very much appreciated.

San Antonio is a very popular conference city. One evening at The Landing jazz club I met a charming couple from California who were there for the National Conference of Bankruptcy Judges. They invited me to one of the conference's official receptions – a desserts party hosted by Price Waterhouse. So there I was eating delicious desserts and hobnobbing with thousands of judges. (There were 3,500 at the conference). At the next evening's jazz night I met a man attending the National Conference of Funeral Directors. He was friendly enough, but rather dull and very sober in manner – the stereotype of a funeral director, I supposed. Sadly he didn't invite me to any social functions (I was pondering what they might do at conferences), and was mildly insulted when I asked, with the environment in mind, whether wooden coffins were ever recycled.

I left San Antonio travelling north to Austin, the capital of Texas, hoping to hear some of the music for which it is so well known. I'd been listening to one of my favourite tunes – 'Boogie Back to Texas' by the Austin-based western swing band Asleep at the Wheel – and felt inspired. Western swing is a style of country music with jazz influences. It is great for dancing and originally created by Texas musician Milton Brown, but made famous by Bob Wills and His Texas Playboys in the 1930s. I really loved it.

An amazing coincidence happened on the way to Austin. I was approaching the outskirts of the city and thought I'd turn the radio on to a local station. The first voice I heard was my brother, John Hull, who lived in England and had recently published *Touching the Rock*, a book about coping with losing his sight in midlife. He was being interviewed on American public radio at that very moment. I could hardly believe my ears, and pulled off the road to sit and listen. What an extraordinary coincidence – and it reminded me of how much I missed him and the rest of my family.

Austin's Sixth Street is famous for its music bars, so that's where I headed. There was some good music and plenty of people around. One of my first stops was Joe's Generic Bar, where I noticed a sign on the wall behind the bar: *'Try our delicious sandwiches. Nobody likes a coward!'* Many of the revellers were from out of town and determined to enjoy themselves, so the atmosphere was extremely lively. I was asked to dance a few times, but on this occasion I declined. The music was usually blues and mostly good, but many of the men in the audience appeared to be in an advanced state of inebriation. I'd had my share of being dragged around a dance floor by a drunk, and wasn't prepared to go through it again.

I'd often thought I could get away with sleeping in the van just about anywhere, because if I was discreet nobody would really *know* I was inside. If it was late at night, I could just pull up and hop straight into bed without showing myself at all. My funds were especially low now because the tenant in my house in Australia had walked out owing several weeks rent, so I decided this would be a good time to try it out.

I found a quiet suburban street not far from the university, but didn't have a very peaceful night. I was worried that somebody might break into the van expecting it to be empty, even though a local policeman had told me that potential car thieves would always knock first! (Could this be true?) So I was very aware of other vehicles passing or stopping nearby, and kept peeping through the curtains to see who might be lurking outside. Nobody ever was, but after that I thought it would be better to put up with having to pay to camp. At least I'd get a good night's sleep and not put myself at any unnecessary risk.

The annual Great Taste of Austin Festival was in full swing on the banks of the Colorado River, so next day I went to hear more music and taste some local food, and met a rather gorgeous African American man called Richard. We arranged to meet again and he took me dancing (oh bliss!), then we heard more music at the festival and went for long walks along the river. We had a lot in common and I enjoyed his company – especially being with somebody who shared my interest in music. He was originally from Austin, but had lived for many years in a remote area of Hawaii, recently returning to the city. He had a small apartment not far from where the festival was held, and a few days later invited me to stay there. It had a rear garden, with a parking area where I was able to sleep in my van.

Richard was having problems settling down to city life, and I was surprised to see a tent set up in his living room. Apparently he used to sit in it and imagine he was elsewhere. His family owned a property about twenty miles from Austin, with a house where his brother and sister-in-law lived. It was just a few acres of uninspiring mesquite scrub, and Richard was renovating a dilapidated barn for a home for himself. He decided to move there while I was visiting. As our friendship was blossoming into something more, I was invited along too. It was a peaceful place and he cooked us delicious dinners, which we ate out in the open. One particularly memorable one was a southwestern American dish called nacho soup, with black beans, onions, green peppers, lots of cheese and sour cream, and served with tortilla chips on the side. Yum!

The weather was warm and humid when I arrived there, but suddenly changed and became much colder. There was even some sleet. During the day I helped with the renovations. Richard found an old bath which had been used to water livestock. He cleaned it out and set it up on blocks, lighting a fire underneath to heat the water. It was great lying in this under the stars, just as long as I kept away from the area directly above the fire!

Richard claimed to be a hairdresser, but he gave me the worse haircut I've ever had. Thank goodness I had a selection of hats to cover up the mess. One thing he did really well was tie-dye clothing, which he sold at markets. Some of his work was lovely.

Although we did get on well, I sensed that he really preferred to be mostly alone. Also, I felt that for various reasons there could be no future with him, so I said goodbye and dragged myself away from this delightful interlude. Sadly I never saw or heard from him again. Travel always involves lots of meetings but also lots of goodbyes, and I felt a bit depressed.

I didn't have much time to dwell on that because before I could drive any further, I had to find a vehicle repair shop. I'd suddenly noticed an ominous rattle around the van's rear wheels. Just as well I did, as apparently the disk brakes were just about falling off. While waiting for this latest repair, I called my friend Barb in Australia to check on my finances, telling her I was in Austin, Texas. She misheard and exclaimed, *'What? Lost in Texas?'* My time with Richard *had* felt a bit like that.

Taking the back roads on the way north to Fort Worth, the van had a flat tyre and despite vigorous efforts I couldn't loosen the nuts to remove the wheel. After an hour or so of fruitlessly trying to look as appealing as possible, and hopelessly in need on the roadside, I sought help from a nearby farmhouse. A burly and cross red-faced man reluctantly agreed to help, but only after I offered him $10. Eventually it was all fixed and I was ready to leave.

It was then that I discovered I'd been standing on a nest of fire ants. These creatures have been steadily migrating north from Central America and live up to their name. They had migrated in their hundreds inside the legs of my trousers and co-ordinated their attack. Thank goodness the farmer had left, because I just whipped my trousers off without a second thought in a desperate effort to remove these invaders. Apparently they always sting in unison – well, actually one stings first, and when the victim flinches, the others sting in response. They sting with their tail and usually seven or eight times in either a circular pattern or a line. It feels like that part of the body is on fire – hence their name. I developed a terrible reaction to their bites, suffering for weeks afterwards, and finding little caches of them in the cabin of the van where I'd thrown my trousers.

Texas Bluebonnets

Fort Worth

Fort Worth is interesting. There is a lot of music and it's high on cowboy culture. It was one of the main settlements on the Chisholm Trail, along which longhorn cattle were driven from the southern Texas grasslands to the railhead at Abilene in Kansas. It was named after Jesse Chisholm, who had a Scottish father and a Cherokee mother, and was an ancestor of the actor/writer Will Rogers. He established a trading post near present day Wichita in Kansas, and blazed the trail south to Mexico through the Indian Territory which is now Oklahoma. Luckily I was there during The Chisholm Trail Roundup – a three day festival celebrating this history. It was good fun with armadillo races, Handsome Ham-Hocker's Hustle (pig races), a parade (of course), BBQ cook-off, cowboy poetry, gunfighters, lots of live music including a fiddlers contest, professional rodeo and chuck wagon races. Best of all for me was the Chief Quanah Parker Comanche Pow-Wow, which included two very special and colourful dance groups – the Apache Fire Dancers and the Comanche Tu-Whee Dancers. Warriors wearing huge feathered head dresses and exotically painted faces performed a scalp dance. It looked incongruous to see one listening to rap music through his headphones in between dances, and another chatting on his mobile phone.

At the little Stockyards Museum I met Winston, an elderly volunteer who was born right opposite the stockyards when they were in full swing. Sadly his old family home had been knocked down for a fast food restaurant. He gave me an impromptu guided tour and told me some of the area's history. Without the railway line, Fort Worth wouldn't have existed. When it was being built in 1873, money ran out 26 miles away at Dallas. Locals finished building the line themselves. Everybody who could swing a pick or drive a mule rallied because it had to be completed in a hurry before the Land Grant expired in 1876. The restored 1896 steam train, 'The Tarantula,' still does short trips from here.

Although no longer in use for auctions, some of the old stockyards area has been preserved with its wooden pens and overhead ramps. There's even a brick-lined tunnel which was for hogs, sheep and goats to pass under the road. Winston told me that more than 160 million head of livestock were sold from here, and during the First World War 40,000 animals were processed *daily*, then shipped off to Europe to help feed the troops. A few longhorn cattle are kept now just for the atmosphere. Part of the area has been turned into restaurants and shops, selling saddles and ropes and other western gear and souvenirs. I was lucky to be at one of the very last cattle auctions. I couldn't understand a word but it was fun watching the action. I learnt that cattle are sold by weight. At that time, from what I could make out, it was about 75 cents a pound.

The stockyards area also regularly hosts re-enactments of western shootouts and I was 'held up' by a couple of colourful men in full cowboy costumes, carrying guns which I presumed weren't loaded – but you never know in Texas! I was eating an ice cream and they insisted I hand it over.

One of the area's star attractions is the historic old Cowtown Coliseum built in 1908, and home to the world's first indoor rodeo. I went there one evening to see Pawnee Bill's Wild West Show – an authentic revival of the 1909 show. Pawnee Bill was a partner to Buffalo Bill and the show included some fancy trick riders and ropers. Roper J.W. Stoker had trained his beautiful white horse, Hot Diggity, to spin the rope with its mouth. A bull-whip cracker used his whip to cut a straw into four pieces, which a woman held in her teeth. A six-shooter shot balloons from around another woman who was on a revolving wheel. (On writing this, I ponder about why the targets are usually women!) There was a mock stagecoach hold-up using an original stagecoach, a little herd of buffalo and some longhorn cattle, and wonderful Indian ceremonial dancers with Quanah Parker, the last chief of the Comanche nation represented. Timmy Brooks took the part of Bill Pickett, the black cowboy accredited with originating the rodeo sport of bulldogging (steer wrestling). Apparently he used to bite the sensitive lip or nose of the steer to help bring it down. I didn't particularly enjoy watching this happen. It made me squirm.

The longer I stayed in the U.S., the more I realised the importance of religion – Christianity really – in many people's lives. Turning on the television in Fort Worth at eight one Sunday morning, I was surprised to discover that of the thirteen channels available, eight featured religious programmes, mainly television evangelists. I also came across an organisation called Cowboys for Christ. They published *The Christian Ranchman* with the banner *'We're not trying to build an organization. We're trying to fill the Kingdom of God.'* Part of their statement of position said, *'Supreme authority over this organisation and all its activities is vested in God's own Son, the Lord Jesus Christ, and exercised by the Holy Spirit. This must be recognized and practiced as laid out for us in God's divinely inspired Word, the Holy Bible.'* Their publication included testimonies by cowboys, information on theological conferences and Christian radio, plus ads suggesting members give donations: *'If the Lord is dealing with you about helping with financial support, please be obedient to the spirit.'*

I saw advertisements in various parts of the U.S. for a 'God and Country' concert, 'Christian's Independence Day in the Park,' a '30 Day Tent Revival' with preaching, singing, worshipping and healings, and lots of gospel singing conventions. Another Christian publication was *The Dallas/ Fort Worth Heritage*, with political commentaries and news. A notice for a National Day of Prayer read, *'It's time we tapped into our most powerful natural resource. A single drop (to our knees) can change the world.'* Also ads for Christian hospitals, schools, conferences, Bibles – 'The Red Letter Study Bible in which all words of God and words of Jesus are printed in red' – and business opportunities. One I especially noted was advertising hair and skin products with a gospel message printed on each. An article calling for 'Christian Capitalists' was about a publisher of Christian books and music offering *'a unique ministry with financial reward …'*

On a similar note, I was surprised to receive a letter from a chiropractor I'd only visited *once*. It was on Season's Greetings letterhead: *'This time of year makes us remember God's blessings in our lives. You've been a blessing to me in that you've allowed me to participate in your healthcare during the last year.'* All of this was interesting for me, coming as I did from a rather secular country and, of course, from a religious background.

There may well be similar publications and attitudes in Australia but I had never seen any, and of all the people I know today only *one* goes to church. I stopped attending when I left home. Until then, it was church twice on Sunday, with Sunday school in-between and no possibility of going to any other Sunday event which wasn't connected – cinema, concerts etc.

Despite this, I realised when I was in America that I really have a fascination with religion, especially Christianity in its various forms. As a young child I had disappointed my parents by refusing to become a member of our church or to take communion. Dad occasionally preached 'revival' sermons, asking people to *'give themselves to Christ.'* He would sometimes tell me that he would be especially praying for *me*. I spent the hour or so counting the bricks in the church walls so I didn't have to listen. I also became rather good at fainting and dropping from the pew to the floor! I think that part of this was acute self consciousness at being the minister's daughter and all the expectations that this brought.

My ever hopeful parents even took me to a Billy Graham crusade and, although I found him impressive, I just felt it wasn't right for me. Also, I saw a certain amount of hypocrisy in some of those churches. Our religious upbringing was strict and very narrow – no alternatives were considered. Now I was discovering for the first time that not all Christians or churches are the same, and that my parents' way of practising Christianity was only one of many. I was becoming more open minded.

It was great visiting Fort Worth's old and not-so-old bars and saloons. The posh Stockyards Hotel bar called Booger Red's Saloon (1913) had leather saddles for bar stools and an original belt-driven ceiling fan. At the Longhorn Saloon there was a country band, a wooden dance floor and plenty of dancing partners. The White Elephant Saloon, one of the oldest bars in the area, had a huge collection of elephant ornaments from all over the world. Filthy McNasty's Saloon (yes that really is its name) had live music and 'famous margaritas.' At a pleasant little pub called The Watering Hole, the owner provided all patrons with a free thanksgiving dinner of smoked turkey with cranberry and bread sauce. As I was Australian, I was also given a couple of free drinks.

And of course there's 'The World's Largest Honky-Tonk,' the 100,000 square foot Billy Bob's Texas, housed in what was originally an open air complex of cattle pens for holding prize animals for the Fort Worth Stock Show. During the war it was used as an aeroplane factory, and after that a department store so large that staff used roller skates to get around. It now has an interesting rustic interior – with a 'Texas-size' dance floor, more than 30 liquor outlets, plus restaurants, pinball machines, pool tables and tourist shops. The whole venue holds over 6,000 people. Country singer Merle Haggard once made the Guinness Book of Records here for buying the largest round of drinks – 5,095 whiskeys for the whole club (40 gallons!) Live indoor bull riding is held every weekend in an old auction ring, and there's a mechanical bull for those who want to get an idea of what it would be like to ride the real thing. Although fascinating to see, I found it a bit too touristy and not very friendly. Nobody *ever* asked me to dance there.

After discovering I was Australian, people in some of the other bars in the area often presented me with a yellow rose. (Think 'The Yellow Rose of Texas,' made popular in the 1950s by singer Mitch Miller – although the state flower is actually a bluebonnet!) I eventually had a row of them in the van, and the flower seller tended to hover near me, hoping for a sale. At one honky-tonk I was given a special T-shirt and a little shot glass shaped like a cowboy boot. I still use it to measure out my gin and tonic. I was also inadvertently collecting soft toys because lots of bars had those 25 cent machines where people try to pick up a prize by manipulating a kind of grabbing device. Many of the men liked to show off their skills at this game and sometimes presented me with the results. I now had four rabbits, a pig and two bears, and the van was getting a bit crowded. Eventually every little nook and cranny of that vehicle was stuffed with my possessions, including what had become an extensive collection of (mostly secondhand) clothes, with something suitable for practically every occasion.

My dancing repertoire was also expanding and now included the Texas two-step, three-step and waltz. I even had a go at various swing dances. Unfortunately, steps and styles for all of these still varied widely from club to club. The line dancing was fascinating, especially at Billy Bob's where it was the fashion to dress up and show off. The young men were particularly athletic, often dropping to the floor in the middle of the dance. I enjoyed watching them. The women generally seemed to be out there to let the men size them up. There was a lot of bottom wiggling in tight jeans. When the band took a break, troops of little kids entertained us with synchronised clogging. All the girls seemed to be dressed up to look like Shirley Temple.

Most of these night clubs or honky-tonks had wooden dance floors and occasionally they were of a 'racetrack' design – an oval dance floor with a bar set in the middle. Sometimes there was a live band, but mostly a DJ played country music. He would announce the type of dance; e.g. waltz, two-step, line dance etc. There was a strict protocol about when, where and what you were allowed to do. No cigarettes or drinks were permitted on the dance floor. For obvious reasons, everyone must dance in the same direction – usually clockwise. Line dancers were banned in some clubs and only permitted in others when invited by the DJ, and swing or jitterbug confined to a certain area – normally the centre or a corner – so the flow of dancers moving around the floor wouldn't be interrupted. The floor was usually spread lightly with a powder which helped feet to glide over the wooden boards. There were often little heaps of this in the corners, so dancers could dip their shoes into it. You had to be careful because too much could be very slippery and cause embarrassingly spectacular falls. Walls were often covered with enormous video screens, showing films of rodeos, and just about everyone in the bar wore western clothing. Sometimes couples would dress in identical outfits with matching hats, boots, shirts and trousers. There was a fairly sexist atmosphere, with tight jeans contests for women, men riding the mechanical bull and lots of ladies nights with free drinks for women. One feature of most of these venues was the neon signs, both inside and outside of the building, and sometimes, as in the case of Billy Bob's, in the shape of the State of Texas – 'The Lone Star State', so named to signify its former status as an independent republic, and as a reminder of the state's struggle for independence from Mexico.

I found a marvellous book called *Honky-Tonks: Guide to Country Dancin' and Romancin*. It was written by Eileen Sisk and gave addresses of the clubs in each state, the size of the dance floor and whether it was wooden or not, the kind of music played, average age of patrons, and if the club was of the 'new breed' or more traditional. She also gave useful hints, particularly to women. For example, never accept a slow dance with someone you don't know. I ignored this advice a few times! She also poses the question, *'How many times can you dance with someone before they think they* own *you?'* The answer was twice! The book states that, *'Texas is unarguably the honky-tonk capital of the world,'* and I certainly agreed with that.

Despite studying up on dance hall protocol, I sometimes found myself sitting out most of the dances and wondered why. Plucking up the courage to ask men to dance occasionally proved successful but they often refused, and I discovered that before I asked it was wise to make absolutely sure a prospective partner was there alone and not with his wife or girlfriend. One day I was asked if I was a school teacher and I realised that, although I always dressed up as well as I could, I looked different. I wasn't from *'round there'*. People were either shy of me or thought I wouldn't be able to dance. The solution was to fit in by buying some Texan clothes – my 'dance uniform.' New western clothing was quite expensive, so I went off to a secondhand charity shop and found some marvellous stuff – tight jeans ($4), little leather boots ($3), and a western shirt ($2) which had a striking design on the back to be seen while dancing. I wondered if the jeans were too tight, especially for a woman no longer in the bloom of youth. I had to lie flat on my back to force the zipper closed. But the shop assistant said, *'Hell no. You're in Texas.'* Anyway, this outfit made all the difference and I started getting loads more invitations to dance. I gradually acquired a whole wardrobe of western gear (including that gorgeous red suede jacket Eddy had given me) and enjoyed dressing up, although I didn't go to the lengths of a cowboy hat. This clothing was particularly useful when, later on in my travels, after I began my radio show, I was invited to act as compere at some of the Bluegrass music festivals. I already had my 'stage uniform.'

As well as noticing that older and often larger women had absolutely no qualms about stuffing themselves into tight jeans, I discovered a particularly active industry cashing in on women's insecurities about ageing and looks. In addition to the usual range of foam-filled bras and tight girdles, you could buy what I referred to as 'strap-on bottoms,' which are actually knickers or girdles padded out to give you the appearance of rounded firm buttocks. Then there is a device which is hidden under your hair (or wig!) with little pincers which pull up the skin from each side of your face, ironing out some of the wrinkles and droops. These might help a women attract a man initially, but what would happen when they got home and she removed all those extras? Maybe it was just to help to get more dance invitations.

Not far from the Fort Worth Stockyards I found the Stagecoach Ballroom, which had live bands several nights a week and free dance lessons on Sunday afternoons. It was a good place for me as it attracted an older crowd, who mainly came to dance, and there were lots of men on their own. One night I was persuaded to try my hand at pool and shocked everyone by easily beating my opponents, despite never having played before. Luck never to be repeated!

I called back into the Stockyards Museum several times to see Winston, the volunteer I'd met a few days earlier. He invited me to his home for lunch and to meet his wife Mary – a lovely couple who I kept in touch with for a long time. I still wear a beautiful wooden pendant that he specially carved for me.

He also introduced me to another older man, Bill, who invited me to base myself at his home, and so I always had a place to stay whenever I was in Fort Worth. Bill lived alone and appreciated the company. He was a *very* keen dancer. In fact, some years later he died the way I think he would have wanted, by dropping dead of a heart attack on a dance floor! He loved cooking up marvellous Tex-Mex breakfasts. These consisted of fried eggs and potatoes with a hot avocado/ chilli sauce, re-fried beans, bacon, and 'armadillo eggs,' a kind of deep fried batter filled with jalapeno peppers stuffed with cheese – also called poppers. Sometimes waffles with butter and maple syrup were added. Thank goodness I was doing all that dancing or I definitely would have grown out of the new jeans in a big hurry.

Bill enjoyed introducing me to his friends and, as usual, none of them had ever met an Australian before. I often thought they were a bit paranoid about my safety. Once Bill said, *'She's from Australia and has spent nearly twelve months driving around and living in her van.' 'Well,'* they said, *'she couldn't do that in this country. She'd be murdered.'*

I quickly learnt to avoid any talk about politics, as my views were often vastly different from most people I met in America, particularly in the south. If somebody asked me what I thought about their president or about a particular political view, I learnt to say something like, *'Oh, I never comment on other countries' politics.'* Many people assumed Australia would be 'behind the times' compared with the U.S., and were surprised to see pictures of our cities with tall buildings! Very few that I met had travelled to other countries, even Canada, so had no firsthand experience of another culture. The media doesn't help much. I found it quite difficult to learn what was going on in the rest of the world. In some areas it was impossible to find a copy of a decent newspaper, like the *New York Times* or *Chicago Tribune*. Television news was generally quite local. I was once told by a friend in New York, *'Well of course the news is mostly American. This is where it all happens.'*

One night Bill and his friend Betty invited me on a 'healthy' walk. We drove 20 minutes through peak hour traffic to an oval with a paved running track, crowded with people walking and jogging, right next to a huge busy freeway with all its pollution. On the way home we stopped for enormous ice creams. The whole episode was interesting but didn't seem very healthy to me. I realised that, unlike Melbourne where I lived, most people in America don't walk around their own suburbs. This is partly because there are usually no footpaths, partly because people are more worried about crime and personal safety, and maybe also because they are used to relying on the convenience of a car and are a bit lazy. I noticed that people will often get into their car to travel 50 yards from one store to the next. In some areas, the sight of somebody walking on the street, even during the daytime, is so unusual that when I did it, people in cars would often stop to ask if I was OK, thinking that perhaps my vehicle had broken down somewhere.

Bill was a great collector of things – almost anything really, as *'you never know when you might need it.'* His house, shed and large garden were packed with all manner of things, including seven vehicles – a little pickup truck, a racy modern sports sedan, a vintage sports convertible, a VW beetle needing repairs, a fairly large motor home, another car being built, and a brand new Harley-Davidson motorbike. He also liked collecting electrical gadgets and the kitchen was absolutely overflowing. In fact it was almost impossible to find anywhere to sit down in the whole house. Fortunately not much of it spilled into the spare bedroom where I slept.

Another intriguing thing about Bill which I definitely *couldn't* get used to was that he almost always carried a little concealed pearl-handled pistol – loaded, of course. When at home, he used to leave it lying all over the house and spent a lot of time looking for it, often asking me if I'd seen it anywhere. I refuse to touch any gun, so it always stayed where he left it until he found it again. Sometimes when we went out he would throw it under the seat of his car, because it was illegal to carry concealed weapons into public places like bars or clubs. (That has changed, and now Texas is one of the American states where people can legally carry concealed weapons, even into churches.)

If Bill was out of town when I was due to arrive, he used to leave a key for me and I would make myself at home. The spare room was always ready. He once came back after I'd been there for several nights and asked with great amusement if I'd felt a lump under the mattress. One of his loaded guns was hidden there and he'd forgotten to warn me. It seems that guns in bars has always been an issue in Texas. The Fort Worth historic cemetery has a special section just for bartenders who apparently were often killed by stray bullets during shoot-outs in the late 19th century.

One day in Fort Worth my van decided to stop and refused to restart. This happened right outside an automotive service shop, but they weren't able to help and suggested it must be an electrical problem. I called the American Automobile Association and was towed to an electrical repair garage where I left it. Fortunately this was within walking distance of Bill's. He very generously offered to loan me one of his vehicles while I waited for parts to arrive. I can't recall exactly what the problem was, but I think it was something to do with a computer chip. This made me think that the older, simpler motors were *possibly* less likely to break down or at least easier and cheaper to repair. This particular problem cost about $500. I only had it back for a couple of days when the odometer stopped working, but I decided I'd deal with that later. In any case, it wouldn't hurt the van's resale value if all the miles weren't recorded for a while!

Bill had a little blind poodle called Percy. He was an old dog and used to mainly bumble around the house and yard, bumping into things. Bill's son was about to go on holidays and Bill agreed to mind his young female chow, a big fluffy dog who happened to be on heat. There was some discussion about whether old Percy would be a risk, but as he was barely able to get around and was so small compared to the chow, the idea was dismissed. Percy immediately fell in love and much to her annoyance followed the chow everywhere, curling up next to her whenever she sat down. Bill was still convinced nothing could possibly happen between them, and at that time I went away for several months. When I came back I laughed to see a sign outside his house: *'For Sale. Chow/Poodle pups.'* Percy had managed somehow, but was extremely annoyed with the results, which were balls of fur not much smaller than him and who wouldn't leave him alone.

Of course, Fort Worth is not all about honky-tonks and cowboy culture. There are many wonderful museums. I spent ages in the Kimbell Art Museum, which is often described as America's Best Small Museum. The beautifully proportioned building, designed by the great American architect Louis I. Kahn, is considered one of his finest creations. The artworks include paintings by Picasso, El Greco, Goya, and Cezanne. The Amon Carter Museum has a fine collection of American art, as has the Sid Richardson Gallery and there is also a Modern Art Museum and some lovely Japanese gardens.

Winston had a special interest in circuses and invited me to watch the famous Carson & Barnes five ring tent being erected very early one morning. I have exciting memories of the annual visit of a travelling circus when, as a young child, I lived in the Victorian country town of Charlton. My two brothers used to rush down to the showgrounds to help erect the tent, and there was a wonderful parade through the town featuring various animals, including an elephant. I suppose we couldn't afford tickets to the performance, but once I crept into the tent with my older brother Keith and some of his friends, under the canvas behind the seats. At 60,000 square feet, Carson & Barnes' tent was the largest in the world. Made in Italy at a cost of $250,000, it needed to be replaced every two years. The circus operated for eight months of the year, travelling almost every day to a different location, and had been doing this since 1937. During winter they would build, repair, train, practice and otherwise prepare for the next season. Fortunately, their 20 elephants (*'the world's largest herd of performing circus elephants'*) helped with the tent, and it was wonderful to see them working with their handlers. Most of the rows of seats were mounted on trucks, which were simply driven into position inside the tent.

That night I went to the performance and saw all the usual marvellous acrobats, jugglers, flying trapeze artists and contortionists. A quote from their literature: *'In the Center ring we gasp in amazement as we watch Miss Carmen suspended in space – hanging only by the hair of her head.'* It also advertised the *'World's Largest Traveling Circus Menagerie,'* which, in addition to the elephants, included a rhino, hippo, lions, monkeys, camels, zebra, giraffe etc. I hated seeing these animals in cages and found it especially difficult to watch the magnificent big cats 'performing.' It seemed so demeaning for them, and I subsequently heard reports of poor treatment, especially in their training routines.

It was also African American History Month in Fort Worth. I went to a couple of the events, including a lecture on black filmmaking where I met a school teacher, Lois Watkins, who invited me to speak to some of her classes at the Careers Day of Polytechnic High School. She was impressed by the travelling I'd done alone and the fact that I'd worked hard to make it all happen, and thought the teenagers might benefit from hearing about it. 98% of the students at this school were black and the rest Hispanic – and 97% of all of them were poor enough to be on food vouchers. I enjoyed speaking to the three classes and they were completely intrigued (of course!) as I was the first Australian they had ever seen. They were aged between 15 and 17, full of vitality and intelligence but, like so many of the Americans I met, not high on knowledge of the world. They asked lots of questions including whether I'd *driven* all the way from Australia and if I knew Crocodile Dundee. If only I had a dollar for every time I'd been asked those things! They also asked me to *'say something in Australian'* and were very surprised when I said I was speaking the way we normally do at home. It appeared that their education was largely about their own country.

One day when I was visiting the Stockyards Museum I met Billy Joe Gabriel, Editor of the *Fort Worth Stockyards Gazette*. He asked to interview me for the newspaper and we arranged to meet again. He never actually got around to the interview but instead took me to my first (and only) ice hockey game – The Fort Worth Fire playing The Memphis Riverkings. It moved at lightning speed, and I was impressed by the players' expertise at skating while manoeuvring the puck across the ice, being tackled etc. I'd had a go at ice skating in my teens, but never mastered it because I was terrified of falling and making a fool of myself. I thought it must be a dangerous game and noticed in the team's magazine an ad for HCA Medical Plaza Hospital – *'proud to keep Fort Worth Fire on the ice'* – and one for Fort Worth Sports Rehabilitation Center.

Billy Joe's idea was to feature me in a new section he was about to start in the paper: 'Visitor of the Month.' I was looking forward to this but the interview was continually postponed, so in the end I wrote the article myself and they published it word for word! On a trip back to Fort Worth the following year, I submitted another article: 'Visitor of the Month Returns.' They published that as well, along with a photograph of me taken at the stockyards wearing a borrowed cowboy hat, sitting on a longhorn cow!

Conversations on first meeting people outside the large cities became fairly predictable. First they'd ask where I came from, then they'd say, *'Oh, I always wanted to go to Australia.'* Then they'd ask me if I knew Crocodile Dundee. I got a bit tired of that sometimes, and used to invent answers when the people asking were especially annoying. One was to say *yes* I did know him and that he used to be my gynaecologist, but gave up his practice when wrestling crocodiles became more lucrative. The frightening thing was that sometimes I was believed. Naturally I didn't spin this tale to the school kids. People continued to ask me if I drove all the way from Australia and once I was asked what colour the sky was in Australia. I said it depended on the weather! Another person asked if it was true that we had Christmas in summer. I explained the differences between northern and southern hemisphere, but this didn't seem to sink in because she said, *'Oh, just imagine having Christmas in July.'*

Sometimes I was asked how long I'd been in America and then congratulated on learning English so quickly. In elevators, my accent was generally a conversation stopper and sometimes people said almost accusingly, *'You're not American!'* On one occasion, I had several men asking me to speak for them. This made me feel like a performing parrot and when one said, *'I love the way you say yes,'* my reply was, *'I don't suppose you hear many women say that.'* Fortunately he wasn't offended and they took it as the joke I more or less intended. Irony is often not understood in America, and so the British or Australian sense of humour can be misinterpreted.

I thought a lot about why so many people I met in America, particularly in the south and the more rural areas, knew so little about the rest of the world. I supposed the education system was to blame and there wasn't the culture of travel that exists in Australia. I saw T-shirts advertising a band's 'international tour' listing a number of U.S. cities, and *sometimes* one in Canada.

I also found much more patriotism than I had encountered anywhere else in the world. Often people welcomed me to *'the greatest country in the world'* and it was usually assumed that, if I could, I would naturally want to live there.

After Fort Worth, I travelled across to the eastern part of Texas, spending a few days in Angelina National Forest camping beside a lovely little lake. This is called the 'Piney Woods' area of the Texan Deep East, and the forest is a beautiful mix of tall longleaf pine, cypress, loblolly pine, dogwood, magnolia and other deciduous species. I was the only person there and, as usual, enjoyed the isolation. Apart from the peace, what I most loved about camping in these places was the chance to see wildlife. As they were mostly around at the beginning and end of the day, I would probably miss out if I stayed in a hotel. It was warm and I spent an enjoyable afternoon lazing on the edge of the lake, watching little turtles trying to sunbake on a floating log. If they were *very* careful and *really* lucky, two could climb on and stay there, but if any more attempted to join them the log rolled over and tipped them all into the water. The funny thing was that they never gave up and that log was rolling all day.

During my extended time in Texas I had danced my way through Lubbock and Amarillo in the west, and as far as Lufkin and Beaumont in the southeast. The state exceeded my expectations. It was more diverse and certainly more interesting geographically than I'd imagined. There are mountains, deserts, fertile areas with rolling hills, forests, lots of rivers and, of course, a coastline which I never saw.

Texas is home to 5,000 species of wildflowers. Depending on the season, the freeways were lined with acres of them – sometimes just a single species, and sometimes several mixed together like a meadow. Administered by the Department of Transportation, they are a big tourist attraction, and mowing is delayed while flowers are in bloom. It was wonderful to be driving past carpets of bluebonnets, Indian paintbrush, etc.

As I was leaving Texas, country singer George Strait's 'All My Exes Live in Texas' (written by Sanger D Shafer and Lyndia Shafer) felt rather appropriate to be playing!

On a Longhorn Cow, Fort Worth

At Comanche Indian Pow Wow, Fort Worth

Bill with his Harley-Davidson, Fort Worth

Fort Worth Stockyards, Chisholm Trail Round up

Oklahoma

Heading north, I crossed over the Red River into Oklahoma. One of the things that interested me most about this state was its history. Native Americans have had a profound impact on this part of the country. Five tribes were moved from their original lands in the south eastern U.S. The one with which I was most familiar was the Cherokee nation, which was forcibly removed from east of the Mississippi. Many died along the way, which became known as The Trail of Tears. The name *Oklahoma* means red people, derived from two Choctaw Indian words, *okla* meaning people and *humma* meaning red. The state flag features an Osage warrior's buckskin shield decorated with eagle feathers and crossed by an olive branch and peace pipe.

I noticed lots of ostrich farms in southern Oklahoma. They use the skins for cowboy boots. On the subject of cowboy boots, they are also made from snakeskin, lizard, Brahma bull-hide, calfskin, horsehide, kangaroo, alligator, antelope, sharkskin and stingray. There are lots of different styles of course, some named after famous country music singers like the 'Garth' (Garth Brooks). As well as Stetsons and other cowboy hats, the Australian-made Akubra hats are also popular in rural America.

Suddenly the weather changed dramatically. The worst snowstorms in over 100 years hit most of the American north east, with airports closed and over 100 people dying in the cold. It was snowing north of Dallas and well below freezing when I arrived at Little River State Park about 30 miles south of Oklahoma City – much colder than I had experienced up in Wyoming. No electricity was available, so my van was *really* cold. Fortunately the bathrooms were heated and had hot showers so I lingered in there, eventually going to bed wearing just about all the clothes I had, including thermal long johns, woollen hat, gloves and socks. I also had two hot water bottles with cozy covers. One was filled when I went to bed and the other was ready to be filled with hot water from my thermos, to save getting out of bed if I woke up cold in the night. Next morning there was lots of ice on the *inside* of the van windows and various items were frozen solid, including my makeup. A bowl of water I'd left on the picnic table had also frozen, so I popped it into my cooler to save buying ice. The van refrigerator had stopped working fairly early in my trip.

There was only one other person in this campground. He was in a large RV with all mod cons. Astonished to discover an Australian woman camping alone, in fairly Spartan conditions, he insisted on giving me something to help me along the way. As he was at the end of his holiday, he donated the remains of his food supply – a pound of potatoes, three tomatoes and a can of beans – which I gratefully accepted.

 Not being used to sub-zero temperatures, I set out for a long walk thinking it would warm me up, but had to turn back when the icy wind started hurting my face and eyes. It was even painful to breathe. The day was much better spent *inside* at the National Cowboy Hall of Fame & Western Heritage Center. This wonderful museum has an excellent collection of western art and historic artefacts from pioneering days, including a Native American exhibit. The 'Visions of the West' Gallery concentrates on the romanticised views of the west portrayed in Hollywood films. There is also a Rodeo Hall of Fame, where I learnt that women used to successfully compete against the men in *all* rodeo events. Now they are restricted to the barrel race, which is only for women and covers horse riding expertise. It's not as rough as the cattle roping or bull riding, but does require stamina and concentration. Horse and rider must carve figure eights around three barrels, 30 to 35 yards apart.

I also learnt that the cowboy's clothing wasn't just fashion. Trousers were tight to avoid being caught in the brush, and leather chaps worn over them for added protection from thorns and branches. The broad brimmed hat was for protection from sun, wind and rain, and could be used to fan a fire, direct a herd of cattle or even dipped into a river to give you or your horse a drink. Bandanas helped keep out dust, and finally the higher heels on the boots gave a firm hold in the stirrup. The pointed toe made it easy to slip into the stirrup – or out, in the case of a fall.

The herds of longhorn cattle, which were driven from Texas to the railheads in Kansas, passed through Oklahoma on a number of trails. These included the Great Western Trail, the West and East Shawnee Trails, and the Chisholm Trail, which I had encountered at Fort Worth. As a legacy of these, Oklahoma City had huge working stockyards, certainly the largest in USA and possibly in the world. 10,000 cattle were auctioned the day I visited. I loved the busy, noisy atmosphere. The auctioneers looked extremely smart with bone-coloured cowboy hats, white shirts and large fancy buckles on their jeans. The ranchers, on the other hand, were rugged-looking and chewing and spitting tobacco, and because of the high winds they were wearing baseball caps instead of the usual cowboy hats. Many also sported denim bib and brace overalls. In front of each was a telephone, and it was surprising to see one man ask the auctioneer for a feather duster to clean his! I couldn't imagine a farmer being so fussy. No doubt they all have smart phones and laptops now. Hogs were auctioned in a separate building, with glass between the buyers and the animals. I wondered if this was so the poor animal's squeals didn't drown out the auctioneer or distract the buyers.

That night I went to an indoor rodeo, which was enjoyable partly because it was much warmer than in my van in the campground. Driving home afterwards, I simply couldn't stop shivering and thought the heaters had stopped working, but then it dawned on me that it was just *terribly* cold outside. Ice had formed on the road. I decided to go to a motel and found a cheap one, but then told myself I was being a wimp. I'd managed OK the night before, so surely I would again tonight. I continued on to the campground and repeated the procedure of layers of clothing and hot water bottles.

Next day I was delighted to discover Chastain's Bar with live country bands and a big wooden dance floor. It was Ladies Night, which meant free entry and free drinks for me. I was told the beer was light, which in Australia meant low alcohol, so I felt comfortable drinking a little more than usual before I drove back to the campground. It took me *three years* to discover that in America, at least at that time, light only meant low in calories! Just as well I was careful regarding my alcohol consumption. It was one of my 'travelling alone' rules.

This night at Chastain's I met a young fellow called Doug who was in Oklahoma City on business. He was a good dancer and we just whizzed around the floor. Towards the end of the evening, he tried to persuade me to come back to his hotel to try the hot tub, *'no strings attached!'* I laughed at this and told him I wasn't interested *'strings or not.'* As it was nearly closing time, I suggested that if he wanted to take somebody back with him he'd better look around quickly, because it was getting late. He rushed off immediately, scanning the room, and later I saw him leaving with a woman in tow.

The next night I was at Chastain's again. Towards the end of the evening the club's manager offered me a free room in the motel next door. He had heard I was camping in these freezing conditions and said they always had a room reserved in case the band needed it, but it would be empty that night. I accepted, but hoped he didn't expect anything in return, and that there wouldn't be a knock on the door in the middle of the night. I was probably being paranoid, as it turned out to be simply a kind-hearted offer.

After I'd finished a day's sight-seeing, there was usually some time to fill in before going out dancing. Normally I'd cook my dinner in the van – often in the street near the venue – then go for a walk or rest, but in freezing temperatures I would buy a cup of tea in a cheap restaurant, and spend an hour or so in the safety and warmth, reading or writing up my diary. Otherwise I might arrive early at the venue and take advantage of the free or inexpensive meal sometimes offered.

I met some strange characters at these bars, and was often asked for my home address, sometimes by unsavoury looking men who said they hoped to come to Australia. A couple of hunters declared they planned to visit so they could *'shoot all the wildlife.'* Usually I gave a false address and phone number for my own safety as much as anything else. Although I didn't expect they would actually *visit*, it was just easier and less likely to provoke anger or embarrassment than simply saying no.

I had various ruses to help ensure I remained safe while travelling alone like this. When camping I'd put out two chairs, two cups etc. so it would be assumed I had a companion somewhere. Unless in a secure area with other campers around, I never hung out my underwear or anything else feminine. I always tried to be aware of who was around and often hid in the van when I heard a vehicle coming. I always thought I should buy a huge pair of old cowboy boots and place them in a strategic position by the van door so it would be assumed a large man was inside, but I never got around to it. I was overcrowded with stuff as it was. I have heard that women sometimes put a male mannequin in the passenger seat – also a good idea, but imagine the *room* it would take! When visiting night clubs or bars, I arrived early so I could park outside and not have to walk around any dark corners, especially when leaving. I often ascertained in advance the name of the bar's owner or manager and introduced myself. They were always welcoming, and usually offered to keep an eye on me, occasionally escorting me to my van at the end of the evening. Some of the larger clubs had a security car to deliver you safely to your parked vehicle. I usually left before the venue closed so nobody would see which direction I was headed, and if anyone was bothering me I could either tell the staff or quietly leave, pretending that I was just visiting the ladies room.

Tulsa in north eastern Oklahoma is interesting because, despite the fact that it is hundreds of miles from the nearest coast, it is a major inland harbour. Barges can go all the way from here to New Orleans via a 445 mile navigation system. This part of the country is in the area known as the 'Bible Belt.' One of Tulsa's star attractions is the Oral Roberts University, which boasts The Praying Hands – at 30 tons the largest bronze structure in the world – and a 200 foot glass and steel prayer tower, with an observation deck at the top. One of the main functions of this tower is to house the staff of the Abundant Life Prayer Group, who offered 24 hour prayers via telephone – probably now also available via the internet. A sign told us, *'You are standing in a place where prayer never ceases ... where miracles are happening right now.'* I could hear a babble of voices behind the closed doors.

Oral Roberts was a charismatic Methodist-Pentecostal televangelist who built the university in 1963 *'at God's request.'* When I visited he was chancellor, and his son Richard was president. There is a museum covering Roberts' life. I found it eerie. It was a series of rooms and everything was automated. I was the only person there and as I entered the first room the door closed behind me. It was almost dark. There was no handle on the *inside* of this door and I couldn't see any other exit! A recorded voice described the exhibits and when it was finished, another handle-less door opened automatically, leading me to the next room. It seemed there was no escaping until you had heard all they had to tell you.

This reminded me of my upbringing – of Dad's sermons, as well as lectures from both my parents, and sometimes from family friends, from which I couldn't escape. One of the latter accosted me alone in our living room: *'Janice, have you found the Lord?'* My response was a hesitant *'yes.'* (It was safer than telling the truth.) Then, *'Has your brother Keith found the Lord?' 'I don't know.'*

Occasionally I saw this person in a city bookshop near where I worked. He would trail around after me, pressing religious tracts into my hands. If I saw him first, I hid behind the shelves. A similar experience occurred in a charity shop in Tulsa, when a man asked me if I *'knew his friend the carpenter,'* and gave me his business card – which read *Basic Instructions Before Leaving Earth.* The first letter of each word spelling out 'Bible.' I escaped from there pretty quickly too. It was also in Tulsa that I was surprised to see a church called the 'Going Hard for Christ Church.'

At some stage of my American travels (I don't remember where or when), I was given a four paged brochure headed *'Warning! Nuclear war is like a picnic, compared to people who will suffer forever in the flames of hell.'* Following was a very long closely typed list of actions considered by the writer to be sinful enough to send a person to hell. As well as the usual crimes such as rape and murder, they included: *'disobedient to husband; mother working on a job away from her child; false evolution theory; effeminate male; female bossing man; fearful; married person who had sex with husband or wife but did not want baby; trusting in the government for your needs; putting trust in doctors, medicines and not in Jesus; smoking; female teaching men; anger; not perfect like Jesus Christ said to be.'* Good grief, I thought – no hope for *me,* no hope for *anybody* and how incredibly sexist.

Not being entirely put off by this religious propaganda, the next Sunday I decided to try to find a black church with a choir, and ended up at a

Church of Christ with about 400 people in the congregation, but no choir. They told me they believed singing during the church service was for *everyone* and shouldn't be restricted to a choir. I thought a bit of each might be OK. When it was discovered I was Australian, everyone wanted to meet me and I was invited to a special luncheon, which I think was to celebrate the church's anniversary. BBQ chicken and turkey had been cooked by the men, and vegetables and desserts supplied by the women. Even better, entertainment was provided by two choirs, one a mixed choir singing modern gospel and the other made up of 14 men singing traditional gospel songs, which had us all stomping our feet and clapping. A very warm experience.

I think these African American churches attracted me for a couple of reasons. Initially it was the marvellous music and the joy and enthusiasm of the congregation. But it was also the feeling of never being judged, of being welcome whoever you were. At some of my father's churches, people were criticised for their clothes or other behaviour, and I really didn't feel a lot of joy there.

I made a detour north to Branson, Missouri, because I'd heard a lot about the music – *'more country music than Nashville.'* But I hated the traffic and commercialism, and after picking up a few brochures I drove straight through – so I missed out on all the tourist attractions such as the wax museum with its recreation of The Last Supper, plus a rather ugly looking figure of Elvis (according to the photo), and images of lots of country music stars. Dixie Stampede (A Dolly Parton enterprise) was described as *'a barrel full of music, dancing, special effects and family friendly comedy.'* At one stage the *'North and South join together in a patriotic salute of Red, White and Blue featuring 'Colour Me America,' written and recorded by Dolly herself. The Patriotic Grand Finale soars with flying Doves of Peace, luminous costumes and fireworks, reminding you of the pride and spirit of America.'* That strong American patriotism, evident again. There were also the twin singing stars John and Paul Cody in their Las Vegas-style musical, in which they were surrounded by 40,000 gallons of 'liquid fireworks' called Waltzing Waters.

There really were dozens of shows available. Some were on show boats cruising Lake Taneycomo; some in churches, like the 'Grand Old Gospel Hour' concert. I've heard it said, perhaps unkindly, that Branson is where many faded country music singers go to make a living. Some even buy their own theatres. There are over 50 venues with more seats than on Broadway and up to 100,000 visitors a day – over seven million each year. It is more than just music. There are hundreds of shops, horseback riding, hiking, family fun parks, water sports and The National Tiger Center! No wonder it's called Silver Dollar City.

Gradually heading east, I crossed over into northern Arkansas and started to feel unwell. A doctor diagnosed mild flu, plus a secondary infection and a fractured rib, which must have happened when I slipped on some ice a few days earlier. It was terribly painful, especially when driving or coughing. After a couple of days in bed, though, I decided that resting wouldn't do a lot to heal the rib and that antibiotics would help the infection, so I decided to keep going. Fortunately the weather had picked up. Spring was being heralded by flocks of honking geese flying north, and the appearance of buds and blossoms. The worst thing was that I'd have to put dancing on hold!

At Maumelle near Little Rock, I found a great spot to camp on the banks of the Arkansas River, a tributary of the Mississippi. There I spent two days lazing in the warm sunshine, watching the enormous barges passing by, reading and waiting for my mail to arrive. I just *loved* getting mail from home, but sometimes there were delays which could be frustrating, but at least forced me to rest for a day or two. Collecting mail was the only thing in my trip which dictated where I had to be at a particular time.

After a few months I was so fancy-free I found it really difficult to make *any* decisions about where I might be within the next week or two. I wondered if my love of this almost complete freedom came partly from the fact that I'd married at 18, moving from a strict and controlling home environment to live with a man who also wanted to control me. Although I'd been out of that marriage for 20 years, other choices had tied me down.

My friend Barb – being the daughter of a Baptist minister – had a similar upbringing to me. We met when we were about 16 and used to get up to mischief together. I would tell my parents I was going to see Reverend Millar's daughter and she, of course, said she was going to see Reverend Hull's daughter! In fact, we usually skipped off to hear some music, or go to a jazz cafe for a glass of claret. At one stage we both worked every Saturday night at a coffee lounge not far from my home. After work we hung out with our boyfriends until the early hours. An obliging milkman agreed to run his horse-drawn milk cart past my house a couple of times so all the bottles would rattle and my parents wouldn't hear us coming in!

Barb was also a woman who loved the challenge and adventure of travelling alone, and sent me this poem:

When I'm overseas:

Take me there by ocean liner

take me there by plane

there's places to discover

and places I must see again

A stranger in a stranger land

footloose and fancy free

When I'm overseas

I always carry it in my passport, but have never been able to find out who wrote it or where Barb found it. Sadly she died some years ago.

Memphis: Elvis and The Blues

Exploring Memphis had been one of my dreams, so it was exciting to be finally wandering up Beale Street with all its blues clubs, cafes and street music. In the early 1900s lots of musicians travelled to Memphis from the south, hoping to leave behind the extreme poverty and make a decent living. At that time Beale Street was lined with theatres, bars and brothels, and many musicians busked out on the street.

It attracted lots of shady characters, and before long the city was known as 'the murder capital of the U.S.A.' According to Christiane Bird's guidebook, *The Jazz & Blues Lover's Guide to the U.S*, one of clubs, The Monarch Club, was nicknamed the 'Castle of Missing Men' because *'gunshot victims killed here could be quickly disposed of at the undertaker's place out back.'* In the 1950s the mayor decided to clean the place up and most of the establishments on Beale Street were closed down. Now the area is classified as a national historic district and once again has a very lively nightlife.

Entry fees to each club were high. I don't quite know how I did it but I managed to persuade one of the club's doormen to let me in free. (He said it was because I was a redhead!) This led to introductions to other door staff, and soon I was lucky enough to be able to visit most of the clubs free. One night I met a group of surgeons who were in Memphis for a conference and being entertained at a blues club by a medical supply company. I took up their suggestion of tagging along for the free drinks. I can't remember where it was or which band was playing that night, but gosh I had fun. On another occasion I was sitting at the bar of B.B. King's nightclub when a man came in to collect a take-away meal. He was standing right next to me and we started chatting. My accent was such a surprise to him that when he paid for his food he paid for my drink, too! There was plenty of dancing in these clubs. It was fun but was of the 'anything goes' freeform kind – quite different from the western style I so loved, which closely resembles ballroom dancing.

Unfortunately Beale Street had become rather commercialised and, although I found lots of good music, there was very little in the way of authentic blues. An exception was The Center for Southern Folklore, which had a bar and restaurant which regularly featured local blues and gospel artists. A private non-profit organisation, its purpose was to document and help preserve the grass roots culture of the south. It's still there and conducts cultural excursions; produces the annual Memphis Music & Heritage Festival; has an extensive archive of photographs and slides, films and video documentaries, audio recordings, television and radio programmes; a book library and lots of folk arts and crafts. Its walls were covered with handmade quilts and colourful murals painted in the naive style. You could ask to see any of their films and the one I chose was *Hush Hoggies Hush: Tom Johnson's Praying Pigs*. Produced by the Center, it shows Mr. Johnson demonstrating how he taught his pigs to wait while he said grace over their trough. They seemed to manage it better than some people I know. I met documentary filmmaker Judy Peiser, who co-founded the Center in 1972. Intrigued by my extensive solo travels, she interviewed me for a weekly television programme she hosted, mainly asking me about where I'd travelled and how I coped on the road alone.

I went to Memphis for the music, most of which I enjoyed, but the highlight for me turned out to be the National Civil Rights Museum. Part of this museum is housed in the old Lorraine Motel where Martin Luther King Jr. was assassinated in 1968. It was chilling to see his car and that of his assistant parked exactly where they had been at that time. I remembered them from the newspaper photographs. You can see the room where King stayed and the balcony where he was shot. The museum traces the history of slavery in the U.S. and the struggle for equal rights – sit-ins, freedom rides and the Montgomery bus boycott for example – with lots of very powerful and moving audiovisual displays and exhibits. To me, one of the most appalling accounts was that of Emmett Till, the 14 year old black boy from Chicago, who was lynched and horribly mutilated in 1955 while visiting a southern town. He was apparently considered a little fresh with a white woman serving him in a shop. His killer is quoted as saying, *'What else could I do? He thought he was as good as a white man.'* I find it hard to understand such arrogance and cruelty. It was all so emotionally overwhelming that I could only stay for an hour or so, making several visits to see the whole museum.

It was thrilling to be in Memphis on the 25th anniversary of King's death, which was marked with a large rally and tribute concert called 'March On.' Held in Mason Hall where he gave his last talk, it was full to overflowing. A choir of 150 made a very exciting and moving entrance, appearing simultaneously from various sides of the hall and down the four aisles and balconies, singing and carrying 'March On' red and black banners. This hall holds many thousands, and mine was one of very few white faces. I started chatting with a man named Eric sitting next to me, who insisted that I mustn't leave Memphis without trying some of its famous BBQ. Next day he and his wife took me off to a marvellous little smoky restaurant for BBQ ribs which were very tasty. Typically, servings were absolutely *enormous*. I don't know why most American restaurants offer such large meals, but I think it has now become so common that anything less is considered poor value, and taking home half your dinner in a 'doggy bag' seems to be the norm.

About 55% of Memphis' population is African American. When I was there it also had one of the highest poverty rates in the country. Some of the public housing was a disgrace and appeared barely habitable. I'd never seen so many cars falling apart, patched up with wire and duct tape but still being driven. There were also lots of vehicles in pieces along the roads and in people's yards, often being worked on by groups of young men.

For the first few days I camped in T.O. Fuller State Park, which is named in honour of a Dr. Thomas O. Fuller, who spent his life working to empower and educate African Americans. It was the second State Park in the country which was open to African Americans, and was in a fairly poor part of town just south of the city. I did my shopping around there and was always the only white face in the supermarket. I enjoyed the experience and everyone was friendly, but once when I was storing my purchases in my van, a white fellow stopped in his car to ask if I had broken down. He advised me not to hang around there as it was considered dangerous. I don't know if this was true or whether he was paranoid, but I certainly didn't have any problems. However, I was always very cautious wherever I went. It was easy when travelling in unknown cities in the U.S. to suddenly find myself in a *very* undesirable looking area. I just hoped that my van didn't decide to break down at those times or that I didn't get completely lost or run out of fuel. No sat nav or mobile phone then!

I soon discovered some very large 24 hour truck stops over the Mississippi River in West Memphis near the intersection of two large interstate highways. To save money I started spending the nights in my van parked in one of these. They are amazing and have absolutely everything a trucker could need, starting with the basics of fuel, extra-large automated truck washes and repairs, plus a shop selling spare parts, CB radios, CDs, souvenirs, batteries, coffee, packaged foods, books, clothes etc. There is also always at least one restaurant and sometimes even a night club with a bar, live band and dance floor. Other facilities are showers (which I couldn't afford, because they cost $5 unless you were buying hundreds of gallons of fuel), laundry, phones, barber, shoeshine and truckers lounge. Although I never identified any of these, I was told that there are often prostitutes specialising in working truck stops. They are referred to as 'lot lizards.' I always parked in a well-lit spot outside the shop, and away from the lines of trucks with their air conditioners running and drivers sleeping in little bunks behind the cabin. I was curious to see these sleeping quarters but was never able to ask in case my intention was misinterpreted. I might have been mistaken for a middle-aged 'lot lizard'! Truck stops are noisy places to sleep as vehicles come in and out all night, so I used my earplugs. Other than that I never had any problems.

It was Sunday morning and I decided to get up early from my truck stop 'campground' to go to another African American church. I thought again about my Methodist minister father, who would have been amazed to see me *willingly* attend church! I was feeling a bit lonely and now knew I would be warmly welcomed, and that the singing and preaching would probably be entertaining and possibly even inspiring.

I tried the New Salem M.B. Church situated in a middle class black area of Memphis. The service started with warm-up singing and a long prayer by a deacon in a kind of rap style, which had a couple of elderly ladies jumping to their feet and shouting *'amen.'* This was followed by the 35 voice choir, with their very hip conductor leaping around and flinging his arms in what appeared to me to be *all* directions. Every part of the service was enthusiastically clapped by the congregation, including that first prayer which was also accompanied by embellishments on the organ and drums. The charismatic preacher, Pastor Frank E. Ray, delivered his sermon with heaps of humour, which had everyone in tears of laughter. He was a great singer, too.

The whole experience was a bit like attending a concert and was certainly a polished performance. As usual I was the only white person, and was literally welcomed with open arms and given a printed card: *'The members of this church welcome you today. We consider it a privilege to have you worship with us and sincerely hope you get a blessing from the service. We hope you will feel at home with us during your visit.'* (Good PR!) When reference was made to passages from the scriptures, the woman sitting next to me shared her bible, which I noticed was a well-worn edition with lots of bookmarks and many passages underlined with red and blue ink, along with hand-written explanations in the margins. I knew many of the hymns, including 'When the Roll is Called Up Yonder,' which always used to be included in our annual Sunday School Concerts. My brother John and I often reminisced about these concerts, which were quite exciting for us. Tiered rows of seats were set up behind the pulpit, and we children practically took over the service, belting out the hymns we had been practicing all year.

Of course, while in Memphis I couldn't miss visiting Elvis Presley's home, Graceland. Most of the interior is (to my taste) rather ugly, especially the Jungle Room with its shag carpet and grotesque carved furniture. But then apart from his music, Elvis was never considered to have good taste. His choice of food was testament to that – the most famous of his favourites being deep fried peanut butter and banana sandwiches!

The grounds of Graceland are lovely and contain the family cemetery. Two of Elvis's horses were still grazing in the paddock, and you can see many of his cars and planes. I have a Boarding Pass to one, the 'Lisa Marie: The Pride of Elvis Presley Airways,' a Convair 880 which was originally a commercial airliner for Delta. He bought it in 1975 for $250.000, named it after his daughter and spent over $800,000 having it customised with a queen size bed, 24 carat gold flecked bathroom sinks, a conference table, games tables and gold plated seat buckles.

Next door to Graceland was The Heartbreak Hotel. You could stay in various Elvis themed suites which included The Graceland Suite (a scaled down version of his mansion), and The Burning Love Suite, described as *'over-the-top romance, with a preponderance of crimson velvet upholstery.'* I didn't try it out. Might have been fun if I had somebody to share it with!

At the historic Sun Studios where Elvis made his first recording, I saw the original microphone he used. His 'Heartbreak Hotel' and 'That's All Right Mama' were the songs I was listening to as I drove around here.

One of Elvis's planes named after his daughter

March On brochure, Memphis

Blues in the Mississippi Delta

I continued south on Route 61, well known as the road the African Americans took to escape to the north from the poverty and discrimination in Mississippi. I was soon driving through the Mississippi Delta with its wide river flats, raised roads and high levies. It is rich farming country with cotton plantations, wonderful antebellum (pre-Civil War) houses, and rough shacks and cottages. The latter were presumably occupied by the black workers. Many of these workers were still tied to the plantations. Their low wages made it impossible to save enough to move elsewhere. In recent years, huge casinos have sprung up in this area. I considered them a blot on the landscape, but I guess they provide some much needed revenue and jobs in this very poor state. I wasn't sure what to make of a sign for one – which said, rather obviously, *'Nowadays every casino has a theme. Ours is gambling!'*

This was the heart of the Delta blues area and is generally believed to be where the music originated. Many of the most famous blues musicians came from here and it was exciting to be right where it all started. Following my *Jazz & Blues Lover's Guidebook*, I found the tiny town of Robinsonville where the legendary Robert Johnson spent time and grew up on a nearby plantation. The larger town of Clarksdale has a Delta Blues Museum, which had recently moved to the old railway station where Muddy Waters bought a train ticket for his first journey north to Chicago. W.C. Handy lived in Clarksdale from 1903-1905, and Bessie Smith died in the G.T. Thomas Hospital here after a car accident in 1937. This hospital later became the Riverside Hotel and was home to many other famous musicians, including the legendary Sonny Boy Williamson, Robert Nighthawk and Ike Turner.

Clarksdale still had some interesting bars. These black bars – or juke joints, as they are more commonly known – were often in windowless dilapidated buildings made of concrete or tin. The interiors can be colourful and are always full of character. A railway line usually runs through these southern towns, dividing them in half with the more affluent whites on one side and the poorer blacks on the other.

Margaret's Blue Diamond Lounge was a juke joint owned by Margaret Palmer on the 'wrong side of the tracks.' I went to check it out early in the day, and had problems finding it because there was no signage at all, not even a beer advertising sign. I was driving very slowly along the street looking for numbers, when a seedy-looking fellow asked if I needed help. He pointed out the lounge, a ramshackle place with the front door hanging off its hinges, and as I looked up to thank him he leant over and, to my surprise, said, *'want a fuck?'* I was shocked. This was a bit scary. Nobody had ever spoken to me like that before, and I hadn't even got out of my vehicle. What would it be like on the street after dark or *inside* the bar? Jim O'Neal, owner of local record shop Stackhouse/Delta Record Mart, and founder of the record label Rooster Blues, had recommended this juke joint because it was considered reasonably safe and tonight there would be local blues band – Stone Gas Band. He had also given me the name of the owner, Margaret.

I decided to go ahead later on and was able to park right outside. Inside, the brightly painted walls were in an advanced state of decay, and lots of the tables and chairs were in similar condition. The toilets were basic to say the least, although relatively clean early in the evening. Christmas lights helped to brighten up the dimly lit, smoky main room. Beer and soft drinks were sold and people brought their own hard liquor in brown paper bags. I was the only white person there and one of only several women. The men were a bit pushy and sometimes upsettingly crude, especially after a few drinks, and the women slightly hostile towards me. I suppose they viewed me as a threat or rival, or just an annoying, curious tourist. For the first time in my trip I felt a bit nervous. In other states people had always responded well if I was open and friendly, but

African Americans have had a particularly tough time in Mississippi and to me seemed to be more suspicious. Strangers are carefully watched.

I introduced myself to Margaret. She was kind, invited me to sit at her table, and made a point of looking after me. Really the main problem I had in Margaret's Blue Diamond Lounge was understanding the local accent. When I was approached, I rarely knew what I was being asked and how to respond! I usually smiled slightly while shaking my head, or said, *'Mmmm.'* Although I did feel uncomfortable, I enjoyed the music and even danced occasionally. For safety, I quietly slipped out just before the band finished.

Despite asking at the local police station, I hadn't been able to find anywhere safe to camp at Clarksdale. I ended up driving miles and sleeping in the van at a small all-night fuel station, which was probably the safest place around. The staff were friendly and there was a bathroom I could use.

A day or so later, I met a young American woman from Wyoming who was also interested in blues music. She was travelling in a van with two large dogs, and we went to a club together and then camped on the grassy banks of the river right in Clarksdale. It felt much safer with her – mainly because of the two dogs, I suppose – and it was good to have some company, especially female company.

It wasn't easy to hear live music in the Mississippi Delta at that time. There were still some musicians around, but many had gone north to Chicago or Memphis where they had a better chance of making a living. Those who remained were pretty casual about their gigs, and nobody seemed to know when and where the bands would play.

I once travelled fifty miles to the Mississippi River town of Helena, Arkansas, to hear a band playing at Club 41. Once again there was no signage outside the club, and I had difficulties finding it. I stopped to ask directions at a local garage where the white attendant said with some dismay, *'But that's a black club.'* I finally got there only to discover that the lead singer Lonnie Shields had arrived, but most of his band *hadn't*, so right at the last minute the event was cancelled. Lonnie invited me to his parents' home for supper to make up for my disappointment. They were charming, but I spent an embarrassing evening because once again I could hardly understand a word they said, and I think they had a similar problem with my accent. Americans often commented on my accent, but when I in turn commented on theirs they were often surprised, as they'd never considered they had one!

I also visited legendary blues musician Junior Kimbrough's Juke Joint at Holly Springs, Mississippi. It was in an unmarked, unpainted, rusty wood and corrugated iron building which took a bit of finding. In contrast, the interior was colourful with interesting wall paintings. I was in luck because also performing was his friend, R.L. Burnside, another well-known Mississippi bluesman who lived right next door.

Back in Clarksdale I phoned Early Wright, a local radio disc jockey known as 'The Soul Man,' who had been presenting his blues and gospel radio programs six days a week for 50 years. He was on air at the time and immediately invited me up to the studio for an interview, rushing down a couple of flights of stairs to unlock the front door. Over the years many famous musicians had performed live on his show. They included B.B. King and Muddy Waters, and he told me that one day Elvis Presley had turned up in the studio.

Ignoring prepared scripts, Early had a particularly colourful style in his treatment of local advertisements: *'A laundromat where many thousands of people have the opportunity to wash and dry their clothes between the hours of 8 am and 10 pm each day.'* Or, *'at the grocery and market, the aisles are so big that two shopping carts can pass each other and never run into each other.'* He died several years after my visit, aged 84.

Greenwood is another town with strong blues associations and a Delta Blues Museum. B.B. King first broadcast from local radio station WGRM in 1940. The town was also a centre of protests and voter registration struggles during the civil rights movement. Happily my visit coincided with The First Mississippi Crossroads Blues Festival, featuring top musicians such as Taj Mahal, R. L. Burnside, Willie Cobbs and Howard Armstrong. It was a small festival, so I was able to meet all these luminaries.

I went back to Helena on the Mississippi River, Arkansas, for the King Biscuit Blues Festival – the largest free blues festival in the south, which attracts many thousands of people from all over the world. At one time Helena was thriving with dozens of saloons featuring blues, but had been struggling for many years. The city decided to host this festival to help restore some of the economy – lost in part to the decline of river trade. The first was held in 1986 and it has since become a lifeline for the whole area. It's named after the world's first live blues radio program 'King Biscuit Time,' which was started by Blues legend Sonny Boy 'Rice Miller' Williamson in 1941, on what was then Helena's new radio station KFFA. Another local bluesman Robert Lockwood Jr. was also involved, and it was hosted by 'Sunshine' Sonny Payne and sponsored by a local company, which made the King Biscuit brand of flour. It helped to sell lots of flour and is still on air. During the festival it broadcast from inside the historic railway station, which is now the Delta Cultural Center. Sonny Payne was still at the helm, and on that day Robert Lockwood Jr. was one of his guests! I introduced myself to Sonny and he asked to interview me, which was exciting. I stood by waiting for ages, but to my great disappointment he ran out of time because the Governor of Arkansas unexpectedly arrived and of course got priority over this unknown Aussie.

A huge camping area had been designated between the levee and the river within walking distance of the stages. It was run as a fundraiser by the Helena Fire Brigade, and was very crowded and somewhat primitive, but fun and a good place to meet lots of people. Late one night, George, a contact I had from the New York Blues Society, escorted me back along the dark levee to my van. As we looked down on the sea of tents, vans, people sleeping on the ground, campfires, makeshift toilets and showers surrounded by mud, it looked a bit like a refugee camp. George was utterly dismayed and viewed me with a mixture of sympathy and amazement, perturbed that I should be living unafraid and by choice in such conditions. He simply couldn't believe that I was actually *enjoying* it, and when we ran into each other again the next day he insisted on buying me a hot meal.

The weather was very hot and humid, and despite late nights I couldn't sleep in as the sun rose early, heating the van to an unbearable point by about 8 am. My neighbours rigged up a private solar shower using plastic sheeting and two hula hoops, and invited me to use it. You simply stood inside the hoops and pulled the top one, with the plastic attached, up around you, securing it to a flimsy pole. To survive the day's heat I wore a bandana around my neck, wrapped around a plastic bag full of ice.

The main festival stage was on the edge of a park facing the levee, which provided a natural slope for the audience. The normally rather dilapidated main street of Helena was alive with food and merchandise stalls, many run by local schools or charities raising much needed funds. A lot of the food was barbecued over wood fires, so the air was heavy with smoke. One shop was doing a roaring trade supplying passes to use their toilet ('potty passes') to anyone who bought merchandise – much nicer than using those awful plastic portable toilets, especially in such hot weather. There were also a number of street buskers. Mike from Seattle was a singer/guitarist with a gorgeous little black and white dog who was part of his act, taking the dollar notes proffered by listeners and placing them in a hat. After I'd spent some time patting her, she *removed* a bill from the hat and presented it to me!

One of the many musical highlights of the festival for me was the Neal family. The patriarch, Louisiana blues harmonica player Raful Neal, chose to stay in the south rather than follow other musicians north to Chicago. His ambition was to have a big family and to teach them all to play music. He went on to have 11 children and they *are* all musical. The eldest, my personal favourite, is Kenny Neal (singer, guitarist and harmonica player), who has recorded a number of albums, often with a band comprised entirely of his own brothers. He has a great voice and stage presence. Then there was drummer Willie 'Big Eyes' Smith, who used to play with Muddy Waters, blues pianist Pinetop Perkins and the flamboyant Sonny Rhodes, who played lap steel guitar and wore a brightly coloured jewelled turban. Some Australian musicians were performing there too – guitarist/vocalist Geoff Achison and harmonica player Harper.

Of particular interest due to its historical connections was the Othar Turner Family Fife & Drum Band. First recorded by folklorist Alan Lomax in 1942, Othar was 92 when I saw him. Along with various members of his family, he was helping to preserve what some researchers say is the *'most African of all surviving southern music'*. Apparently a blend of African rhythms and European instrumentation from the British colonial era, it represents a musical style which has existed for hundreds of years. Musicologists have suggested that some of these musical skills may have come from the military as, until the 1650s, all slaves were compelled to undergo military training. Othar played a five hole fife, which he made himself out of cane. He learned the music from a much older man, providing a link right back to pre-Civil War black slave music. At the time of my visit, he was the oldest and possibly the only living African American fife player in the country. The fife is usually accompanied by a snare and a bass drum, and sometimes musicians tap danced emulating the rhythms of the drum. This type of band was generally confined to the Mississippi area.

After hours, the local juke joints featured many of the top festival performers. At Eddie Mae's Cafe on the corner of Frank Frost Street, I saw the legendary Frank Frost himself. He actually lived there. He was a wonderful harmonica player and had learnt from Sonny Boy Williamson. With him was Sam Carr (son of bluesman Robert Nighthawk) on drums. They had been playing together for many years and in my ignorance I'd assumed they were long since dead. Sadly Frank did die in 1999 aged only 63, but Sam lived until 2009, dying at 83.

Eddie Mae's Café is one of those colourful bars with some very interesting clientele. One night I was one of just three or four white women, the only one alone and, not surprisingly, the only Australian, and I had a great time dancing with everyone. Southern African Americans have a particular way of dancing, especially to blues music. It's rather sexy and is referred to as 'low down and dirty.' I couldn't quite manage this, but despite my clumsiness and inhibitions I received *two* marriage proposals that night! Alcohol consumed by my suitors must certainly have played a part in prompting these exaggerated displays of affection, but I wondered if 'marriage' in this case was really just a euphemism for sex.

Each year at the festival, a number of teams compete in the King Biscuit BBQ Cook-Off. It's a serious business and I learnt a little about it when I became friendly with The Crispy Critters, an all-male team of 13 from different states. Covering three generations, they'd been competing for 18 years. A sign outside their tent read, *'Danger. Men Cooking.'* They don't own restaurants and just do this for fun. After talking to them about it, I decided that it's really an art form. A couple of the team are engineers. They had designed a special iron oven to cook whole pigs, complete with temperature control monitors to record temperature of inner chamber, ambient air temperature and meat temperature in the shoulder and ham. It also had a timer to remind them to baste and add wood every 30 minutes, and was mounted on a trailer so it could be towed around the country. Of course, a whole pig takes many hours to cook, so they worked in shifts throughout the night. Years of experimentation and research had gone into their basting sauce.

The Critters offered me a glass of wine and let me stay while the judging took place. At this stage they were one of three finalists. A member of the team was elected spokesperson and described cooking procedures to the four judges, but the sauce recipe is a closely guarded secret, never disclosed to anyone. That night the winners were announced from the main stage and The Crispy Critters were declared Grand Champions, coming first in all categories except sauce, where they were second. They were presented with enormous gaudy red and gold plastic trophies, depicting a pig standing on something resembling a small building. Their barbecue pork ribs were the best I'd ever tasted – absolutely mouth-watering, and I'm not much of a meat eater. They told me the largest barbecue cook-off in the U.S. is held at the Memphis In May Festival with more than 250 competitors, and the previous year they'd come second.

I back-tracked on my travels quite a lot, and attended King Biscuit Blues Festival several times. After I began my own radio show in Australia in 1997, I was eligible for a backstage pass. This gave me access to the musicians and lots of other interesting people. I was able to interview some, and to stand behind the barriers in front of the stage, almost at their feet while they performed. This particular spot was a great place for photography but to get there I had to walk right in front of the enormous speakers, which were deafening. I'd run out of earplugs and rushed down to the chemist to buy some, but despite ordering in large supplies they'd sold out within a couple of hours! I had to make do with little wads of cotton wool. Fortunately there were other smaller stages, including one which was totally acoustic and another devoted entirely to gospel music. One memorable day, that backstage pass gave me access to a VIP tent with complimentary food and wines.

Frank Frost at King Biscuit Blues Festival

"Getting Down" to the Blues in Eddie Mae's Cafe. (Frank Frost in check shirt)

With Blues Musician Kenny Neal at King Biscuit Blues Festival

At King Biscuit Blues Festival

With Sonny Rhodes at King Biscuit Blues Festival

Early Wright, "The Soul Man," in studio, WROX, Clarksdale

Jnr Kimbrough's Club, Holly Springs, Mississippi

Deeper South

After weeks of chasing music, I needed some respite and looked for a nice place to camp. I eventually settled into the Great River Road State Park, which is right on the Mississippi River in Mississippi. I couldn't see the river from the campground, but a short walk took me to a viewing platform, from where I was able to watch a beautiful sunset while huge barges slowly passed.

Next day the weather was lovely, and in no time I had loads of laundry strung up to dry in the warm sunshine. I even washed the van, which was wearing six months of dirt. Days like this every week or so were important to keep things under control! I was constantly checking to see if there was anything I could do without, but at the same time I couldn't seem to stop myself collecting stuff along the way. After catching up on the usual diary and letter writing, I spent the rest of the afternoon lying in my hammock, dozing and reading. I was one of only several people camped in this large area, so it was very quiet. After cooking the usual boring pasta dish for dinner for the fourth night in a row, I took it down to the river with a vodka and tonic. In America, gin and vodka are much cheaper than wine if you buy them in those plastic half gallons. I could often pick one up for nine or ten dollars. The tonic was more expensive!

Soon I was on the road again, heading even further south past the rotting remains of old cotton gins and plantation houses, and some squalid looking villages with tumbledown shanties and lots of poverty. The faces I saw in the street were mainly black. These scenes contrasted with attractive towns such as Lexington, with its lovely old square and historic buildings.

Florewood River Plantation State Park near Greenwood is a working re-creation of Mississippi Delta cotton plantation life from about 1850 when cotton was king. I gathered all the buildings were original – the beautiful big house and a plethora of outbuildings including planter's office, cookhouse, tutor's room, smokehouse, laundry, poultry house, sewing/loom room, barns, commissary, sawmill, sorghum mill, cotton gin, domestic servants quarters and slave quarters. Some of the larger plantations had several thousand slaves, but this one, owned by Greenwood LeFleur, cultivated about 100 acres with 50-60 slaves. In season, visitors can have a go at picking cotton. I had a marvellous afternoon wandering around and lingering in these old buildings. It gave me a real feeling for the period.

Tired after a long day of exploring, I stupidly managed to back the van into a tree in a campground. The bumper bar was crumpled but, even worse, was some damage to *me*. My neck was painful, but it wasn't until next day that I realised I must have suffered some kind of whiplash injury. Driving on a freeway I suddenly felt very faint and nauseated. I just managed to pull over but couldn't park safely as the road was raised up with narrow verges. After activating the hazard lights, I flopped on to the floor hoping the highway police would come along, but nobody stopped. After about an hour I was able to continue. This incident was scary, but as I was feeling a bit better I found a place to camp at Puskus Lake and went straight to bed.

I woke up at 5 am suffering from vision loss, nausea and the worst headache I'd ever had. My first migraine! Medication had absolutely no effect and I knew I must find a doctor to check out my neck. Nobody else was in the area, so as soon as daylight came I packed up and somehow managed to get to the nearest town about half an hour away, stopping every few miles to be ill on the side of the road. What a miserable experience.

Fortunately, I found a chiropractor who treated me immediately. He told me to spend time resting. I drove back to the lake and slept for 18 hours. Two more treatments and I was almost ready to go on the road again. This wonderful and kind chiropractor insisted on charging for only the first visit: *'If you turn left out of here, and drive under the railway bridge you'll see a liquor store on the right. Instead of paying me, treat yourself to a decent bottle of red wine which will help you relax and cheer you up.'* He was right, and I consider him one of the real treasures I was to come across on my journey.

After a couple of days I was ready to continue my travels and also contemplate the damage to my poor van. The bumper bar was badly dented. I spent some time trying to replace it with a secondhand one. However, Volkswagens were fairly rare in this area so I gave up on that and took the van to a garage to see if it could be repaired. A nice fellow bashed out the dent and he also refused to charge me. People were so kind, especially when they discovered I was from another country and travelling alone. I sometimes thought that perhaps they were so willing to help because I was doing something they'd dreamed of themselves, but hadn't had the opportunity.

On this trip I occasionally had marvellous luck. Once I decided to make a rushed drive to Jackson in Mississippi, with the idea of attending the Jubilee Jam Music Festival. I arrived tired and late, wondering if it was worth buying a ticket for the couple of hours left on that day or to wait until next morning. As I hovered near the gate, someone leaving offered me a ticket for the whole weekend, as they had a spare. Of course I accepted, and saw some great musicians including Percy Sledge, looking rather like a circus ringleader dressed in red, blue and white and singing his hit song 'When A Man Loves A Woman' (written by Calvin Lewis and Andrew Wright) to his latest wife. I also tried some southern food – deep fried catfish with hushpuppies, which are fried cornmeal croquettes. They apparently got their colourful name because they were often cooked and thrown to the dogs to keep them quiet while the main meal was being prepared out in the yard.

It was at this festival that I found my view blocked by a very tall African American man, wearing a large cowboy hat. I wondered out loud to the woman next to me about whether I should ask him to remove his hat. She suggested it wouldn't be a good idea, but I decided to anyway. Very politely I said, *'Excuse me Sir, but would you mind taking off your hat?'* Turning around, he replied, *'For a voice like that, I'd do anything.'* So my accent was still having a good effect!

At a small supermarket I stocked up on groceries for the next week or so. In the more rural areas it was hard to find the kinds of food I like to eat. For example, bread was usually the soft, spongy, white packaged variety, and the selection of fresh fruits and vegetables was limited, but there was always enough to make pasta sauce or a vegetable curry. I made my own muesli in large quantities whenever I found appropriate ingredients. Beer and spirits were readily available, except in the occasional 'dry' county. Wine was harder to find and often rather pricey. At that time, most people in the south didn't drink much wine and so knew little about it, often keeping good quality red in the fridge – understandable in a way, because in hot weather cool drinks are more sensible; iced tea for example. I once took a very special bottle of aged Australian Shiraz to friends in Tennessee, and was shocked to see them mix it with *sweet fizzy lemonade*.

That night was spent in the 'primitive' section of Holmes County State Park near Durant, in a lovely hilly area with lots of forest. 'Primitive' in American campgrounds usually means no laid out or levelled sites, no electrical hookup and sometimes no picnic tables; and the bathrooms are a short drive or long walk away in the main camping area. They are cheaper than the fully equipped area and often quieter, and I like their more rustic setting.

On this occasion it was hot and humid, with plenty of mosquitoes and sparkling fireflies after dark. I was the only person in the area. It wasn't gated and access was freely available from a public road nearby. Usually in these situations I was careful not to be seen by any passing vehicles. This evening I was a little careless and didn't even have the usual two chairs out. Just on dark, I was walking around when a car unexpectedly arrived and slowly drove through several times. I couldn't see who was in it, but they could clearly see me. They eventually left and I went to bed feeling slightly uncomfortable. I'd just got to sleep, but woke in a terrible fright to feel the whole van rocking and the tarpaulin covered box on the roof being tampered with. I peeped through a crack in the curtains but couldn't see anybody around, and it suddenly occurred to me that it might be an animal. I sounded the horn a couple of times and a huge racoon leapt off the roof and scurried into the bushes.

Racoons are gorgeous and highly intelligent animals, but can be a real nuisance in North American campgrounds and homes. They are often referred to as 'masked bandits'. Most people know not to leave any food lying around outside – even in closed coolers – as these creatures are pretty clever at opening most things. I met a party of 15 school children with two teachers camping in a State Park. Their coolers were rifled on their first night and their *entire* supply of food eaten – enough for 17 people for three days! No food was stored in my rooftop boxes, so I have no idea what enticed it up there that night. Probably just curiosity. They are very inquisitive creatures.

I decided to explore the Natchez Trace Parkway. This National Parks road roughly follows the historic trail or roadway, which was originally a trail used by the Natchez, Chickasaw and Choctaw Indians, and then the main north-south route for over 200 years. It became quite busy and by 1820 more than 20 inns were operating along its length – from Natchez on the Mississippi River in south east Mississippi, to the Ohio River Valley. The modern road which I drove along was started in the 1930s and now extends for about 450 miles from Natchez to just south of Nashville in Tennessee. I joined it near Jackson, Mississippi, and travelled the last 80 miles south to historic Natchez. It's like driving through a beautiful park, with grassy edges covered in wildflowers and lined with wonderful trees, including dogwoods which were in full bloom. Large white flowers covered their branches and carpeted the ground underneath.

No commercial vehicles are permitted on the parkway and speed is limited to 50 miles per hour – a leisurely pace after the hectic freeways. Along the way are nature trails (some following the ancient and sunken trace), historic sites and even some free campgrounds in natural settings. I camped at one of these – Rocky Springs, which in 1860 had a population of 2,616. All that remains are a couple of wells, a cemetery and the Methodist church built in 1837, still in use. There are pleasant walks through the area. These free campgrounds along the Natchez Trace have only basic facilities – no showers – but there are toilets and water, picnic tables and fire rings at every site. The hilly forested settings are delightful and piles of cut wood were usually placed near each site. I was lingering in the picnic area here when a large African American family invited me to share their barbecue lunch. It was great fun, but in return I had to submit to being filmed speaking *'in Australian.'*

This whole region of south western Mississippi is gorgeous. There are absolutely hundreds of restored antebellum houses, plantations and other historic buildings. In the 19th century Natchez had more millionaires than any other area in the U.S. This was partly due to the many thousands of slaves working the plantations, providing wealth for their owners. Melrose Estate is an imposing mansion – a blend of Greek revival and Georgian architecture – with beautifully proportioned rooms, Italian marble fireplaces and two unusual *hand-painted* English floor cloths.

I loved Springfield Plantation with its restored slave quarters and handsome 1786 mansion built entirely by slaves using clay from the land. President Andrew Jackson married Rachel Donelson here in 1791. When I visited it was still a working plantation of 1,000 acres. Its main house is one of the very few mansions of this era in which the interior is entirely original. I spent some time quietly soaking up the atmosphere in an old wooden rocking chair on the first floor verandah. I could picture 18th century women sitting there sipping mint juleps, enjoying the evening breeze and the view across the field, which is probably much the same as it was 200 years ago.

The house which intrigued me most was Longwood. It's the largest octagonal house in the country and has a Byzantine style onion-shaped dome. However, most of the interior was never finished due to lack of skilled labour and money around the time of the Civil War. Only the ground floor was ever occupied. The original workers' tools were still lying around upstairs, more or less where they left them. The gardens here were very pretty, with azaleas in bloom and huge trees draped with Spanish moss.

Before heading to Louisiana – New Orleans in particular – I spent a couple of lazy days camped in Homochitto National Forest right in the southwestern corner of Mississippi. Again the camping was free and there were few other people around, so I had the peace I always wanted after driving and sightseeing. I walked and lay in my hammock reading.

The rangers noticed I was alone and kindly visited me once or twice a day to make sure I was OK (or maybe it was to hear my accent!) On the second day, they said a tornado could be coming through, and if it got a bit wild the best place for me would be in the bathrooms a mile or so away. At this stage of my trip I hadn't experienced a tornado so was a bit anxious, but fortunately it changed direction and my day of leisure wasn't disturbed. I wondered what I *would* do if I happened to get caught in one with no shelter around. The weather seemed to be all over the place. One day 84 degrees and extremely humid, and next a rainstorm and down to 40 overnight. My ideal of around 70, clear and sunny was rarely achieved.

It was in this area that I first heard a Christian radio station. Programs included *'Lifestyles of the Resurrected and Faithful'* and *'Interpreting the news in the light of God's word.'* (*'Storms are God's way of telling us we're sinning.'*) As far as I knew, no similar stations existed in Australia at that time.

I was surprised at how much forest there is in Mississippi. There are even some black bears, although sadly the only one I saw there was lying dead on the side of the road. This mix of music, relaxing in the forest campgrounds and exploring historic places was very enjoyable. I still loved the complete freedom to do just as I wished, despite the fact that I was sometimes lonely, especially when I wasn't feeling well. Although I didn't want someone travelling with me all the time, I did miss a friend with whom to share some of my experiences.

I developed various strategies to cope with this. One of the most successful was writing to my family and friends, because it felt as though I was *talking* to them. Telephone calls were a rare luxury, although I did occasionally do battle with the telephone company AT&T. In order to speak to an operator to make a collect call to Australia, I had to say *'operator.'* Their automated service did not understand my accent. I tried different pronunciations, but often had to grab somebody walking past to ask them to say it into the telephone for me! When realising I wanted to call Australia, the operators then often asked, *'Ma'am will they be able to speak English?'*

I continued to keep my daily diary, and when I felt really down I read through it to remind myself of all the wonderful experiences I was having on this trip. Of course I *did* meet lots of people, most of them very nice and almost always amazingly generous, but we often had little in common so conversation was usually superficial.

Once I was visited by two women camping nearby. They were slightly odd characters, selling some kind of device which they claimed would clear the air of radiation. On discovering where I was from they rushed back to their camp, returning with two cans of food which they presented to me *'in the interest of international sisterhood!'*

Reading was something I especially enjoyed when travelling, and I usually tried to have books about the areas I was exploring. Some were *Trail of Tears: The Rise and Fall of the Cherokee Nation* by John Ehle, *My Bondage and My Freedom* by ex-slave Frederick Douglas (published in 1855), and *Telling Memories Among Southern Women* by Susan Tucker. But I also read books on the civil rights struggle, the Oregon Trail and sometimes classic novels by American authors like Mark Twain and William Faulkner. Then, of course, there was the music I was discovering, and the growing number of tapes I was carrying with me – Little Milton, Red Steagall, Mary Chapin Carpenter, Brooks & Dunn, Johnny Gimble (a Texas fiddler), Asleep at the Wheel and many more.

Racoon

The Family who shared their lunch at Rocky Springs Natchez Trace

Elma P. McCoy outside her shop

New Orleans and All That Jazz

I was now in the Deep South and on my way to New Orleans. The drive was scenic – first over the Homochitto River with its wide sandy banks, and into Louisiana on the large and impressive Interstate Highway 55. About 40 miles of the highway is raised on concrete pylons over water. I loved the bayous (swampy creeks) with the little boats and shacks perched on the banks, and then the huge lake Maurepas and the absolutely enormous Lake Ponchartrain with its 28 mile causeway – the longest in the world. At one stage I camped near the end of this causeway and regularly drove over it into New Orleans. At first I found it exciting to be driving across the longest causeway in the world, but by the third trip I realised it was actually quite boring. The only vaguely interesting part was wondering if there would be a police car at one of the little emergency parking spots and then seeing the high buildings of New Orleans come into view through the haze. Once I saw a racoon walking along the road, miles from land. How could it have got there? Maybe in or on somebody's vehicle.

At that time New Orleans was known as 'the murder capital of the world,' and when it subsequently lost that infamous claim some residents were disappointed. I didn't encounter any safety threats, but arrived feeling over-tired after a very long day's driving, and lost my way as soon as I encountered the city's freeway system. I was trying to find the main post office to collect my mail. There were lots of roadworks, which I discovered later was fairly normal for New Orleans. It's difficult trying to navigate a new and complicated road system when you are also the driver and when the signage is terrible. As usual, I had looked up directions in advance and written them in bold ink on a piece of paper attached to the dashboard. I did eventually find my way downtown and collected some letters, but got lost several more times before crossing the huge Mississippi River to camp in Bayou Segnette State Park.

When I arrived there, now utterly exhausted, I was shocked to discover it was closed due to a problem with the availability of water. The bathrooms would be closed between 7 pm and 7 am, and only those people with their own toilet facilities would be allowed in. Evening was approaching and I felt far too tired and stressed to try to find anywhere else at that stage, so I talked the rangers into letting me stay, telling them I'd manage between those hours.

 I loved this peaceful park and I often wonder how it fared during Hurricane Katrina. It's only 12 miles from the bustle of downtown New Orleans, but felt like a tranquil oasis. The banks of the bayou were interesting to walk along. There were lots of birds and even alligators. I saw one sunning itself on a log right in the campground. They are much smaller and less dangerous than the crocodiles we have in northern Australia and they don't tend to bother people, but it's wise to be cautious. A stunning Yellow Crowned Night Heron, in its full mating plumage, reminded me of some of the men I would see on stage at the New Orleans Jazz & Heritage Festival!

It was hot, humid and thundery, and rained very heavily all night, so I appreciated being able to sleep in my cozy van. One of the major problems here – and in many places I camped – was the clouds of insects, particularly mosquitoes, and even when it was not raining I had to retreat into the van just before dusk. The humidity, along with cooking inside, led to a healthy growth of mould on the ceiling, which nearly drove me crazy. I ended up treating it periodically with diluted bleach, inadvertently leaving splotchy marks on the fabric lining. The other problem with this dampness was that to prevent the canvas sides from rotting, the van roof was only supposed to be lowered if they were completely dry. I tried to keep the roof closed if it was raining, as drying it out before I left wasn't always possible.

It was at about this time that I decided to fetch some of my best clothes, including my long dancing skirt, out of a suitcase, which I had carefully wrapped in a large plastic garbage bag and stored on the roof rack, covered with a tarpaulin. Unfortunately both the tarp and the plastic had torn in places and water had leaked in. This had obviously happened some time ago as everything was mouldy. I tried washing the clothes but the damage was done, and I had to throw everything away. The only thing salvageable was my rucksack, which I hardly ever used anyway. Obviously I should have been checking the suitcase from time to time. I decided to get rid of it completely and use only purpose-made, properly-sealed plastic containers, which proved to be the right answer.

New Orleans is a beautiful and fascinating city, and what better time to be there than during the Jazz & Heritage Festival. I collected my festival ticket and decided to do some sightseeing. Parking in the historic area of Algiers on the southern bank of the Mississippi River, I took the passenger ferry across to the city, then a cruise on the Steamboat Natchez with its exotic 32-note steam calliope – a mid-19th century steam-powered organ. Wood is normally used to boil the water to make the steam, which is pushed through the pipes or whistles operated by a keyboard. As well as being used in churches, they were popular with travelling fairs and circuses. Only about 75 were ever built and, of the less than 20 which still exist, four are on steamboats operating on the Mississippi River. The Natchez was only christened in 1975 and its calliope is a replica – sounding a bit like a train whistle playing a tune. There were synchronised coloured lights which came on each time a note was played.

I also learned some interesting facts about the river on this trip. The fourth longest in the world, the Mississippi carries approximately 685 million tons of sediment into the Gulf of Mexico every year. Of its 2,500 miles, only about 850 are commercially navigable. I thought that later I would try to explore some of the upper Mississippi River with its many locks.

We passed a huge concrete barge, loaded with recreation vehicles parked side by side. Apparently this is a popular way to travel. No facilities are provided, but you can cruise the river with all the comforts of your own motor home. I didn't see any chairs or people on the deck, and wondered if they watched the passing scenery from *inside* their vehicles.

After my cruise I explored the French Quarter. This is a city which has definitely preserved its original centre, and there are streets of picturesque historic buildings. It's quite commercialised in parts with tacky souvenir and sex shops. Some bars had bored-looking musicians belting out New Orleans jazz standards. Entry was usually free, but patrons had to buy at least one (over-priced) drink per set or face being thrown out. One venue I did love was the famous Preservation Hall. This non-profit establishment for serious lovers of traditional New Orleans jazz opened in 1961 in order to, as its name suggests, preserve the music. It has its own house band and record label, and is a small, intimate, totally acoustic venue. I remember it being rather dark with lots of character, and that I had to sit on the floor. Others were standing at the back and just a few managed to get a seat. The audience could make requests, but had to tip $20 to get the band to play 'When the Saints Come Marching In!' You hear that song rather too often in New Orleans, and no doubt the musicians were a bit sick of it.

New Orleans is famous for its food and there are many wonderful restaurants in this area of the city. I'd been to some on a business trip a few years earlier. In one of the souvenir shops I saw an entire wall of hot sauces with fascinating names such as 'Road to Hell,' 'Halfway to Pure Hell,' 'Pure Hell,' 'Ragin' Inferno,' 'Global Warming,' 'Dave's Insanity Sauce,' and 'Dave's Total Insanity Sauce.' There's even a guidebook devoted *entirely* to Louisiana hot sauces. When having a coffee in the cafe of a large hotel, I noticed that a number of different staff came to ask me if I needed anything else. I commented on this when the fifth person arrived and was told, *'Oh, I'm sorry ma'am, we just want to hear you talk!'*

Later I crossed over the river again to Jean Lafitte National Historic Park and Preserve for a ranger-led walk on the Bayou Coguille Trail in the Barataria Preserve. Almost all of the trail was on a raised boardwalk through swamps and across the Kenta Canal to a marsh overlook. We saw lots of alligators, birds, snakes, fish, squirrels and large irises in bloom. There are also plenty of frogs, including bird frogs (I couldn't distinguish their calls from birds), and sheep frogs, which really do sound *exactly* like sheep.

There are various fur-bearing animals in the bayou areas of southern Louisiana – muskrats, minks, beavers, nutrias (swamp rats) and even bears.

The only one I saw was a nutria swimming around in the water. They were introduced from South America and have proven to be extremely destructive of the habitats in some areas. Weighing up to 25 pounds with twenty sharp teeth including four big incisors, they have large appetites and can fairly easily destroy whole plant species. Unusually, the females have teats high on their sides so the young can feed while the mother is swimming. The ranger who led the walk was Bruce 'Sunpie' Barnes, considered by many to be the best blues harmonica player in New Orleans. I made a point of seeing him at the festival and noted that he is also a wonderful zydeco accordionist, and gives a very spirited and sexy performance on stage.

The New Orleans Jazz & Heritage Festival was one of the highlights of my American adventures and I went to it three years in a row. That first year was probably the most exciting as I didn't know what to expect, but the second year my sister came with me, so that was special, too.

The festival at the fairgrounds ran over seven days with a break of three in the middle, which was welcome as the whole event was huge and could be exhausting. The fairgrounds were open from 11 am to 7 pm, but there were also lots of evening concerts in the city and with all those visiting musicians in town, the bars and night clubs had special events. The atmosphere all over the city was one of infectious excitement.

All the publicity suggested that parking anywhere near the fairground venue would be impossible and everyone should catch a special bus from the city. I wanted to be independent and decided to risk driving. Leaving early, I found a parking spot only two blocks from one of the main entrances. It was in the street right outside a house belonging to Myrtle, an elderly woman who offered to watch over my van which she did every day, even using her rubbish bin to reserve a space for me. I think she liked a bit of company, and enjoyed inspecting my van and the novelty of sitting in it to have a cuppa while I ate my breakfast. This was one of a number of cases when my *van* was the drawcard – not me or my accent. Most of the residents in that area enjoy the festival atmosphere, and many cash in on it by renting parking spaces in their yards, selling food, sun hats, cool drinks and insulated can holders. Some of these holders had straps so you could hang them around your neck, leaving your hands free to clap.

One day Myrtle wasn't there and my parking spot was gone, but I found an even better one right next to a Hari Krishna temple. As soon as they saw me parking, they came out with breakfast and provided free vegetarian meals for the duration of the festival for me and anyone else passing by. Sometimes they even insisted that I take a plate home for later. They also kept an eye on my van and once, out of respect, I took part in one of their services. At the end of every day I went back to Jean Lafitte National Park to camp.

The Jazz & Heritage Festival is huge with an average attendance of half a million. When I was there it had 14 music stages and various other cultural happenings, including Louisiana cooking demonstrations, art and craft stalls and a Louisiana folk village. An African area offered African food and clothing and the Congo Square stage. This was where I saw the colourful Free Spirit Stilt Walkers – a local group carrying on a tradition which was thought to originate in West Africa and later brought to the Caribbean. They dance on their *stilts!* I tried various local foods, such as fried catfish po-boy (a long bread roll), boiled crawfish, jalapeno bread, shrimp etouffee (a spicy stew with Creole seasoning – usually paprika, cayenne pepper, thyme, basil, oregano and lots of garlic), jambalaya (a spicy one-pot rice dish with prawns, sausage and chicken), gumbo (similar to jambalaya but more of a stew served over rice), and the best fried green tomatoes I've ever tasted. Another delicacy was fried alligator with turtle sauce, which was a bit tough and got stuck in my teeth. *Well*, I thought, *better than the other way around!*

New Orleans is famous for its parades and several wove their way through the crowds at the festival every day. They usually consisted of a brass marching band, accompanying members of Social Aid & Pleasure Clubs. These clubs were originally formed in the mid-1880s to provide some benefits to the African American community in the form of payments for families of fee-paying members who became ill or died, like a kind of insurance. This is no longer such an economic necessity so, as far as I can gather, they are now mainly for pleasure, and march on major holidays, events and at jazz funerals. First in line are the club members and marshals, dancing and prancing their way along blowing whistles, waving fans (lots of feathers) and umbrellas and wearing colourful co-ordinated outfits – usually smart suits with snazzy hats, often in primary colours. They are followed by the brass band and then members of the public known as the 'second liners.' There are modern takes on these traditional brass bands, sometimes featuring young musicians with more of a funk influence, like Dirty Dozen Brass Band. They have helped to keep this style of New Orleans music alive.

When my sister visited, we danced our way around the festival grounds. She was enthusiastically following a marching band when she fell and had to be treated in one of the first aid tents. This didn't dampen her spirits at all, and when I finally found her she was in the process of having the staff take photos of her bandaged foot for her souvenir album. At one of the shops we both found earrings we wanted, but couldn't bring ourselves to be so self-indulgent. Our solution was to buy them for each other as gifts!

The gospel tent was particularly exciting. It held thousands of people. The performers I saw were all African American, and varied from groups of three or four members to choirs of a hundred or more. Some were families of several generations like the Johnson Extension. Others had colourful names – The Mighty Chariots, Famous Rocks of Harmony, Soulful Heavenly Stars, The Famous Mighty Imperials, Mighty Clouds of Joy, Zulu Ensemble Male Chorus, New Orleans Headstart Singing Angels, The Mighty Sensations, and Holy Name Singers of the Institute of Divine Metaphysical Research. Above the stage was a sign: *'Let's Jam for Jesus.'* The audience, which included lots of church groups, was usually very excited, almost frenzied, with people clapping and leaping to their feet shouting out, *'Amen,' 'Praise the Lord,'* and, *'Tell it to us, sister.'* When you have so many people behaving like this it's easy to get swept up into it, and I found myself on my knees, hanging on to the fence surrounding the stage. I was on my knees because really I didn't want to block others' view! The entire tent rocked, spurring on the already enthusiastic performers until they sometimes went into a trance and had to be held down to prevent injuring themselves. Security staff weren't seriously concerned with keeping the audience in its place, as the metal barriers across the front of the stage were quite effective. Their main problems were keeping the musicians *on* stage! As it was steaming hot, a local funeral parlour handed out cardboard fans advertising their services.

Among the most exotic performers in New Orleans are the Mardi Gras Indians. All African American males, they wear extraordinarily extravagant attire modelled on Native American dress but much more exaggerated, with *enormous* brightly coloured feathered headdresses and elaborately beaded costumes. They make these themselves at vast expense – often taking a whole year to do so – and because they never wear the same costume for more than twelve months, they have to make a new one every year. They named themselves after Native American Indians who often supported escaping black slaves, and date back to the 18th century when the black neighbourhoods of New Orleans, unable to participate in the official Mardi Gras, held their own celebrations. Each area or ward of the city formed a Mardi Gras Indian 'tribe' with a Big Chief. There was a lot of violence, as the parades were often used as a time to settle old scores. This tradition continues today, but the exchange of insults is stylised, and the emphasis is more on competing with dress and stage performance. Some of the tribe names reflect their heritage. For example – Golden Arrows, Creole Wild West, White Cloud Hunters and North Ward Hunters. They each have their own tribal songs and ceremonial dances with drums. Those heavy beaded costumes are far too hot to be leaping around in the New Orleans humidity, so as the show progresses the Big Chief gradually discards one piece after another until he is down to an ordinary T-shirt or singlet and trousers. I was thrilled to have my photograph taken with one whilst he was still in his full regalia, and a prized souvenir is the large yellow feather he pulled out of his headdress for me.

One marquee concentrates on the more traditional side of jazz, with bands such as Wallace Davenport and his New Orleans Jazz Band. It's here that you see more 'second liners,' like the Double Nine Highsteppers. They didn't follow the bands, but danced their way down the aisles, with many of the audience joining in. Some were holding beautifully decorated umbrellas. Umbrellas seem to play a special part in all New Orleans parades. I thought that might be because they had to be carried due to frequent heavy rain, so were incorporated as a feature. They are often fringed, feathered or frilled and covered with embroidered musical notes or instruments, and can be real artworks.

I learnt a lot about music in New Orleans and I particularly liked the local Cajun and Zydeco bands, and the chance to see some big name artists like Bob Dylan, Buddy Guy, Lloyd 'Mr. Personality' Price, Nina Simone, Aretha Franklin, B.B. King, Pete Fountain, Willie Nelson, Clarence 'Gatemouth' Brown, Lionel Hampton and Sonny Rollins. Little Richard stood on top of his piano and shouted, *'Look at me, I'm 61 and still beautiful.'* Eccentric bluesman 'Ironing Board' Sam got his name because he always set up an ironing board on stage on which to play his keyboard. Rhythm & Blues pianist Dr. John was described in the program as *'insanity with a respectable name.'* He started off as a New Orleans session player and later developed a persona based on a legendary New Orleans voodoo figure.

At the outdoor stages, which featured Cajun and Zydeco bands (Eddie Le Jeune, D.L. Menard, BeauSoleil and many more), I discovered that most Cajun people are as crazy about dancing as I am. Their history and music is interesting. They are descendants of the Acadians, a group of French who migrated to what is now Nova Scotia in Canada, but were expelled from there by the British. Many eventually settled in Louisiana in the 1760s, which at that time was owned by France. It was bought by the Americans in 1803 under what is known as The Louisiana Purchase. Their lively music – perfect for dancing – largely evolved during their time in Canada and remained virtually unchanged for nearly 200 years. In the 20th century it absorbed aspects of jazz, western swing and blues. Traditionally it is all acoustic and features a fiddle, guitar, small button accordion, a metal triangle struck with a metal rod, and sometimes the large string bass. They apparently brought the fiddles and triangles with them from France, but I think German emigrants were responsible for the introduction of the accordion or melodeon – a smaller instrument. When the factories in Germany were destroyed in WWII, the Cajuns started building their own. Vocals are in Cajun, a dialect of French, and their singing is often almost a shout, with an occasional 'Cajun yell,' which sounds something like *aaaeee*. They taught me how to do that and in return I taught them the Australian call of the bush, the *cooee*. They are a fun-loving group, and even when rain made the festival a quagmire, they danced on and on until they were absolutely covered with mud. They were happy to teach any onlookers the main steps, and I was keen to follow up on this after the festival finished.

Zydeco is, I think, a kind of Creole adaptation of Cajun music, with a heavier beat more inspired by blues and reggae. It features the large piano accordion rather than the smaller Cajun button variety. There are also drums and electric instruments (as opposed to the acoustic of traditional Cajun), and a 'rub board' of corrugated metal, worn like a vest and scratched with spoons or forks or metal finger picks to provide percussion. Zydeco is usually played by black musicians so attracts more of a black audience, and dancing to it is generally quite different to dancing to Cajun. It *is* possible to dance the Cajun jitterbug (a kind of swing dance) to Zydeco, but often there are not such complicated steps or manoeuvres. The couples I saw at a Zydeco festival in country Louisiana tended to just hold on to each other and sway, or even bounce in time to the music.

I went to an evening concert in the city and saw a popular young gospel singer. His was not the traditional gospel I had expected, but more modern Christian music, and to my surprise he attracted a huge crowd of teenage girls who screamed and practically threw themselves about in a frenzy, behaving in much the same way as any young girl might in front of her rock idol. Once again, my restricted Christian upbringing affected my expectations.

I also went to a famous music venue called Tipitina's, got lost on the way and asked directions at a garage. The conversation went like this: *'Is Tipitina's on Chapatoula?' 'Yep.'* We could have been speaking a foreign language!

At Tipitina's, Bruce Daigrepont's Cajun band was playing, and lots of people were dancing. A local invited me to dance and then bought me a drink at the bar. We got along well, and towards the end of the evening he wrote a list of what he considered was necessary for a perfect relationship. He went though it with me point by point! Was he checking me out as a possibility? First on his list was *'mutually compatible goals.'* I diffused the situation a little by mistakenly interpreting that as *'mutually compatible* goats.' Others on his list included *'many similar interests,' 'fabulous sex,' 'similar ethics and etiquette,'* and *last* of all, *'love.'* I decided he would certainly not be on *my* list.

After a day or so at the rainy festival, I decided to give up trying to keep my shoes clean or even on my feet at all! I squelched barefooted through the ankle deep mud, glad that glass was banned from the area, but wishing that everyone wouldn't throw their spiky crawfish claws and shells on the ground. It rained and rained. The mud was spattered up to my knees, and one day warnings of a dangerous thunderstorm closed the festival down early. At the end of each day, long lines of people were trying to clean themselves at the water taps, and outside the fairgrounds enterprising locals offered a hose-down for 50 cents.

A day or two later, a huge storm dumped seven inches of rain in just over an hour. I was driving and had to stop on the side of the road. It was impossible to see through the windscreen. A couple of feet of water covered the supermarket car park, but it soon all drained away and things were back to normal. These extraordinarily heavy storms and the high water table are the reasons local cemeteries have the graves built above ground. When people tried to dig the pits, they filled with water before the coffins could even be lowered.

That first year I stayed on in New Orleans for a few days after the festival finished. I had met Frank, an elderly man who was a good dancer and who offered me the use of a wonderful vintage 'Airstream' caravan parked in his driveway – one of those much sought after rounded silver vans, probably from the sixties. It was hooked up to electricity, had air conditioning and a small bathroom with a shower, so I was comfortable, self-contained and glad to get away from the annoying insects at the campground. I was covered with bites and my hands and feet were swollen. To welcome me, Frank had cooked an enormous upside down pineapple cake and dozens of pralines – that fabulously rich New Orleans sweet made with sugar and pecans. He also took me out dining and dancing a few times, which was great. Sometimes we went to Cajun dances and sometimes Western. At one dance hall the band played nonstop from 7 pm until 2 am, with just a change of one or two musicians from time to time so they could rest in turns. Although in his seventies, Frank must have been very fit because he never wanted to sit out a dance. It was beginning to feel like a repeat of my experience in Roswell, where I had to bandage my blistered feet before every evening out.

As I was getting ready to continue my travels, Frank asked me if I liked squirrels. I said I did as I had often watched their antics when I was camping. *'Good,'* he said, *'because I've got two in the freezer and you can have one to take with you!'* So it seems that in Louisiana they really *do* live up to their reputation of eating anything which moves. I declined this offer, but later on in my trip I was offered a cooked squirrel leg. It was a tiny little thing and to be polite I made an effort to nibble at it. Although it tasted a bit like chicken, I somehow couldn't enjoy it, especially when I was told the locals called them tree rats.

The Westbank Steppers Social and Pleasure Club

Mardis Gras Indian

Mardis Gras Indian

Young Member of a New Orleans Social and Pleasure Club

Dressed for the New Orleans Jazz and Heritage Fest

Cajun Dancers in the mud

Cajun Dancing, New Orleans

This coupon entitles you to
50¢ OFF
CITY PARK CATERING
SHRIMP JAMBALAYA
LIMIT ONE DISCOUNT PER COUPON

AREA II
BOOTH # 31

Frank's Airstream Caravan, New Orleans

Rural Louisiana and More Cajun Music

After New Orleans I decided to explore more of southern Louisiana with its marshes, bayous, and antebellum mansions, by following the famed Great River Road – a tourist route winding along not far from the Mississippi River. Many of these old mansions had avenues of wonderful old live oak trees draped with Spanish moss. Some trees are nearly 600 years old. They are called *live* oaks because, unlike other oaks, they are evergreen. The older trees are protected and many belong to the Live Oak Society, which has its headquarters in Lafayette. To be eligible for membership, trees must be at least 100 years old and pay an annual fee of 25 acorns.

I spent a day on Avery Island which is not actually an island, but a dome composed of salt deposits eight miles deep surrounded by wetlands. Hot chillies are grown here and the salt is harvested for Tabasco pepper sauce. I took a tour of their factory, which was started by Edward Avery McIlhenny who also cultivated the Jungle Gardens – 170 acres of local and exotic plants, lakes, bayou and lawns. Within the grounds is a major breeding site for the snowy egret, which McIlhenny is attributed with saving from extinction. There were no egrets when I was there, but I did see the specially constructed platforms for the 20,000 nests which are occupied each spring. Thirty truckloads of twigs for nesting are dropped in the area every year.

Feeling hot and tired I sometimes had to force myself on, but some fascinating discoveries kept me going. For example, I found out that in 1980 an oil drilling company accidentally broke into a salt mine tunnel

1,500 feet under Lake Peigneur, west of New Iberia. All the water was sucked out of the lake and blasted up from the mine. A new house plus 65 acres of land ended up *in* the lake, which refilled in only two days.

For dinner one night I bought a huge pile of freshly cooked crawfish. The elderly man selling them told me that $100 million of these crustaceans were harvested every year in Louisiana. Their existence is celebrated at the 'world famous' Breaux Bridge Crawfish Festival held during the first weekend of May, where you can eat boiled crawfish, fried crawfish, crawfish etouffee, crawfish dogs, crawfish jambalaya, crawfish boudin (sausage), crawfish pies, crawfish bisque, crawfish gumbo etc. There are also crawfish races, a crawfish eating contest and a crawfish etouffee cook-off (etouffee is a spicy stew, a bit thicker than gumbo.) Of course, Cajun music and dancing is also a feature of the festival, and a requirement is that all bands must have an accordion.

By now I had started to learn a variety of Cajun dance steps. It's different from western dancing, even though some of the dances share the same names. For example, there is a Cajun two-step and a waltz (both are variations of ballroom dances done with a partner) and an extremely energetic jitterbug, which nearly did my knees in. In some venues, I saw dancers preparing for this jitterbug by doing a series of warm-up exercises. It was as if they were about to go for a lengthy jog. They even wore jogging shoes, shorts and towelling headbands. For the more traditional Cajun dances like the waltz or two step, the women usually wore long skirts which gracefully swirled around as they turned.

There are lots of little places in Louisiana which hold Cajun dances, but they tend to be scattered around the countryside and have to be hunted down. Some are in dilapidated looking shacks miles from anywhere, and others in smart restaurants in the centre of a town. I even found one in the middle of a campground. In the smarter establishments, most of the dancers were regulars who all knew each other and, although they were friendly, they were not particularly interested in dancing with a stranger, especially one who was still learning. Once the only dance I got was with a 90 year old ex-priest who could barely totter around the floor, but apparently enjoyed holding the women. He had a tight grip!

The little town of Eunice, right in the heart of Cajun country, hosts 'Rendez Vous des Cajuns' at the historic Liberty Theater every Saturday evening. It's a live television show with Cajun comedians and bands, and a disturbingly sloped dance floor right in front of the stage. Most of the show is in Cajun French and there are usually three bands with comedians in between. Locals translated some of the jokes for me. At the time I thought they were very funny, but when I recently tried to decipher my notes – *'bloated bull, bugle and a drawbridge'* – they just didn't make sense, so I can't tell you any!

Near Eunice I visited the famous Savoy Music Center. Marc Savoy has played the Cajun accordion for about 60 years and is considered by many to be the best. He also builds them, and every Saturday morning hosts an acoustic jam session. Some of the finest Cajun musicians play at this little shop. The Savoy family is very welcoming, and visitors are encouraged to bring food to share, particularly the boudin sausage.

The small town of Mamou, a little further north of Eunice, was great because there were at least six bars in the main street and most offered live Cajun music and a free dinner on different nights of the week. Fred's Lounge was run by the delightfully warm and friendly Tante Sue. It was only open on Saturday mornings and had a live radio broadcast with a Cajun band – Steve Riley & The Mamou Playboys – which filled most of the tiny venue. Busloads of people arrived, so it was packed with little room to dance. I won the prize (a delicious selection of Cajun sauces and spices) for having travelled the furthest. Not many could compete with Australia for that. When Fred's closed for the day, people moved next door for another Cajun band and more dancing, and then further up the street for a free catfish dinner or some of that tasty boudin sausage.

Everyone I met in these little towns was extremely friendly and kind to me, but I noticed complete segregation. Even though it is not unusual for 50% of the population to be African American, I never saw a black face at a Cajun bar or restaurant. I commented on this to a bartender, who told me they would not be welcome. I suggested that surely it would be illegal not to admit them, and what would he say if I arrived with an African American friend. He said he would ask *me* to leave and assume my friend would go with me. On the other hand, I always felt welcome at the Louisiana black clubs, which often had Zydeco bands.

I hunted down one little Cajun nightclub in the backwoods. A dance featured a local band. They were amazed to have me arrive unexpectedly and immediately called one of the managers – an Australian married to a local woman. He was off duty, but rushed in to meet me. He hadn't spoken to anybody from his own country for ages, and insisted that I come back to his home, meet his wife and camp on his property. But first he took me to a Zydeco club. He was a nice fellow, but I was glad I had driven my own vehicle there as he drank quite heavily, and when it was time to leave was too intoxicated to drive. I dropped him at his home and escaped!

Alabama to Nashville

The next state I visited was Alabama, east of Louisiana, and my first stop was at a campground on the shores of Tombigbee Lake. This lake is part of the Tennessee-Tombigbee Waterway, built in the 1970s. With a canal, locks and various dams, it enabled goods to be shipped directly from ports on the Tennessee River in the mid-south such as Chattanooga to an ocean port in the Gulf of Mexico. I camped right next to the water and all night long enormous barges passed by, often eight lashed together. They were mostly empty going up river, and full of cut timber and wood chips coming back. I particularly liked watching them at night when they picked out the banks with huge spotlights. I took my sister there several years later and we camped in the same place. She was really looking forward to seeing a barge, but even though we waited until well after dark none came through, so we gave up and went to bed. Half an hour later we could hear one coming around the bend, and without thinking twice we both rushed out in our bare feet and flimsy nighties and stood on the bank, waving while the enormous spotlights played over us!

Near Mobile, Alabama's only port, I camped at the exotically named Chickasabogue Park a few miles north of the city. I chose a lovely site in a forested area. As it was Friday and I thought the place might fill up for the weekend, I left a few items, including my wash up bowl and chair, to show that the site was occupied and went off to explore the city.

Mobile has lots of interesting historic buildings, including Fort Conde, right on the waterfront. Originally built in 1735 it was occupied first by French troops then English, Spanish and American. I was disappointed to discover that like a lot of the buildings in the area, it was actually a reconstruction on the original site. Much of the town had been destroyed by fires in 1827 and 1839.

Arriving back at the campground in the early evening, I discovered that everything I'd left there had been stolen. This was disappointing, inconvenient, and of course cost money to replace. It was the only theft I experienced during all my travels in America. The people in the camp office were most apologetic and gave me two nights camping free of charge. They also got their maintenance staff to fix the table in my van which had come apart from its base, so all of that more than made up for my losses.

However, that night I was kept awake for hours by a young group of revellers nearby. I should have moved, but was too tired to pack everything up and drive away. I just kept hoping they'd eventually shut up and go to bed. It crossed my mind that maybe they were the people who stole my things. I got my revenge early next morning by driving past the now-slumbering group with my radio blaring, which set their dogs barking!

I was keen to go to another African American church, so on Sunday I found one that had been recommended by one of the park rangers. As usual I was the only white person there, and felt a bit self-conscious. There was some great singing which I enjoyed, but then it turned into the longest church service I'd ever attended.

The sermon just seemed to go on and on and on. I was reminded *again* of all the years I had been forced to sit in church, feeling uncomfortable while my father was preaching sermons which I was sure were directed at me and my wayward behaviour. I could never walk out then, and I felt just as trapped here. I was in the middle of a row in the middle of the church and thought it would be insulting, disruptive and rude to leave. I tried to be patient by thinking about what I'd do after the service and by practising my pelvic floor exercises.

I finally made my escape after *three and a half hours*. The congregation was filing up to the altar to take communion. I walked in the opposite direction straight out the door and into my van. My instinct to get away was so strong that I drove and drove until I got to Florida and Pensacola Beach, where I had a stiff gin with lunch (almost unheard of for me) and a brisk walk on the beautiful white sand.

I felt that my trip was being dominated by insects (as usual I was covered in bites) and my poor van, which was giving more problems. The fresh water pump had stopped working again, but worse was the fact that despite my letting the engine warm up for some time before setting out in the morning, it often just stopped without warning after about 20 minutes of driving. It would start again, but not until I'd turned the ignition off and then on again. This usually happened in extremely inconvenient spots – when I was in heavy traffic and there was nowhere to get off the road, or when I was just entering a freeway, and once when I was driving up a steep narrow winding road with an enormous coal truck right behind me.

This continued for weeks, and despite calling in at garages every few days or so, nobody seemed to be able to do anything. Every morning I'd be saying, *'please don't stop now, please don't stop now,'* but the cantankerous beast almost always did. It was so unsafe, but it seemed there was absolutely nothing I could do except hope it wouldn't happen at a *really* dangerous moment on the road.

I came across a brochure for the Association for Applied & Therapeutic Humor, *'committed to advancing the knowledge, understanding and use of therapeutic humor to enhance healing …'*

I knew laughter could be great therapy, but had never heard of an association solely dedicated to it. A three year course was offered, each level qualifying for a graduate or undergraduate college credit. I thought I could do with something to lighten things up. However, dancing could be my therapy, and I decided to drive north to Nashville where I was sure I'd find lots of suitable night spots, and possibly a VW dealership where I'd have a better chance of having the current problem diagnosed and fixed. I wasn't in any rush and just ambled, sightseeing along the way and staying in some pretty State Parks.

On the second morning the van wouldn't start at all and I had to call the American Automobile Association. The mechanic jump-started it and said he couldn't find anything wrong, but next morning the same thing happened. This time the park ranger got it going and I found yet another garage, only to be told the starter motor had burnt out *again*. Of course I had to tell the mechanics to go ahead and replace it.

On I went again, feeling more and more anxious about my van and its lack of dependability. Of course I was driving huge distances and often in very hot weather.

Almost the final straw was when that night – 3 am actually – I heard rustling sounds in the biscuit packet on the shelf next to my head. I put the light on and yes, there were mouse droppings and a little piece gnawed out of the packet. My heart dropped. I had visions of a repeat of the pack rat experience in the desert. I set another trap with cheese and managed to catch him in a few minutes, thank goodness.

I found another historic theatre in one of the little towns I passed through. The door was open so I thought I'd check it out. Inside I was greeted by several people and asked to sign their guest book, which I did – *'Jan Dale from Melbourne, Australia.'* Then I was conducted to the main theatre upstairs where, much to my embarrassment, I realised a wedding was taking place. I discreetly left, but often wondered what that bride and groom thought when they came across my signature in their wedding guest book!

Nashville lived up to expectations with plenty of live music and dancing. I found a campground within walking distance of a number of venues, including the famous Grand Ole Opry. There was even a nightly concert in the campground's 750 seat music hall. It was a thrill to be able to get a front row seat at the Opry (a cancellation, surely) and have a close up view of some of the great old traditional country artists, such as Grandpa Jones, Wilma Lee Cooper, Hank Snow, Bill Monroe – the father of Bluegrass music – and Little Jimmy Dickens, who was very short and quipped: *'When I pull up my socks I blindfold myself.'*

The Opry Square Dance Band with the Melvin Sloan Dancers was especially fun to watch. This concert was started in 1925 by George D. Hay as a one hour 'barn dance' on radio station WSM. It's now the longest running radio broadcast in U.S. history, and showcases a mix of traditional and contemporary country, bluegrass, folk, gospel and comedy performances in front of a live audience. Hundreds of thousands of visitors are attracted from around the world. I saw it at the purpose-built hall opened in 1974, seating 4,400. Its home used to be the beautiful Ryman Auditorium, originally built as a religious tabernacle and recently renovated. The Opry returns there for three months over winter.

The newer venue is a little out of town and alongside it is Opryland USA, a theme park presenting all kinds of American music in stage productions, and showboat cruises on the Cumberland River etc. The posh Opryland Hotel has over nine acres of indoor gardens, including a wonderful conservatory enclosing a tropical garden with fountains, cascades and a two acre water garden with waterfalls. Of course I couldn't afford to stay there but once, on finding the campground full, I slept in the hotel car park. Next morning I used their facilities, bought some postcards and, supplying my own orange juice, drank it in one of the gardens while writing to various friends, telling them I stayed there last night, which was more or less true!

Getting back to my apparently growing obsession with churches, I found a copy of *The Church & Christian Support Guide to Metro Nashville*, with its many ads for a huge range of Christian denominations, many of which I'd never heard of. There was also a multitude of ads for Christian owned and operated businesses, including a Dial-a-Prayer. I thought this guide might be useful to help me find an African American church with music. In contrast, while walking downtown I came across the Wildhorse Saloon, *'dedicated to Boot-Scootin' Good Times'* and *'The most fun you can have with your boots on!'*

That Nashville VW dealer *did* find the engine problem. It cost a fortune, but by now I was practically past caring. I just wanted to feel safe on the roads. I called Barb in Australia to check on my finances, and she assured me all was well and I could even afford a treat. A treat then was buying a $3 chicken burger instead of cooking!

My garage had a chauffeured van available to drive people to and from their work or home while their vehicles were being serviced. Nashville is the centre of the business side of country music with record company headquarters, lots of recording studios and many musicians. It reminded me of Hollywood, where every service person is an aspiring actor waiting to be discovered. Here of course they are all musicians or songwriters. As well as Volkswagens, my garage also dealt with other foreign cars such as Mercedes and BMWs, so a lot of the successful record company executives or talent managers were customers. It's really difficult for musicians to have access to such individuals, but the driver of this vehicle was a songwriter and when he discovered he was driving an appropriate person, he would play a tape of his songs to his 'captive' audience. I imagine his success rate wasn't very high or he would have been making a living from songwriting instead of driving.

'Music Row,' a few minutes from Nashville's downtown, had the Country Music Association's Hall of Fame, George Jones Gift Shop, Country Music Wax Museum and various studios and record companies, including Warner Brothers, EMI and Universal. At Hendersonville, a few miles away, was the Twitty City entertainment complex – an unfortunate name, I thought, but it was actually the home of singer Conway Twitty.

One of the campground staff heard I loved to dance and invited me to dinner, then dancing, with a promise to teach me some local steps. He seemed OK, so I accepted.

The 'date' started off well. He collected me in his pickup truck and presented me with a pair of earrings which, although a bit trashy, were fun. I put them on immediately. Dinner was a nasty surprise – the 99 cent special at a fast food place. Still, I thought I shouldn't be too picky.

Then we went on to a large honky-tonk just north of Nashville called Denim & Diamonds. The rest of the evening was a complete fiasco. Not only did he not know *how* to dance, but after downing copious quantities of beer at a dangerously fast rate he oggled every other woman in sight, eventually spotting one he obviously preferred to be with and dumping me for the rest of the evening. I caught a taxi home, but not before managing to find at least one very nice person who *could* dance. I vowed that if I ever again accepted any invitation like that I'd take my own vehicle (if it was running). Next day he came to my campsite to apologise and ask me to give him another chance. Surely he wasn't serious.

Before leaving Nashville I went to a nearby shopping centre only to find the car park roped off, as a woman had been shot outside a bank an hour or so before. I was glad I hadn't got up any earlier or it might have been me. I headed east out of Nashville on the big Interstate 40, which cuts through the city and stretches thousands of miles across America – from the South Carolina coast to California. Tennessee is a beautiful state, hilly and green with lots of lakes and scenic areas and lovely parks for camping and walking. At Edgar Evins State Park, my site was a railed wooden deck like a patio, jutting out from the steep side of a hill overlooking the picturesque Center Hill reservoir. I was able to drive the van right on to it and there was still plenty of room for the wooden picnic table and my folding chairs. In fact, two or three vehicles would have fitted. What a great place to sit and watch the sunset. I stayed three days and read two whole books, and there were absolutely no biting insects! Perhaps it was a little late in the year for them.

I started to feel a bit lonely again and couldn't decide what I wanted to do next. In the end I continued east to The Great Smoky Mountains National Park, where I was thrilled to see a black bear crossing the road in the early morning mist. The campground was in lovely forest, with a stream running right through the middle and some great walking trails. I enjoyed this very much but still felt a bit depressed, and wondered if I was getting tired of this kind of travel. It was hard work, all that navigating and driving, worrying about the van, hanging around garages, looking for a new place to camp almost every day, and rarely able to afford little luxuries like eating out instead of cooking my basic meals in the confined space of the vehicle, or even occasionally staying in a motel. I missed having someone to discuss things with and I just couldn't decide what I wanted to do next. Nothing appealed and although I toyed with the idea of going home, I didn't really want to give up.

An added concern was that I had apparently walked through some poison ivy and had a terrible allergic reaction. Both my heels were covered with large pustules, which were incredibly itchy and leaked a ghastly yellow fluid. I could only wear sandals and even they were uncomfortable. Before I realised what it was, I had managed to transfer it to various places all over my body. The pharmacist told me that I should change my clothes and bedding every day to avoid this happening because it is very contagious. Fat chance of that, the way I was living! I couldn't think how I had picked this up because I had always been so careful not to walk through any forest unprotected, but if you are allergic to it a trace in cut grass can be enough. Somebody told me that even patting a dog which had been in contact with the plant can cause an allergic reaction in some people. I applied various lotions and ointments, and swallowed bottles of tablets, but it still took weeks to heal.

Music and dancing usually cheered me up, so when I was able to get into some shoes I went to a honky-tonk near Knoxville. It was called Cotton Eyed Joe and was a pleasant place, and although I found a couple of people to chat to, nobody would dance with me. A man told me he was a guard at a nearby atomic bomb production plant. This was unsettling as I hadn't even realised it was there. He invited me to come home with him, saying he was lonely because his wife had recently walked out after 32 years! It certainly didn't seem like the kind of situation to cheer *me* up.

Two-stepping at Wild Horse Saloon, Nashville

Campsite on Tennessee-Tombigbee Waterway, Alabama

Camping- Edgar Evins State Park, Tennessee

Falling in love with Bluegrass Music

Continuing on, I left Tennessee and drove through that little pointed sliver of Virginia wedged in between eastern Tennessee and Kentucky. I'd heard that Breaks Interstate Park in the Appalachians – partly in southeastern Kentucky and mostly in Virginia – was spectacular, so that's where I went. I loved the pretty camping areas with their beautiful trees, and the numerous scenic trails with wonderful views of deep gorges cut by winding rivers. It was mid-week and few people were around. I was able to watch a very cute trio of little racoons playing in a hollow log.

At the information centre I noticed a brochure advertising Timmy Cline's Bluegrass Music Festival at Elkhorn City, in the heart of the coal region of Eastern Kentucky. Perhaps this could be the boost I needed to get me out of my doldrums. The drive to Elkhorn City was difficult – down narrow, winding mountain roads busy with big coal trucks, and in temperatures of over 92 degrees. I passed lots of ramshackle mobile homes and broken down vehicles, but fortunately mine was performing OK for a change. It appeared to have responded well to all that recent mechanical attention! I eventually found the site without any problems.

People at this festival varied from coal miners, farmers and truck drivers from this region, to retired couples from other states. Lots of them were amateur musicians. I felt a bit self-conscious rolling up on my own, but they were all very friendly, especially when they discovered where I was from. As was often the case, they could hardly believe I was travelling all alone in the van and that I'd managed to find this fairly isolated little town. (I did have maps!) Again I was asked if I'd driven all the way from Australia. I was invited to share their food and many went out of their way to make sure I was happy and looked after. This was especially generous as they were certainly not well-off people. They also explained the intricacies of the music and introduced me to all the musicians. I was presented with T-shirts, baseball caps and CDs to take home as souvenirs, and personally welcomed from the stage, with songs often dedicated to me. I was being thoroughly spoilt and I loved it. It was just what I needed.

I immediately fell in love with Bluegrass and the people involved with it. It is acoustic stringed music, often played very fast (sometimes referred to as *'country music on steroids'*), and with fine three or four part harmony singing, which usually includes a high tenor 'mountain' voice. It has its roots in the music brought in by early British emigrants, which then evolved into Old-Time or early country music. The genre is attributed to Bill Monroe, who started playing this way in the late 1930s. I had recently seen him at the Grand Ole Opry, and was later thrilled to meet him several times and even *dance* with him.

Traditional Bluegrass generally includes a fiddle, guitar, mandolin, banjo and double bass, which is often referred to as a 'doghouse' bass because it's big enough to house a medium sized dog! Sometimes there is a resonator guitar, an instrument originally designed by John Dopyera and also known as a Dobro™, which is now a Gibson Guitars registered trade name. It has a wooden body with a metal sound chamber specially built to make the instrument louder (it has to compete with a banjo!). It also gives it a beautiful melodic sound similar to the Hawaiian guitar, as it's played with a metal slide and finger picks. Like jazz, the instrumentalists take turns to play solos and usually improvise. As Bluegrass is often played at a fast tempo you need to be extremely good to be successful. To quote Richard D. Smith in his book *Bluegrass: An Informal Guide*, it is *'a highly disciplined American Art Form. Devotees appreciate crisp instrumental playing and tightly structured harmonies from a bluegrass band, as classical music audiences value the virtuosity of a top chamber orchestra.'*

Festival organiser Timmy Cline had his own band and, like many of the people I met, comes from a long line of musicians. The event was in honour of his father, Curly Ray Cline, a famous fiddle player. A highlight of one memorable evening was being personally entertained by a band called The Brickey Brothers in their bus, and then trying to stay up all night watching the jam sessions around the camping area and waiting for the Kentucky sunrise.

Flatfooting is a style of dancing traditional to the Appalachian region and was a mystery to me, so I was very much hoping it would be part of this festival. Not only did I *see* it here but in no time at all I was on the dance floor learning how to *do* it. You don't need a partner to flatfoot and it's not usually synchronised like line dancing or square dancing. It's hard to describe as there are lots of variations, but I think it comes from the dances brought by early settlers from Ireland, Scotland and England, and possibly even includes some Native American influences. It can also be called clogging, buck dancing, step dancing, hoedowning or back stepping. Like the music, the dances are passed down from generation to generation, and there are regional variations and lots of variety in the steps, which of course must be in time to the music. Some dancers wear metal taps on their shoes and if they aren't in time it can put the band off. Steps include heel kicks, foot and heel thumps, thigh slaps and sometimes even jumps. Clogging seems to be the more energetic version, but people of all ages flatfoot and the elderly seem to be among the best. I once saw a 90 year old champion performing on stage at a festival. One of my main dance teachers at Elkhorn City was an 84 year old local character who arrived at the festival with his enormous pet rooster, which he tied to the leg of a chair!

I don't think I have ever learnt how to flatfoot or clog properly, but had a lot of fun trying and spent half the festival on the dance floor. When there is no dance floor, people often bring a large wooden board on which to dance and everyone loves to watch.

An American politician called Bob Wise was called 'The Clogging Congressman' because he used to clog at political rallies and in parades. He is quoted as saying: *'A woman once said to me, I'd rather see you clog for one minute than listen to you talk for ten.'* Strangely, my horoscope in the local paper next day said: *'you will find the urge to dance almost overwhelming!'*

One thing I did learn is that it is never OK to dance to gospel music at a Bluegrass Festival. It is considered disrespectful, and musicians often remove their hats when playing a religious number. If somebody remains on the dance floor or leaps to their feet, they are quietly asked to resume their seats. This is quite different from the African American gospel I saw in New Orleans where the audience was positively encouraged to take part and often leapt to their feet in the aisles.

Lots of people at Elkhorn City told me about other festivals so off I went, starting with Meadowgreen Park at Clay City, also in Kentucky. It's held on a lovely private property bordered by a river and with a gently sloping hill dotted with shady trees, leading down to the stage. Run by the Kentucky Friends of Bluegrass Music, which had about 400 members (I was made an honorary member and proudly wore the T-shirt for years), it was a much larger festival, with more bands and a bigger audience. This was where I met many more of the first generation of Bluegrass musicians, including The Goins Brothers, Ralph Stanley, The Osborne Brothers and the flamboyant Jimmy Martin, self-proclaimed King of Bluegrass. Television evangelist Freddy Clark and his wife Sylvia were also performing with their family band. They had eleven children, which included two sets of twins and at that time the eight eldest, ranging in age from about seventeen down to four or five, played in the band. They were all pretty good. Again I camped on the property along with dozens of others, met just about everyone there, was welcomed a number of times from the stage and had various songs dedicated to me. I was still enjoying all the fuss!

One thing I really couldn't get used to was tobacco chewing. Although I thought it was better environmentally than smoking, I didn't enjoy seeing people chewing on enormous wads and then spitting into the receptacles they carried around. Chewing bubble gum and blowing bubbles was also very popular. I even saw ads for *'the official motorized refillable bubble tape dispenser'* – Power Gum Dispenser – which people clipped on to their belts. You just had to press a button to dispense a measured amount. You could also buy chewable bubble gum 'credit cards', 'mobile phones' and a Monopoly set with gum or chocolate pieces. The winners can bankrupt other players and then *eat* their houses, hotels and playing pieces! I also saw a candy jewellery kit: *'make your own jewellery and then eat it.'*

At Meadowgreen Park I was given a free ticket to the even larger Poppy Mountain Bluegrass Festival, which was then in its second year and already becoming a success story. It's held on a very hilly 1,000 acre farm property, just outside the college town of Morehead in central eastern Kentucky. I saw some familiar faces from the previous two festivals, and once again people encouraged me to share their food and drinks. One evening a fellow invited me to his van for a 'fuzzy navel'. This conjured up some startling images until I discovered he was talking about a drink made from peaches (fuzzy), oranges (navel) plus vodka and peach schnapps. I tried one. It was delicious, but very alcoholic.

Poppy Mountain Bluegrass Festival has lots of amusements apart from the music. These included vintage vehicle rides, hay rides, horse rides and a pig roast. I have a photo of myself on stage holding a huge and handsome (live) python. Her name was Hazel. She weighed thirty pounds and you paid to have a photo taken with her around your neck. As just about everyone else was scared of her the owner wasn't making much money, so he often invited me to hold her to demonstrate she did no harm. She must have got sick of this, because once she started to wind herself rather tightly around my neck and had to be hurriedly extricated!

Another surprising experience was to see someone there clogging on roller skates! He was equally surprised to meet me and insisted that we have our photograph taken, together with Hazel the python. As a bonus, I happened to be wearing my snakeskin patterned jeans! For the rest of the festival, he proudly carried that photo tucked into the band of his fancy straw cowboy hat.

I'll never forget learning to drive a four-wheeler at 3 am (probably after one of those fuzzy navels), and walking back to my van in the early morning mist with the distant sound of stringed music floating across the valleys. A little bus regularly took people touring the Poppy Mountain property, and when it was discovered that an Australian woman was there my camper van became a stop on the tour. The guide would say: *'and here in this little van is a woman all the way from Australia.'* If I was in the van I would leap out and give them a couple of words in my Aussie accent and they'd all clap! One evening as I was wandering around the out-of-hours jam sessions, I noticed that a young man appeared to be following me. When I confronted him he said, *'I'm sorry. I just want to hear you talk!'*

I was welcomed from the stage here as well, sometimes even *on* to the stage to draw the raffle or announce winners. Word got around and I was soon interviewed by various radio stations, and generally treated like the celebrity that I wasn't! Lots of people wanted to take my photograph or have theirs taken with me. Awards were offered for the oldest person in attendance, a dance contest winner, best parking lot pickers, best campsite and the person who travelled the furthest, which I won three years in a row.

Little did I realise at the time that I would one day eventually have my own Bluegrass radio programme, and be one of the emcees for this and other large American Bluegrass festivals.

For some reason, people often assumed that visitors from other countries might all *know* each other. For example, somebody once said to me, *'Oh, you're from Australia. I once met a man from Germany.'* Trying to make sense of this comment, I said, *'I'm from Australia, not Austria,'* to which he replied, *'Yes, Down Under. We had a man here from Germany, but I can't remember his name. There was also a man from England who came through on a bicycle. I think his name was George. You might know him?'*

It's hard to know how to answer such questions, but I explained that in fact the United States is actually closer to Europe than Australia. Most of the people I met outside of major cities – particularly in the south – had never been to more than one or two of their country's states, let alone another country. National pride was very evident and people often told me that America was by far the best country in the world. They couldn't quite imagine why I might not want to live there permanently, even when I explained that I loved my country, too.

Heavy rain and deep slippery mud seem to be almost a tradition at American Bluegrass festivals and Poppy Mountain was no exception. Vehicles were sliding all over the place and I was worried somebody would crash into mine, which was parked within several feet of an extremely muddy track. Lots of vehicles had to be towed out when the festival ended, and several tractors were standing by for this purpose. However, when my smallish van got stuck I didn't need one, because six burly men rushed up and more or less lifted it out!

I was amazed to learn that some people spend their whole spring and summer going from one festival to another, and by September were already at their 30th. There is nothing like this at home, largely because Australia's small population doesn't support a lot of festivals – especially Bluegrass – but also because the whole atmosphere at American music festivals is different. I think this is partly because almost everybody camps on site, including the musicians. Various facilities are provided and often include electrical hookup and showers. Campers sometimes arrive a week or more prior to the festival to secure their favourite site and meet up with friends. I discovered a whole culture around these camping areas with some people decorating their site in a particular theme. At Poppy Mountain, one year there was an area called Halloween Alley, where every camp had Halloween lights and pumpkins. There was even a haunted 'house' with appropriate recorded sound effects.

It was also surprising to me to learn that lots of people spend little time near the stage but actually come to jam in the camping area. The term for them is 'parking lot pickers.' They are often fine musicians, and going to these festivals gives them a chance to play with lots of others. Groups of people often parked their caravans or motor homes in a square, covering the area in the middle with tarpaulins – and that's where everybody congregated. Sometimes the playing went all night and was exciting (but exhausting). I was often encouraged to sing along, but my voice always seemed too low for Bluegrass. It was probably better for me just to listen or to dance. I regularly chided myself for staying up late every night, not getting enough sleep, feeling exhausted etc., but I was always so sad when a festival finished and I was on the road again. Many people invited me to visit their homes, so I was building up contacts all over the country.

It was at a Bluegrass festival that I had my first taste of moonshine liquor, which was offered in a large preserving jar in a brown paper bag. Moonshine refers to any kind of distilled alcoholic drink upon which tax has not been paid. The stills were often hidden deep in the mountains and probably many exist today. I had a tiny sip and thought it tasted terrible. This was probably just as well, as it's incredibly strong and because it's home-made nobody is sure of the actual alcohol content. It's also sometimes called Mountain Dew which sounds nice (there's a soft drink of the same name), but one small glass of the real thing can put you right 'under the table.' In fact, people have been killed by it.

There are a lot of myths associated with moonshine and one is that good moonshine whiskey makes better fiddler players. A song I hear occasionally played by Bluegrass musicians is called 'The Moon Still Shines (on the Moonshine Still.)' I don't know who wrote it – its origins are hazy – but I love the title. Strangely, although it is illegal to make it, possess or sell it, it's not illegal to *teach* people how to make it. There are even courses offered.

It was also at Bluegrass festivals that I really became aware of the cost of U.S. health care, especially for people who could not afford insurance or who did not work for companies which provided it free. Expenses associated with a heart attack or other major health issues could mean losing your house or being in huge debt for many years. Collections were often taken up for musicians who had incurred high medical bills.

There is sometimes a kind of raw ignorance displayed at some of these festivals which involves racial discrimination and sexism. When this is combined with alcohol it can be highly unpleasant and even explosive. Although I didn't see anything *really* bad, there was one instance when a drunk man was bothering some of the women on the dance floor. He was chased off the property, but not before guns were produced.

Somebody at Poppy Mountain suggested I should go to the 'World of Bluegrass' Convention held at that time at Owensboro, in northern Kentucky. It was starting in a few days so I drove straight there, arriving without tickets and (of course) with practically no money. I slept in my van in the parking lot outside the hotel. In the foyer I found Pat Hicks, a lovely man who I'd met at festivals like Poppy Mountain. Sadly his wife had died a few months earlier and his heart wasn't in this event. He kindly gave me his tickets to the weekend Fanfest and Annual Awards night. He also taught me a lot about the history of the music and we often sat around in the hotel foyer while he pointed out the various celebrities and I rushed off to get their photographs. So I met a lot more of the Bluegrass legends including Bela Fleck, Eddie Adcock, Earl Scruggs, Doc Watson, Rhonda Vincent, J.D. Crowe and Jerry Douglas.

One day when I was in my van, having a much needed afternoon nap to help cope with all the late nights, I was woken by sirens and lots of yelling. I put my head out to see what was going on only to discover I was camped right next to the Owensboro Gaol, which was surrounded by police and fire engines called to a fire there!

After that, I decided to move a little closer to the hotel entrance. When my situation was discovered, various people offered me access to their rooms for a shower, and one man even had an extra key issued especially for me so I could go in during the day when he was out, and not worry about trying to find him to borrow his key. On the day of the Awards ceremony I took my outfit to his room, ironed it and hung it in his wardrobe. He'd invited me to shower and change there later in the day but didn't know I'd done this, and I didn't know his wife was due to arrive! You can imagine the shock she got when she opened the wardrobe to hang up her outfit, only to discover a dress already in there. It took a bit of explaining but she did believe him in the end, and I enjoyed laughing with her about it later.

Lots of organisations and private individuals hosted hospitality suites for convention registrants with live music, food and drinks. The main purpose of these was to act as showcases for musicians, because the event is attended by record company executives, festival organisers, radio presenters, promoters etc. I especially loved these unofficial showcases. They didn't start until after the main events finished at 11 or 12, then continued until the early hours, with concerts often scheduled for as late as 3 am. One was hosted by the Californian Bluegrass Association (the largest in the world). They rented up to three hotel suites, two featuring live concerts and one for jamming. These were fairly small rooms so the music was not amplified, and listeners practically sat at the feet of the musicians. Most of the bands were top rate, and I think that for me this was the highlight of the whole week.

That first 'World of Bluegrass' week was tremendously exciting. I learnt so much about the music and its history, and had the most fun ever.

With the late night or early morning concerts and 9 am seminars, it was hard to get much time for bed. The event is run by the International Bluegrass Music Association – IBMA – which many people say stands for *'I've been mostly awake.'*

I recall singing acapella gospel with a group of people on the hotel fire stairs at 4 one morning. The acoustics were great, but I'm not sure about the singing. I do love singing and had taken lessons a few years earlier. My teacher felt I had potential, but as my work became more demanding I didn't continue, so no potential ever developed. I regret that now.

I went back to this event many times and it subsequently moved to Louisville, where the entire hotel was completely taken over by Bluegrass musicians and fans. Groups of people formed impromptu music jam sessions in the corridors and foyers, bars, and sometimes even in the elevators. As the doors opened at each floor, people waiting were sometimes confronted with a band in full swing. One evening I was in one of the bars listening to a fairly large and well lubricated jam session when a pizza delivery man arrived. He handed over the pizza and with very little encouragement joined in with great gusto on the hotel's piano! I've found that Americans are inclined to be more spontaneous than the British or Australians, and less self-conscious about letting go a little and having a good time. This, along with the fact that I was away from home and feeling rather fancy free, encouraged me to let go a bit, too.

It was all such fun, but would be terrible for any hotel guests who weren't interested and hadn't been warned. Fortunately the hotel had two separate buildings, so the main one was devoted to music and the other deemed a quiet area. In the public areas of the 'music' building there was a sign: *'No jamming on this floor after 4 am.'* Of course the music doesn't stop then, just on that particular floor!

There used to be a lot of smoking inside the building, particularly in the stairwells, and twice this set off the fire alarms and brought several large fire engines screaming down the street. The staircases were full of people rushing down, clutching their precious musical instruments. Nobody seemed bothered about any other items of luggage.

After a few years in Louisville the event moved again, this time to the much larger city of Nashville, not necessarily a popular move as many felt it would be overwhelmed by all the country music there. By then I didn't have a vehicle, so stayed right on site in the conference hotel.

The Awards Show was held in the Grand Ole Opry building a few miles away, and we were to collect our pre-paid tickets in advance for the concert and shuttle bus. Early that evening I was lazing in the bath, when I suddenly realised I'd forgotten to get mine. I rushed downstairs, but the ticket booth had closed. After trying frantically to locate somebody in the office or in the public areas of the hotel, I decided just to go and see what happened.

I managed to sneak onto the shuttle bus with a tangle of people, but the Opry was a different matter. I pleaded my case *('I've come all the way from Australia for this,'* etc.) but to no avail, and stood at the entrance in despair – when I suddenly noticed one of the Board members inside. Brushing past the ticket collector (*'I'll be back'*), I accosted him, explained my situation and that I'd promised the ticket collector I'd be back. He said, *'well she's far too busy to worry about you, so just come with us and let's see if we can get you in.'* He was with another man and they squeezed me in between them, distracting the usher who didn't notice a ticket was missing. The seating was reserved, but on long benches and as we were small people, we just squashed up together and got away with it. I spent the whole night worrying that I'd be discovered and thrown out in disgrace!

Trying to flatfoot at Elkhorn City

My "camp site" at Poppy Mountain festival

With Hazel the python on stage at Poppy Mountain

My favourite dancer. Bruce – the raincape and umbrella salesman, Poppy Mountain

With Mike Auldridge and Jerry Douglas

With Pat Hicks at "World of Bluegrass" convention, Owensboro, Kentucky

Dancing with Bill Monroe ("Father of Bluegrass music") at Long Hollow Jamboree Tennessee

Back to Texas

After that first visit to Owensboro, I was travelling back through Kentucky towards Lexington when I noticed the back of the van was absolutely covered with oil. A Volkswagen dealer diagnosed serious problems, which would mean a new engine costing about $3,000. I wondered whether I could afford it or whether I should cut my losses and end the trip. There was such a lot to see and do, and I was still really enjoying it, so I decided to go ahead. It took about ten days to replace the engine, and I was able to stay with some music friends nearby in Nashville.

Afterwards I decided to head back to New Orleans to attend another Jazz & Heritage Festival. Within a couple of days problems with the van surfaced again, and by the time I actually got to New Orleans the engine was running very noisily. It seemed that this vehicle really didn't like travelling! Apparently it had overheated, and two pistons had burnt out. What to do now? The engine was still under warranty and this would be honoured by any VW dealer in America, so instead of returning all the way north to Lexington I decided to stay for the festival, then to try to get back to Fort Worth in Texas. My plan was to see some states in the mid-west – Kansas, Wisconsin, North and South Dakota – and Fort Worth was more or less on the way to them. Also, I could stay there with Bill while the van was being repaired. He had again offered me the use of one of his many vehicles.

It took a couple of days to get to Fort Worth, and I had to nudge the recalcitrant van along all the way, sometimes being reduced to tears with the stress, especially when it wouldn't start. One good thing happened on this part of the trip. I was going for a walk through a forest when I came across somebody's forgotten cache of beer – 22 cans – hidden in long grass not far from a campground where alcohol was forbidden. They'd obviously been there for some time as the grass had grown up all around them, but they appeared to be intact. I opened one to make sure and then surreptitiously ferried them all back to my van and into the cooler. What a haul!

The garage in Fort Worth was really helpful. Hanging around was a bit frustrating, though, and I was anxious not to overstay my welcome with Bill. However, not all of this waiting time was unhappy or wasted – I went dancing (of course!), and became familiar with many of the best venues both in Fort Worth and nearby Dallas. One was The Stagecoach Ballroom that I'd discovered on an earlier visit. It was open several nights each week with a good country band. It attracted an older crowd which was serious about its dancing, and I hardly ever had to sit one out. I went there every night it was open, and met a charming fellow who was one of the best dancers I have ever known. He took me dancing four nights in a row and was so good that we sometimes gathered an admiring crowd. I was in heaven. He swept me off my feet in every way, until I discovered he'd just spent seven years in jail! If men only realised how easy it would be to attract women if they knew how to dance properly, surely they'd all rush out and take lessons.

Another of the men I met dancing at Fort Worth was George, who invited me out to dinner. He told me he planned to retire in about eight years and travel. When he heard I'd been to many countries, he suggested that if I was still available we should journey together, with me showing him the world while he paid the expenses for us both! He was also an excellent dancer so this sounded enticing, but I never did get back in touch with him. I imagined it was one of those 'too good to be true' offers.

I had another of these in Kentucky. A fellow told me he was very rich, as oil had been located on his property. He also was fascinated by my travels and asked me to phone him reverse charge from time to time so he could follow where I was and what I was doing. I did this, and upon hearing of the various mechanical problems I was experiencing, he offered to buy my vehicle from me at current market price, have it completely rebuilt and give it back to me free, no strings attached. I must admit this was also tempting. I'd always dreamed of meeting a rich 'Sugar Daddy.' But of course I couldn't accept such an offer, and it was just as well I didn't, because much later I discovered that he was in jail for fraud, and that all the stories about wealth and oil were untrue. He was a real trickster!

Finally there was a message that my van was ready, and their driver would collect me from Bill's next morning. It felt wonderful to have my own vehicle again after almost five weeks, and I hoped that the problems were now behind me.

One of the first things I did after I collected my van was to give it a good test by driving to Dallas and back – about 40 minutes on the freeway. In the historic west end of Dallas, with its large brick warehouses converted into shops and restaurants, I saw the Down Under Bar – one of a chain of bars which appear to be to be portraying a very stereotyped image of Australia. The menu included 'dingo dogs' (corn dogs – which are battered deep fried corn cobs served on a stick), 'Wombat Cheeseburgers', and Vegemite sandwiches.

On the way back to Fort Worth I stopped and, believe it or not, couldn't re-start the motor! An inspection yielded nothing obviously out of place so, feeling a bit apprehensive, I tried again and finally got back on to the freeway. My relationship with this vehicle was now definitely a love/hate one, and it seemed to feel the same way about me. It protected me and took me to wonderful places, but only when it felt like it and on its own terms!

Although Bill was very kind, I'm sure he must have been glad to have his home back to himself. As a parting gift I wanted to give him a book by an Australian author, and the only one I could find was Thomas Keneally's *Season in Purgatory*, which we both agreed seemed appropriate to the circumstances!

On The Way North

Texas had been very hot and humid, so it was a relief to be travelling north into cooler weather. On the first night I stayed in Oklahoma City and naturally went dancing, not getting to bed until 3 am! Then it was Kansas, where the wheat was being harvested by huge machines. I could hear them working right through the night.

I drove over some truly beautiful country roads, through expansive wheat fields and past lovely farms with huge old barns with curved roofs and walls, thinking all the time of that wonderful film *The Wizard of Oz* and singing 'Kansas City Here I Come' by Leiber & Stoller … although Kansas City is actually in Missouri!

One of the things I loved about this trip was that I never knew what or who I might come across. I accidentally found the historical geographical centre of the continental 48 U.S. states at Lebanon, Kansas. Nothing much marked the spot except a sign, a picnic area, a tiny chapel seating four people and a dilapidated closed-down motel. The area is hilly and open with lush grasses and few trees. In fact, the *actual* geographical centre is in a farmer's field, but he didn't want people tramping all over his property, so the memorial was shifted slightly.

After entering Nebraska, I found an attractive place to camp at Ravenna State Recreation Area on a backwater of the Loup River. It was free and I was glad to be the only person there, until right on dusk I accidentally locked the keys in the van. I had noticed several houses within reasonable distance so I walked to one, only to be chased off by a couple of fierce dogs baring their teeth. Further on was a run-down looking trailer and fortunately somebody was home. She was helpful and first drove me back to the van with a piece of wire, which we used to try to break into it. This didn't work so, having no telephone, she then drove me about twelve miles to the town of Ravenna to get the police, who followed us out and had the door open in seconds. They all treated the incident as a huge adventure, as having never even *seen* an Australian before they were amazed that I had turned up alone in this out-of-the way place. Although I never met her again, this kind lady sent Christmas cards for several years to *'my good Australian friend.'*

It was so good to be back inside the van as I'd had visions of sleeping on the ground and being attacked by anything that came along. Something *did* come along in the middle of the night. At about 2.30 am I was woken by a really noisy motorbike. The rider wore no helmet and looked a bit scary. He drove through the area several times, slowing right down when he passed me. I couldn't imagine what he was doing here. Perhaps the word had got around that I was camping alone.

I felt frightened and hid behind my curtains with the keys in my hand, ready to drive off if he stopped. It was such a relief when he finally disappeared – and a reminder of how vulnerable I really was. It kept me awake for a long time and I left as soon as it was light.

Chapel at geographical centre of continental 48 U.S. states

Entering Nebraska

Buffalo Bill

I loved the 'Wild West' history and it was great to find the home of Buffalo Bill: Col. William F. 'Buffalo Bill' Cody while travelling through Nebraska. 'Bill' had acquired this ranch of about 4,000 acres during the heyday of his Wild West Show, and in 1886 built a large handsome wooden home. The restored house is now part of a State Historic Park, together with outbuildings and 16 acres of the original ranch. It contains extensive collections documenting his life and times.

William Cody had a very colourful career, starting work as an ox-team driver for fifty cents a day in 1856 when he was only eleven. At fourteen he joined the gold rush to Colorado and soon after became a Pony Express rider. He must have been incredibly fit, because it is documented that he once rode 322 miles in 21 hours and 40 minutes, exhausting 20 horses! In 1864 he enlisted in the Kansas Volunteer Infantry and served in the War Between the states.

Later he was employed to supply buffalo meat for workers on the Kansas Pacific Railroad, and is said to have killed 4,280 buffalo in eight months. No wonder the poor animals were practically wiped out in a short time. He claimed the title of 'Buffalo Bill' in a buffalo hunting contest near Sheridan, Kansas. He also served with the Fifth Cavalry in various expeditions against the Indians, took part in hunting trips and was a U.S. Army scout.

Eventually Cody became involved in acting, starting the famous *Buffalo Bill's Wild West Show* in 1883. It was a spectacular panorama of cowboys, Indians, trick shooters and various specialty acts.

The show ran for thirty years, touring all over the United States and even to England. Up to 400 people were employed – two of the most famous being Sitting Bull, principal chief of the Dakota Sioux, and the legendary markswoman Annie Oakley. Eventually his show joined with Pawnee Bill's Far East Show, which was the one I had seen recreated at Fort Worth. Cody had been involved in a number of disastrous financial adventures over the years, and in 1911 sold his beautiful ranch to Pawnee Bill. He died in Colorado in 1917, just before his 71st birthday.

At Wichita I later discovered that there'd actually been *two* men called Buffalo Bill. Before Col. William F. 'Buffalo Bill' Cody, the original was William Mathewson – a fascinating pioneer who spoke 14 Indian languages and is credited with rescuing 54 women and children from Indian captivity. He apparently also single handedly rescued 155 men and a train of 144 wagons loaded with government guns and ammunition! He led buffalo hunting expeditions into Western Kansas when a harsh winter threatened settlers with starvation. Later on he was involved in peacemaking between the white community and the Native Americans.

Buffalo Bill Cody's home

Trading Post in Pioneer Country

This really is pioneer country. In Kansas I had crossed over the Pony Express Trail, along which riders carried mail in relays from St. Joseph, Missouri, all the way to the new settlers in Sacramento, California. It only operated for 18 months between 1860 and 1862, and it cost *five dollars* to mail a half-ounce letter – an enormous sum at that time. I also saw traces of the three main trails, which took white settlers across the country to the west – the Santa Fe Trail, the Mormon Pioneer Trail and the Oregon Trail.

At Ash Hollow State Historical Park in Nebraska, you can still see deep ruts made by the heavily laden wagons as they descended, sometimes sliding, down steep Windlass Hill and into the Hollow. With its fresh water spring and plenty of wood and grass, it was an ideal place to make camp. It became an important resting stop on the Oregon Trail, which ran from Independence in Missouri to Oregon City, not far from modern day Portland on the west coast.

As I travelled west through Nebraska I noticed a striking rock formation in the distance. This was Chimney Rock, which the emigrants could see for two days before reaching it. It's about 500 feet high and when they did reach it, many climbed up and carved their initials into the rock. For them it was an exciting and important landmark, as they were now one-third of the way to Oregon. Soon they would be crossing the very difficult terrain of the Continental Divide.

Trading Post in Pioneer Country

I was also reading a wonderful book by Lillian Schlissel called *Women's Diaries of the Westward Journey*, which gave me a clear idea of the terrible hardships faced by most of the quarter of a million people who crossed between 1840 and 1870. Many adults and children were buried on the journey and, until quite recently, items such as heavy cooking pots could still be found where they were discarded along the trail.

The little Museum of the Fur Trade, near Chadron, Nebraska, had a warning on its leaflet: *'The original primitive environment of the trading post has been preserved. Twice in the past 30 years a rattlesnake has been encountered in or around the buildings. Visitors must be aware of this remote possibility. Please govern yourself accordingly.'* I'd have loved to have seen a live rattlesnake – from a reasonable distance, of course – but if they'd only been seen twice in 30 years, you'd have to be pretty lucky!

This trading post was rebuilt on its original foundations using logs, which had been hand-hewn over 100 years ago, so it certainly looked authentic. To help keep inside temperatures manageable, it was partly sunken into the ground and the roof covered with earth and grass.

The original was built in 1833 by the American Fur Company as a wintering house. Fur trading was only done in winter when the furs were in prime condition. Inside was just about everything you might have needed at that time – ammunition, gun flints, powder kegs, bags of coffee and sugar, kegs of 100-proof whiskey – which was mixed half and half with water and dispensed by the cupful – medicines, knives, hatchets, jewellery, mirrors, clay pipes, Chinese vermillion for Native Americans to paint their faces, tobacco, blankets, clothing, cooking utensils, dried meat and much more.

After this wonderful museum, I drove north and into South Dakota through Oglala National Grasslands. Thank goodness some of these prairies have been preserved, as they are gorgeous high rolling plains.

When I was there the grasses were a delicate moss green. Dotted across them were the beautiful pronghorn antelope which I had first encountered in Wyoming, plus herds of bison, and larger than usual black-tailed prairie dogs. These cute relatives of the squirrel are about the size of cottontail rabbits and similar to meerkats. They live in large groups in underground burrows and there's always one standing on a mound outside as a lookout scout. The mounds also act as a dyke to keep out water and a burrow has several chambers, including a listening post closest to the surface, a toilet and a multi-chambered living area. They are called 'prairie dogs' because their call is similar to a bark.

The group I watched was particularly fat, probably because, despite warnings against it, tourists had been feeding them all kinds of rubbish. I thought that if this continued, the poor things would have to enlarge their burrows. Sad to learn they are now endangered in some areas. Considered a menace to ranchers because cattle can trip in a hole and break a leg, they are vigorously hunted, not for food but largely for sport. The Nebraska Outfitters and Guides website says, *'they are a great way to get some practice in with long rifle shots as they are extremely jittery and a long range shot of 100 yards or more is common.'* There is a lot of footage on the internet of shooters enjoying blasting them to pieces, which I personally found really distressing.

South Dakota is famous for its Black Hills, which are clad with ponderosa pines, and the scenery was different from anything else I had seen. Further south, most of the forest I'd explored was deciduous or a mix of deciduous and evergreen. My song here was 'The Black Hills of Dakota,' originally written by **Sammy Fain and Paul Francis Webster** for the film *Calamity Jane* and sung by Doris Day.

The weather was becoming very unpredictable, and when I was walking around Sylvan Lake in Custer State Park I was caught in a huge thunderstorm with lots of hail. It was slippery, and one vehicle slid into a ditch. I was absolutely drenched and nervous about driving in these conditions, so I stayed the night there and tried to dry everything out. The hail was inches deep on the ground and on top of my van. It looked just like snow. When it melted, some water managed to creep in through the fibreglass roof wetting my sleeping bag.

Next day was clear and sunny and I was looking forward to more exploring, but my van had other ideas. It wouldn't start again. The park rangers tried to help, but eventually a tow truck was despatched from a local garage and the van and I were transported six miles to the little town of Custer. They cleaned the distributor cap and spark plugs, and it started without a problem.

Off I went to see the famous Mount Rushmore with those faces of American Presidents carved into the rock – George Washington, Theodore Roosevelt, Thomas Jefferson and Abraham Lincoln. It's spectacular, but I couldn't help thinking about the 'destruction' of the beautiful mountain. The sculptor, Gutzon Borglum, took six and a half years to complete them. Each face is 60 feet high. 400 workers were employed and 90% of the 450,000 tons of granite removed was taken out with dynamite!

I wanted to camp out in a national forest, but my confidence in the mechanics of my vehicle had taken another dent, so I went to a private caravan park in Custer.

That evening I found a local saloon with real sawdust on the floor and a certain rustic Wild West charm. I tried to teach a nice young man to dance. He was willing but not adept, so we ended up playing darts. (I used to be somewhat of a champion at darts, winning many competitions and bets when I lived in England.)

Back at the campground, I was trying to park the van in an appropriate spot. Halfway across a gravel track the motor stalled and wouldn't restart so I simply went to bed there, and had an uncomfortable night worrying that somebody might want to drive through.

At Mount Rushmore

Oregon Trail marker

Repairs in Rapid City

Next morning the wretched vehicle *did* start without problems, but I wasn't mucking around anymore. I drove straight to a Volkswagen dealer in Rapid City. While they looked at it I looked around town. What a nice city. No building over four storeys, and some attractive historic ones, too. I particularly liked the Prairie Edge Trading Company and Galleries with beautiful Native American arts and crafts. To cheer myself up, I bought some lovely silver and copper earrings, and a matching pendant in the shape of the feather the Native Americans regularly depict in their artwork.

Back to the garage to receive the news. It was not good – the compression was down on all cylinders, and particularly on the two which hadn't been replaced in Fort Worth. They pronounced the van almost undriveable. When realising it was my home, they said I could take it, but not to leave town or drive more than necessary. They were booked up for the next two weeks and also had to contact Volkswagen America to get approval to repair or replace the motor, which was still under warranty. I simply couldn't believe this could happen again. I was so angry, upset and frustrated that I was in tears.

I found a decent campground just outside the city limits. Fortunately it was on a hill and there were other campers who I felt sure would help if I needed a push. The van was running so badly that it was something of a problem to actually get it up the hill at all.

I sat down with my evening drink and once again considered my options. My current six month visa would run out before too long, so I had to leave the country. I was due back in Nashville in two weeks, where I was booked on a plane to England to visit my brother and his family, and have a holiday in Greece with them.

Volkswagen gave approval for the motor to be replaced under warranty, so one was ordered in from Canada. I booking a flight to Nashville to connect with the UK flight. So I now had about a week to fill in at Rapid City, which actually turned out to be lots of fun once I'd adjusted to changed circumstances. Naturally, I checked out the local honky-tonks and found one I liked called Boot Hill Saloon. It had a big wooden dance floor and some serious dancers. I met some friendly people there. Martin was one of the best dancers and taught me heaps. There were some great women there, too, and we all went to the usual 2 am breakfasts. I really had a good time – discovering that something good always comes out of something bad.

Martin took me on a day trip to the Badlands National Park, which is a stark, treeless area of deeply eroded canyons carved out of the grasslands. There are plenty of prairie dogs and pronghorn antelopes, plus bighorn sheep and mule deer which *do* look a bit like mules – squat and solid.

The park is bordered by Pine Ridge Reservation, headquarters of the Oglala Sioux tribe. Wounded Knee, site of the infamous 1890 massacre, is not far from there. The walking trails were rough, dusty and slippery and Martin appeared to be wearing his best dancing outfit – black cowboy hat, elegant beige and black western shirt, beige jeans and highly polished boots!

One morning another of my new acquaintances arrived at the campground to take me for a ride on his Harley-Davidson. We explored a little of the Black Hills area.

In addition to all this fun, I had a couple of minor things done to the van while I had the time. One was replacing the pump for the fresh water tank, and the other was buying a bike rack and having it welded to the front bumper bar of the van. Then I found a bike for $20 at a charity shop. The garage kindly raised the seat and handle bars for me, I pumped up the tyres and away I went. At least if I broke down again, I'd be able to transport myself by bicycle.

I loved my new bike, and had to be careful I didn't spend time admiring it when I was driving as I could see part of it through the windscreen. I don't think it is legal in Australia to fit a bicycle to the *front* of a vehicle, but it is in America. In fact, many public buses have bicycle racks on the front. In any case, I couldn't put it on the back because that's where the motor was, and I also needed to access cupboards from the rear door.

Finally, it was time to get the van to the garage, from where they would take me to the airport for my Nashville flight. The campground was a little out of town and I had a few miles to drive through the countryside. About halfway there the engine died. There wasn't a house or building in sight. My heart sank and I sat for about a minute, wondering what to do. My plane left in two hours.

Suddenly I heard a voice with an Australian accent asking directions to Rapid City. I couldn't believe my ears and my luck. A van had pulled up next to me and in it was a man driving himself around America – the only other Australian I had met doing this during my whole trip, and he'd arrived at my greatest time of need! I explained my situation and he immediately offered me a lift.

The garage got me to the airport in time, and retrieved the van later … and I had a wonderful holiday with my family in Greece.

Off Again Through South Dakota

Six weeks later I arrived back in Rapid City and collected the van. I was advised to stay in the area until I had driven 1,000 miles on the new motor, and could have the same garage do a routine check and service to make sure everything had settled in properly. I knew about this. I'd done it twice before!

I drove around a bit, then checked into the same campground and rushed off to Boot Hill Saloon to see my friends there. They all knew I was back because they noticed that my van had disappeared from the garage storage yard. I'd brought back some Greek nougat for them, which stuck to everyone's teeth and was a complete conversation stopper for about 15 minutes. Martin, the friend who had taken me to the Badlands, arrived around 11 pm. He had seen my van parked outside the club and had immediately gone home to change into his dancing clothes. It was a lovely welcome.

To build up that 1,000 miles, I did a lot of driving in South Dakota – through the Black Hills again, where I spent a couple of days camping in the forest and trying out my bike. I managed to get my shoelaces caught up in the spokes and unceremoniously fell off. The only good thing about that was there was nobody to see!

In the evenings I sat outside under a full moon, and listened to that eerie sound of distant coyotes calling. Part of the Black Hills National Forest extends into Wyoming, so I crossed the border and found an incredible 'mountain' called Devil's Tower – a huge stone monolith of 876 feet, with almost perpendicular sides, which are actually fluted columns. About 400 people climb up these columns every month, and it is a sacred site to many Native American tribes.

There are some lovely walking trails around the base of the tower, and a large prairie dog colony near the entrance to the park. I went straight to the campground and spent a couple hours in the late afternoon lazing in my hammock in the shade, drinking cold beer and waiting for the temperature to cool enough so I could cook dinner.

Next morning the air was full of smoke from a wildfire at a nearby reserve. From a vantage point I could clearly see a helicopter with a bucket suspended underneath, dipping water out of a small lake and dropping it on to the flames. This reminded me of unpleasant experiences of fires in the Australian bush, and I decided it was best to leave the area.

On the drive back to Rapid City I visited the historic town of Deadwood, which appeared to be almost completely taken over by gambling. This is apparently just carrying on an old tradition, as in 1876 'Wild Bill' Hickok was shot in the back of the head while playing cards in a saloon. He was just one of the many colourful characters of the area's gold and lead mining days in the mid to late 19th century. His jobs included various tasks which called for a fast gun and no aversion to bloodshed, and at one stage he was a Marshall.

Martha 'Calamity Jane' Canary was another local character. She was a prostitute and performed in a Wild West show. Sadly, acute alcoholism killed her when she was only 53. She claimed to have been Wild Bill's sweetheart, but historians think this was purely a figment of her imagination. Her dying wish to be buried next to him was granted, and their graves still stand in the local Mt. Moriah Cemetery.

Another famous character associated with the town was Nat Love, who was born as a slave in Tennessee in 1854 and is often described as the first black cowboy. He had many adventures working with cattle in Texas and Arizona, and in 1876 he helped to deliver 3,000 steers to Deadwood. The town gave him his nickname of 'Deadwood Dick' when he achieved spectacular results in a fourth of July contest involving horse roping and saddling and shooting.

In 1907 he published an autobiography: *The Life and Adventures of Nat Love, Better Known in the Cattle Country as Deadwood Dick*. This led to a number of 'dime' novels, and the 1940 movie *Deadwood Dick*. The town of Deadwood was actually named after the dead timber on surrounding hills.

I was spending a lot of every day driving because I wanted to build up that 1,000 miles quickly so I could get on with the rest of my trip. One day I drove to the Wyoming border and also halfway to North Dakota, and discovered *another* geographical centre of the U.S. This one is of the entire country, all fifty states, and it's in the little town of Belle Fourche, South Dakota.

My van's engine seemed to be running really well and I was delighted, until I discovered the oil levels were low. I topped up, only to have the red warning light come on again after only 100 miles. I phoned the garage and drove back to Rapid City, spent the night dancing, and took the van in next morning. They had to replace something which I think was called the oil pressure sender, which was apparently faulty, or maybe it was the oil pump. I *had* felt I was on the way to becoming something of an expert in things which could go wrong with an air cooled VW Van, but I was rapidly losing interest. I didn't care what it was, as long as it was fixed and preferably didn't cost me anything.

Fortunately everything else seemed OK so I prepared to finally leave the area, but first I had to renew the vehicle insurance. This proved difficult. I tried lots of different companies – some couldn't help at all, though, because I was an 'alien.' It was the old problem of them not easily being able to check my driving record. Finally I found a great little local company which issued a six month policy on the spot, and it only cost $200 compared to the $640 I'd paid for the previous six months. I had to have a South Dakota address, so Martin let me use his and sent the papers on to me later.

It was good to be on the road again, and now I was travelling back towards the east, planning to see some new sights. One was The Prairie Homestead. Listed on the National Register of Historic Places, it was built in 1909 by pioneers Ed Brown and his wife. It had sod brick walls, a grass roof and was partly dug into a bank. This area of western

South Dakota was one of the last regions of the state to be settled by homesteaders, and this house is one of only several of its kind still standing.

Back past the Badlands, and a sign advertising *'The World's Only Corn Palace'* caught my eye in the town of Mitchell. I couldn't imagine what it could mean — perhaps a museum devoted to humour? I had to stop to see. It turned out to be an amazing building, originally serving as an exposition space where local farmers displayed the fruits of their harvests. Now it's more of a combined entertainment/ convention/ sports centre. It has an exotic architectural style with Moorish minarets, turrets and kiosks, but the most interesting thing to me was the exterior decoration. All of the outside, including the domes, was covered with murals made from corn cobs, grain and grasses, which are native and of natural colour. The grains are tied into bunches and nailed on to the building. The corn is sawn lengthwise and also nailed on — all to the artist's designs and specifications, of course. All these decorations are completely stripped down and redone each year, which cost from $80,000 to $100,000. Crews work on it throughout the summer, so I guess it provides a lot of employment as well as tourist dollars. It looks absolutely stunning.

Having now seen so much of America, it seemed a shame not to add a couple more nearby states. I nipped up Interstate Highway 29 into North Dakota through the city of Wahpeton, where I camped in a fairly basic but cheap municipal campground right on the Red River. Minnesota was on the other side. I was really enjoying my bike, and rode it around the campground and even into town. This meant I was able to leave the van set up for camping while I did the shopping and also, as often happened, nobody else could take my spot when I was away. Having no particular need to be anywhere at a given time meant I could languish in bed reading until noon next day.

Somebody had told me about an excellent truck stop near Fargo — still in North Dakota — and I decided to stay there for the night, partly to save camping fees. The town itself is very attractive, with two microbreweries and a wonderful art deco theatre built in 1926, which had recently been restored. I knocked on the door and somebody let me in for an unofficial tour when I told them I was involved with the film industry in Australia.

Back at the truck stop, I discovered a large bar with a dance floor and live music. There was also a restaurant and all the other usual truck stop amenities. I even found a good dancer. He was a truck driver from Canada, and introduced me to some local women who were fun and invited me to share their table. This was nice, as sometimes in these places the women were inclined to be a little hostile, treating each other more as rivals.

Next morning, despite a late night I was on the road by eight. Even with earplugs, truck stops are too noisy to allow anyone to sleep in. I had my breakfast over the border in Minnesota, and then briefly visited the city of Minneapolis a little further south on the Mississippi River. It has a beautiful sculpture park, but my highlight was seeing Jack Kerouac's original manuscript for *On The Road*, which he typed on an 120 foot continuous reel of paper!

Wisconsin and The House on the Rock

I crossed over the river into the State of Wisconsin and continued south to see a most incredible museum – The House on The Rock.

In the 1940s, local man Alex Jordan decided to build a house on the top of a 60 foot chimney of rock in the Wyoming Valley. He was on a pretty tight budget, so he carried the building materials – stones, mortar and timber – in baskets on his back up the steep sides of the rock, using ladders and sometimes simply scrambling up. When people heard what he was doing, they wanted to see. It became a popular weekend past time, so he decided to charge visitors 50 cents. This enabled him to complete and extend the house, build beautiful gardens (in the first few years he planted 50,000 trees) and add to his various collections. He eventually built 14 rooms, some incorporating part of the rock as their walls and floors.

However, the structure I thought almost *more* impressive was completed 40 years later. Designed but not built by Jordan, it's called The Infinity Room, because it extends 218 feet out over the valley and tapers to a point at the end. There are wonderful views in every direction through the 3,264 windows. Walking right out to the end is a bit disconcerting as it shakes slightly, and some of the windows are in the floor, so you can see right down to the valley 156 feet below.

Surprisingly, Jordan didn't spend even one night in his dream house. He continued living in his town apartment a few miles away. He was an avid collector of many things and a number of large buildings have been erected to display them.

I expected to spend an hour or two there, but ended up staying the whole day and *still* not seeing it all. The standard walking tour through is two and a half miles. Everything is in excess. The original building houses the world's largest collection of Bauer and Coble stained glass lamps, considered by many to be finer than Tiffany's. His numerous other collections include antique weapons, oriental art, thousands and thousands of antique dolls and dolls houses, hundreds of antique wooden carnival horses hanging from ceilings and walls, and a whole street of reconstructed 19th century shops furnished with antiques.

He had a fascination with coin-in-the-slot music-making machines and initially bought some, but then started designing and making his own. He made dozens of them. It seems that his imagination knew no bounds. Some, like the baroque music chamber orchestra, fill whole rooms and include a variety of mechanically operated instruments, played by figures in costumes of the period with appropriate furniture. One is shaped like a giant octopus and plays the Beatles tune 'Yellow Submarine.'

The most fantastic of all is in a building entirely devoted to circuses. A circus band has 120 life size figures each playing an instrument. The whole thing is operated by a single coin in a slot. This extravaganza took 14 people three years to build. There are 37 miles of wiring, 31 blowers and 2,300 pneumatic motors! Also in this building is a circus bandwagon with a 40-piece band, a pyramid of life-sized elephants and the largest collection of miniature circuses in the world.

Then there are the organ and transportation collections, each housed in their own buildings, and the spectacular carousel – largest in the world – 80 feet in diameter and 35 feet high, with more than 20,000 lights. Instead of the usual horses arranged on the deck, there are 269 individually designed and brightly painted figures of animals and mythical creatures, which took more than a decade to plan, construct and hand-finish. Interestingly, Jordan never travelled himself, instead employing others to find and purchase the collections for him.

Viewing all this was marvelous but overwhelming. In a way it was like American materialism gone mad, and reminded me of the many people I met who had an excess of vehicles or wardrobes of clothes they never wore and to which they kept adding – shopping or collecting as therapy. Sadly, Australia seems to be catching up.

Upper Mississippi River

I'd seen the lower Mississippi River in Tennessee, Arkansas, Mississippi, and Louisiana where it empties into the Gulf of Mexico, and now I decided to explore more of its northern reaches, where it is a border to Minnesota, Wisconsin, Iowa and Illinois.

There are 200,000 acres of wooded islands, forest, prairie, marsh and water extending 261 miles south from Wabasha, Minnesota, to just above Rock Island, Illinois. It's a lovely area, but I was surprised to discover that despite it being a designated wildlife refuge, the hunting of ducks, geese, deer, squirrels, racoons etc. is permitted. Fortunately I was there out of season.

I continued into Iowa – another new state for me – and camped in Pikes Peak State Park, sipping my evening drink and admiring spectacular views of the confluence of the Wisconsin and Mississippi rivers with its many islands, until it was nearly dark and time to think about dinner. This pre-dinner drink continued to be an enjoyable ritual, especially at the end of a long and tiring day. Sometimes I stashed it into my backpack and climbed up a hill or walked to a lookout point to watch the sunset. I continued my other daily ritual of writing my diary, usually in the mornings sitting at a picnic table. It was a routine I loved, and perhaps my secretarial training contributed to the fairly meticulous recording of everything! I also usually went for an after dinner walk, sometimes getting caught after dark, but usually remembering to carry a torch!

The Mississippi River was always used for transportation, and during the 70 year heyday of logging in the 19th century seven hundred million dollars' worth of logs were transported on it in rafts. A full log raft was enormous – 600 feet long and 270 feet wide. They were just logs loosely bound together but the men who worked on them (log drivers) could run across them almost as if they were on dry land. They even cooked and slept in tents on the rafts. Of course the chief means of human transportation was the river boats. Their best cabins were named after states in the Union. That's where the name 'Stateroom' comes from.

The traffic today is mainly barges transporting coal, minerals and sand. I knew nothing about barges as we don't have them in Australia, so I was surprised to see how big they can be and that they are pushed rather than pulled. Sometimes many are linked together and the whole thing can be 1,200 feet long. There are 27 lochs on the upper Mississippi River, and barges usually have to go through in two sections. I loved watching this procedure, seeing the water flowing in and out and the barge slowly rising or lowering until it was at the same level as the river beyond. In winter the river freezes with up to four feet of ice, so the lochs must close.

I drove along the Great River Road, now back in Missouri, thinking about and sometimes singing songs which have been written about the Mississippi River, particularly Jerome Kern's 'Old Man River' and 'Miss the Mississippi and You' by Bill Halley. There were wonderful views of the river and, in areas where the road moved inland, I sometimes took side trips back to the banks. On one of these I arrived in a particularly uninspiring area which was prone to flooding and had a deserted shanty town of ramshackle houses built on stilts.

I'd planned to have lunch here, but changed my mind and decided to find somewhere nicer. The van had other ideas and wouldn't re-start. It had been running well since the latest motor, so I couldn't understand what could be wrong. For some inexplicable reason I was always so hopeful about this vehicle. Nobody was around and I thought I might be there for some time, so ate my lunch anyway. Eventually an old fisherman came along in his truck and was able to jump start my van. At a nearby town I had the battery replaced and hoped that was all that was wrong.

I was cheered up by seeing some rather strange place names in Missouri – Humansville, Fairdealing and Tightwad. I wondered about their origins. There are odd place names all over the country. Some others

I noted were Worstville in Ohio, Idiotville in Oregon, Bummerville in California and Monkeys Eyebrow in Kentucky!

Being a great admirer of Mark Twain, I also decided to make a quick visit to the picturesque little river port of Hannibal where he spent his formative years, and which was his inspiration for *The Adventures of Tom Sawyer, Adventures of Huckleberry Finn, Life on the Mississippi and other works.* You can visit his home, a museum which has one of his famous white suits, the law office where his father was a justice of the peace in 1841, and other historic buildings, all now protected from flooding by a levee.

An unexpected heatwave took temperatures well into the 90s and without aircon in the van I was really suffering. The answer was Lake Wappapello in the foothills of the Ozark Mountains, where there is a State Park with a swimming beach and a large, attractive and well-kept campground. It was hilly and I had a whole ridge to myself, with glimpses of the lake through the trees. Being on a ridge had the added benefit of a breeze and a slope to get the van going should there be any problems.

After setting up I walked down for an evening swim. The water was warm and still, like a tepid bath, and I was completely alone there. As it grew dark I floated on my back watching the stars come into view, while lots of little fish nibbled my arms and legs. Later in the evening, the heat and humidity were relieved by a dramatic electrical storm followed by lashings of rain.

Insect bites were again driving me crazy and, despite slathering myself with repellent, new ones appeared every day. One of the difficulties was the campground bathrooms which were nearly always filled with insects, which launched their attacks when I was undressing or in the shower.

Once I had a terrible shock when I felt something tickling my thigh and looked down to see a huge black spider running up it. I nearly brought the roof down with my screams. Of course I knocked it off, but it stayed crouched in the corner of the shower room so I asked the ranger to remove it. He said it was a close relative of the tarantula! I've seen a lot of wildlife in campground bathrooms, but irrationally it's the big spiders I'm most afraid of. I usually checked out the whole area before I started undressing. Occasionally a large scorpion walked in when I was under the shower. I could handle that without any fear at all by just keeping my eye on it and stepping around it. My history of arachnophobia comes, I think, partly from the plague of redback spiders (black widows) in and around one of our homes when I was a child. I had to be taught to be scared of them. Even now, if a large spider appears on the wall of my house I have to leave the room, if not the whole house, until I can arrange for somebody to come and deal with it.

I spent most of the next day at Lake Wappapello following some forest trails, which were a bit spoilt for me as I was continually walking into sticky spider webs. I tried to clear the way ahead of me by waving a stick around. I also cycled up and down the hills, which was hard work but good exercise, and I tried to clean out my fresh water tank, which had become tainted by the old hose I'd used to fill it.

Then I continued east towards Springfield through more attractive hilly forests, and spent the night at Big Spring-Ozark National Scenic Riverways. There were only two other campers and they were some distance away, which, of course, was perfect for me. Once again I unhooked my bike and rode to some of the scenic points. Big Spring is picturesque – an underground river emerging from under a rocky cliff and filled with lovely water plants. The water is warm and very blue where it emerges.

It was time for urban life again, and hopefully some dancing. Springfield was the nearest city. On the way the accelerator pedal stuck down. The engine raced at full speed. This was a bit scary. I was careering through a small town at the time, but managed to pull up safely and locate a mechanic. He cheerfully walked half a mile to where I was parked, fixed the pedal and asked if $5 payment was OK! After all the vehicle problems I'd had, I would have paid him $50 without a qualm. Near Springfield I found a State Park to camp and was surprised on checking in when the ranger asked me how to spell Australia.

At the Springfield Visitors Bureau I enquired about dance venues. They could only suggest the afternoon dance at the Senior Citizen Center, which was not at all what I had in mind. After a bit of sleuthing, I found a branch of the western honky-tonk 'Midnight Rodeo' and went to their

7.30 dance lessons – always a good place to meet people. Somebody offered to partner me, but disappeared immediately after the lesson. My dancing had obviously failed to impress. I did get a number of other dances during the evening, and met a couple of great women who made a point of introducing me to the best dancers. One of them invited me to dinner and dancing the next evening. We arranged a meeting place but, sadly, I went to the wrong spot and we missed each other.

I did, however, discover the amazingly over-the-top Bass Pro Shop in Springfield. The first of what is now a chain of absolutely enormous stores devoted to outdoor activities, it's now called The Grandaddy, and has become a tourist attraction with over four million visitors annually. To quote its brochure: *'Boasting nearly 500,000 square-feet of immersive shopping fun, the Grandaddy offers visitors one of the largest assortments of outdoor gear, apparel and gifts under one roof. Guests can explore the store's seven intricate aquariums, complete with educational sessions on Missouri's native fish, or marvel at the alligators and turtles traversing the in-store swamp.'* Some of its other features are a four-storey stone waterfall, fish and wildlife museum, indoor rifle, pistol and bow range, trout pond, duck pond, a restaurant and, of course, millions and millions of items for sale, including 7,000 lures, camping equipment and the world's largest fishing and pontoon dealership! Another example of American excessiveness and all too much for me.

Next day was the First Greater Ozarks Blues Festival, which involved a free concert with local bands then a 'Headliner Concert' with some national celebrities. This cost $12 but I saw it free from level two of the carpark next door.

Then I did a blues pub crawl, visiting some wonderful old historic pubs, but they were loud and smoky and I ended up in a small, practically deserted restaurant, sipping wine and listening to a great little jazz trio of older musicians. They were so appreciative to have somebody actually *listening* to their music that they came to my table afterwards to thank me!

I drove out of Springfield at midnight, planning to sleep at a truck stop. I couldn't find one, so settled on a well-lit 24-hour supermarket parking lot.

The Tennessee Fall Homecoming Festival

After more vehicle problems, yet another motor was fitted by a great garage in Clarksville who were kind enough to lend me a vehicle. I decided to have some fun at the Tennessee Fall Homecoming near Norris in Eastern Tennessee, not far from the Smoky Mountains. It was an annual event held at the Museum of Appalachia, a 70 acre pioneer mountain village in a beautiful setting, with lots of historic wooden buildings – log cabins, barns, a gristmill, smoke house, underground dairy, sawmill and church. All of these had been relocated from various parts of Appalachia. They even had Mark Twain's family cabin, moved from the picturesquely named Possum Trot in Tennessee.

This museum and the festival were the result of a lifetime of work by founder John Rice Irwin. In the early 1960s he started travelling through isolated parts of Appalachia, collecting pioneer, cultural, antique and everyday items. He was still doing so nearly 50 years later and told me, *'It was my intention not to develop a cold, formal, lifeless museum. Rather, I have aimed for the lived-in look, striving for, above all else, authenticity.'*

I thought it the best museum of its kind I had seen. It really felt that at any moment the original occupants could walk in from the fields. It also housed a fantastic collection of old and unusual musical instruments from the Appalachian region. There were banjos made from ham cans, hub caps, and biscuit tins, and using cat hide or groundhog hide. One was octagonal. A fiddle was made out of a jawbone of a mule and a guitar from a *toilet seat*! An 1833 banjo is believed to be the country's second oldest.

The Tennessee Fall Homecoming Festival celebrated Old-Time traditional music, Bluegrass music, old-time mountain farming, homemaking and arts and crafts. I find Old-Time music hard to define, but it is the folk music which existed before Bluegrass, and on which Bluegrass was actually based. It is also called Mountain or Appalachian Music, and largely has its origins in Britain, where many of the early settlers came from. It was often played for dances or just on the front porch. Banjo and fiddle are the main instruments, and in the early days were frequently homemade. Many of these settlers were very poor and didn't travel, even to the next valley, so before the advent of radio their music developed in individual styles specific to their areas. I love hearing their stories in the legacy of their songs, with names such as 'The Old Doctor That Fell in the Well' and 'Whole Heap of Little Horses'.

There were hundreds of musicians performing at this festival, and some colourful local characters. Reverend Robert Harris described himself as an *'old-time North Carolina circuit rider.'* He came complete with horse, bible and saddlebags, and told me his life was still spent preaching and travelling in this style. Gerald 'Abe' Bestrom specialised in looking exactly like Abraham Lincoln, and he did a good job of it with the appropriate facial hair and a large black hat. Most of his time was spent being photographed with various visitors, but he also stood about giving orations.

Members of the Overmountain Men and the 29th Regiment of the Tennessee Volunteer Infantry dressed in Civil War attire. They had reconstructed revolutionary and civil war encampments, and occasionally gave demonstrations of rifle firing and campfire building. Dressing up and re-enacting historic events seems to be a very popular pastime in America. There were also Pioneer Hunters and Trappers in frontier dress, and Doc Randall's Old Time Travelling Medicine Show, complete with band and an original wagon with stage. Doc was selling some kind of snake oil, which naturally he claimed could cure just about anything. Of course it was all tongue in cheek: *'This medicine contains ginseng, kerosene, benzene, goldenseal and wild cherry. You can brush your teeth and comb your hair with it. It does for undies, the bunions and corns, and if you men have trouble getting up in the night with your kidney problems, take a dose of this and you won't go to bed.'* The band played between the 'doctor's spiel' and also added appropriate musical 'punctuations' when he was talking. It seemed a pretty good recreation. Lots of older American musicians I met on my travels first earned their living working for such outfits.

While I was engrossed in Doc Randall, a little wooden cart went past pulled by five goats all wearing tinkling bells and hats with their names on them (Buster, Tom etc.). They were giving lifts to children. In one corner of the museum, dozens of antique tractors, well-diggers and other odd-looking contraptions were chugging, popping and steaming away, supervised by The Smoky Mountain Antique Engine & Tractor Association. Next to them was an old mill, in which sawyer Milas King was carving up logs using a large circular saw. These were being made into traditional split rail fences.

One of my favourite demonstrations was by the (mostly) elderly Mennonite family, making sweet sorghum syrup using a mule-operated grinder to extract the juice from the plant and then boil it in vats over a wood fire. They still used this method on their own farm.

Many of the other people involved in the traditional activities were also elderly, like the two delightful sisters, aged 89 and 91, wearing frilly pinafores and bonnets and selling home grown apples. Liberty Hill Farms were making apple cider, and a whole host of people were cooking traditional food like apple butter in cauldrons over open fires, carving wood into various objects, whittling, making baskets, brooms, ropes, knives, lye soap, beeswax candles, jewellery, caned chairs, working with leather, pottery, quilting, knotting, tatting, spinning and weaving, painting, and blacksmithing. It was wonderful to see these old arts and crafts being kept alive.

Musical instrument makers were well represented – especially those building Appalachian or mountain dulcimers. A mountain dulcimer is not a true dulcimer (an ancient instrument dating to before the time of Christ and played with hammers), but a traditional American stringed instrument and part of the zither family. Its history is hazy. The word *dulce* is Greek for sweet and *melos* is Latin for song. The German *scheitholt* is thought to be one of its ancestors and mentioned in German writing as early as 1618. But the Appalachian instrument seems to have originated in the 18th century, and has had a resurgence in popularity in recent years. It normally has three or four strings, and looks like an elongated fiddle or zither with an attractive hourglass form, but is sometimes made in other shapes such as teardrop or oval or even rectangular. It has frets and is strummed or plucked while being held in the lap or on a table. To my ear it has a delicate and pretty sound.

Gathered near the makers were small dulcimer bands. These were mainly women and one of them gave me a brief lesson. It seemed fairly easy to produce a simple tune, but I suspect it would take a lot of practice and skill to play well.

There were a number of stages, and little groups of musicians were also playing on the porches of the old homesteads and cabins, just as they would have when the houses were occupied.

At the daily gospel singing in the log church, I found myself in the middle of a wonderful choir of voices. No musical instruments accompanied the singing. Hymn books were passed around, and a leader started by singing the words of each line of the hymn in a kind of chant. This is called 'lining out', and is said to have originated in England to help those who did not know the tune or are unable to read.

Shape-note or sacred harp singing is another method. Shapes are used to represent the notes on the scale and special hymn books were published. These hymn books were called *The Sacred Harp*, and so the music also uses that name. To promote this method, teachers travelled the country holding singing schools and selling the song books. Until very recently, shape-note singing could only be heard in rather remote areas of the Appalachians, but now there is a resurgence of interest and some singing schools are keeping the tradition alive. It has even arrived in Australia. That day in the little log church at the museum, with everyone around me singing lustily and in natural harmonies, I felt transported back to another time and found it deeply moving.

I was thrilled to be invited as a guest to sit on one of the chairs placed on the back of the main festival stage. Watching the musicians from just a few feet behind them was an interesting perspective. I could observe their discrete communications and better understand how a band works together. I was also able to meet them all backstage and watch some very famous people, such as Bluegrass and Old Time musician Ralph

Stanley and legendary guitarist Doc Watson, warming up. It does seem strange to have guests sitting right *on* the stage and I rarely came across it, but it is also a feature of the Grand Ole Opry and probably other venues as well.

I camped in Norris State Park, a few miles from the Museum of Appalachia in a hilly area not far from a large lake. The festival finished about five o'clock, and one night I went into Knoxville about 16 miles away to look for somewhere to dance. I *did* find a place, but it wasn't really what I wanted. There was a good country band, but the crowd yelled for rock 'n roll, so I gave up.

Arriving back at the campground, I noticed one of the large shelters was full of musicians. There were three or four mountain dulcimers, a couple of autoharps, a banjo, double bass and fiddle, and they sounded wonderful. I was warmly invited to join them – as a spectator, of course. A cosy fire was burning and next to it sat a man whittling a piece of wood. It could almost have been a scene from the 19th century.

Back Stage, With Mac Wiseman, Tennessee Fall Homecoming

Doc Randall, The Medicine Show Man.

Rev. Robert Harris & Gerald 'Abe' Bestrom

Mennonite family making sorghum syrup

Back to Nashville

Back in the Nashville area I was intrigued by The Tennessee Walking Horse National Celebration at Shelbyville. I'd never heard of Walking Horses and had no idea what they were, so I went to see. These beautiful horses are specially bred for their smooth gaited, rather flashy walk. They lift their front legs high and wear tall heavy shoes so that they and their riders are tilted backwards. There are various events in this competition, and this high-stepping action of the front legs is called 'big lick' movement.

It's fascinating to see, but looks so unnatural that I checked out comments from the Humane Society and discovered that although some trainers are kind, others are not and carry out a process called 'soring'. This uses various methods to inflict pain on the horse so it lifts its legs higher. One is to apply chemicals such as mustard oil, diesel fuel, kerosene, salicylic acid, and other caustic substances to the horse's legs, and then often a heavy chain around its ankle or nails in those heavy shoes on the front legs. The high stepping is the horse's way of trying to avoid the pain. These cruel practices are banned, but it seemed they were often still carried out.

I drove back to the Clarksville garage to have the van serviced. Everything was working properly as far as they could see and I was so happy. The van was finally behaving itself – what a relief. But within three miles I couldn't get past second gear, and limped back to be told the transmission had collapsed. A replacement would cost $2,000 plus labour. This *really* put a dent into my optimism and I didn't know what to do. They kindly lent me a vehicle while I came to a decision.

Once more I removed all my stuff, including my bike in case the van never ran again, and drove back to Nashville in shock. How could I be so unlucky? Over the next few days I tried to decide what to do, going over all the usual options – trying to sell it, etc.

I felt depressed and couldn't make a decision. I tried to put it out of my mind for a few days and booked in for some dancing lessons, went for long walks in the country and had some long overdue swimming lessons. I'm slightly embarrassed to admit that I also resorted to some shopping therapy. American department stores have absolutely marvellous sales. I bought a pair of snappy bathers for $12, reduced from $85 – then a lovely winter coat and leather gloves trimmed with rabbit fur. It's odd, but despite not being a big consumer, quite often when the van broke down and I knew it was going to cost me money I shopped! Perhaps I just badly needed a treat.

One night I went to a bar about 40 miles north of Nashville. I had heard that a good band was playing there. The bar was called The Zoo and looked great with animals painted on the walls, but it turned out to be very rough. A woman abused me for dancing with a man who she didn't even appear to be with (he had asked *me!*), and when the band took a break, the elderly scrawny bar-maid wearing a tiny mini skirt jumped up on stage and lifted her skirt so we could see the unattractive sight of her stomach and brief bikini. Lots of people got *very* drunk, and in the end a terrible fight broke out which continued in the street, with people running up and down the road and bottles being thrown. One woman wound up with a broken nose. She was sitting on the edge of the gutter, crying and covered with blood. The bar owner ushered me into the refuge of his office, locked the door behind him and sent out a large fierce dog, which I presumed he trained for such occasions. Finally the police arrived, and it was safe enough for me to get away. Although I did want to forget about my problems for a while, this was not the kind of distraction I needed.

A much nicer experience was going to Long Hollow Pike Jamboree at Goodletsville. The "Father of Bluegrass Music" Bill Monroe lived nearby and I was thrilled that he was there that night. Not only was I able to meet him but he even danced with me.

I was worried that I had overstayed my time with my Nashville friends, but I had no vehicle at all now (the garage needed it back), and certainly couldn't afford to rent one or to stay in a motel for more than a couple of days. They reassured me but I did try to keep out of their way as much as possible. It was an unhappy time for me, but eventually I had a re-built transmission freighted out from Oregon. It had a two year warranty and cost $750. I could hardly wait to regain my independence and get on the road again and, just *maybe* this time, I had a vehicle in good running order. I had refused to give up and perhaps my persistence was finally paying off. After all this pampering, the van might actually behave and see me through to the end of my travels.

I often wonder why was I continually optimistic, and think that I'm either terribly naive or that it must be part of my nature. Mum and her sister Lorna were like that – glass half full people always trying to look on the bright side.

I'd never named my van, but at this stage I thought Horace might be appropriate – and so it was christened. This was a name I usually used for large scary spiders inhabiting my space!

I had recently read John Berendt's fascinating account of life in Savannah in his book *Midnight in the Garden of Good & Evil*, and was keen to visit this Deep South city on the Savannah River near the Georgia coast. I drove the 500 miles there without incident, and fell in love with the place. I spent ages exploring its beautiful streets, many cobbled with wonderful 19th century buildings and lovely squares. A real feature of the city are the large live oak trees draped with Spanish moss. Some are 300 years old.

On Sunday morning, wearing a recently acquired velvet 'leopard skin' hat with matching sleeve cuffs, I went to a service at the First African Baptist Church. It dates from 1788, and I think it was the first church in the United States built and owned by African Americans. At one stage it was used as a safe house for escaping slaves. As usual, the congregation was very welcoming and several women complimented me on my outfit. I always noticed in America that people were very generous with their compliments. If they thought you looked good, they would often tell you.

Even passersby in the street commented when I was walking around looking at the shops and restaurants, and it made me feel wonderful.

Travelling north again into South Carolina, I discovered Hunting Island State Park. It has a campground in a marvellous maritime forest right on the ocean. My site was surrounded by huge old trees with Spanish moss and I could clearly hear the sea. There are lots of hiking trails with bird hides, and I was also able to ride my bike for miles along the hard sandy beach without encountering a soul, then along a lagoon lined with palms. It was exciting to see a pod of dolphins frolicking in the open sea, and to walk on the beach at night with a full moon glistening on the water. I even had time to sit and do absolutely nothing, except pig out on a $5 pound of prawns.

One night I went for a twilight walk around the campground and stepped over something lying on the road. I'd assumed it was a stick, but looking back I saw that it was a large snake with its head raised in a striking position! It *probably* wouldn't have been poisonous, but you never know. I'd obviously become careless – something which I could never let happen in Australia, where most snakes are *very* poisonous and occasionally aggressive.

At one of the Bluegrass festivals I had met Bob. He was intrigued and impressed with the fact that I was travelling alone, and amused at all the adventures I was having. I laughed at his comment when he saw me driving – *'Golly, a manual and not even power steering. What a woman!'*

He invited me to visit his home city of Detroit. I'd never been there and I liked him a lot, so decided to accept. He suggested that I could store my van somewhere there while I went home for Christmas. It was getting colder and I thought I'd better continue driving as Detroit is much further north – right up near Canada – and I didn't want to be driving in snow and ice.

Congaree National Park in South Carolina was on the way and it sounded worth visiting, so I decided to stay the night there and explore next morning. On arrival I discovered they had no camping area, but the ranger said I could sleep in my van amongst a few trees just outside the gate. It was freezing. Ice formed on the inside of the windows and twice I woke up shivering and had to refill my hot water bottle. In the morning I retreated into the visitors centre to warm up and they kindly gave me hot tea. A six mile boardwalk took me right through the swamp, which has the last significant stand of old-growth flood plain forest in America. There are 90 different tree species, including loblolly pines over 300 years old and up to 170 feet tall. It's one of several pines native to the American south and is much valued for lumber.

Nashville was also more or less on my way, so I called in at the garage again because I'd noticed a bit of oil leaking from the engine. They replaced some oil seals, but discovered the transmission oil was leaking. I didn't know what this meant, whether it was serious or not, but they didn't have time to fix it.

When I was thinking about this, I began to feel unwell and realised there was a problem with one of my teeth. The gum was swollen and painful, so I found a dentist who diagnosed an abscess. Something would have to be done quickly. First was an antibiotic course which took a few days, and then the tooth had to be removed. As it was connected to a bridge, that had to come out, too, and a temporary one had to be put in. This cost about $900, and frantic calls to and from Australia finally confirmed that my travel insurance would cover it.

I was beginning to feel unlucky to say the least, and for the first time on the trip I was *really* keen to get back home and reconsider this whole damn travel business. My hair looked terrible so I had a perm to cheer myself up, but it turned out too short and too curly, ageing me by at least ten years. Thank goodness for hats, and thank goodness the oil leak was fixed by the tightening of a few bolts – apparently a normal procedure. Finally I left Nashville once again.

It was getting *really* cold now – well below freezing at night. Camping was a bit uncomfortable, so I thought I'd better get to Detroit as quickly as possible. But I noticed oil leaking *again* and yet another garage discovered it was coming from the right hand head. They were a VW dealer, but didn't have the expertise to do the work and advised me to go to a garage with a mechanic who *could* work on an air cooled engine. I did this, and learnt that the oil was leaking because the head had most probably not been torqued down properly, and the engine was also losing compression. At this stage I simply didn't know whether to laugh or cry.

Eventually another dealer went ahead and did the job. Volkswagen offered to give me money towards the purchase of a replacement vehicle, provided I bought it from that particular dealer. A generous offer, but sadly there was nothing remotely suitable for me. Packing my things in and out of Horace was getting extremely annoying, but I did it once more.

Detroit and a Visit Back Home

I finally arrived safely in Detroit. It's a city of contrasts, its prosperity being during the height of the American motor vehicle industry. This was long past and there were many visible signs of decay. Disused lots were covered with rubbish and once grand mansions were deserted and falling apart. Many roads were also in terrible condition, and a magnificent old railway station building sadly appeared to be deteriorating beyond repair.

Since my visit the city has been going through a process of regeneration. I'd love to see it now. It has a rich musical history, particularly in Blues, Rhythm & Blues and Soul. Motown Records was originally an African American owned label, and did a lot to foster the racial integration of popular music. Some of the most famous Motown artists are Stevie Wonder, Aretha Franklin, Smokey Robinson, The Temptations, The Supremes, Four Tops, Bill Haley and The Jackson 5.

My friend Bob organised a fantastic visit. He knew I'd been roughing it on the road for a long time, and treated me to a room at a bed and breakfast in a lovely 19th century building. It seemed so luxurious and I enjoyed every minute of my stay there. Then there were dinners out, a concert with the Detroit Symphony Orchestra, great evenings in blues bars, and flowers delivered to my room. He'd even arranged for me to be interviewed by Ken Calvert, one of the city's top radio personalities who had a morning talk show.

As Bob knew I loved to dance, he'd searched out suitable venues and had even taken dancing lessons. What a man! At one bar I was surprised that a number of men asked me to dance. Later, I discovered he'd called in there earlier in the evening to word up some of them up! I'd never been so spoilt in my whole life. This was the kind of generosity which kept me going in America, despite the dreadful behaviour of Horace.

In addition to all this pampering, Bob had found a reasonable place for me to store my vehicle while I briefly returned to Australia. It was a yard surrounded by a high fence right next to the owner's bakery, and guarded by a fierce looking Rottweiler. I felt confident it would be pretty safe.

Whenever I went back home, I spent some time sorting through everything in the van and making lists of what I had and where it was stored. I did this for a couple of reasons. One was because I left various clothes and toiletries, and didn't want to have to bring more over. The other was so that if at any time I found I couldn't return, and needed to ask somebody to dispose of the van for me, I knew exactly what I would like to keep and just where it was stored. I also had to make sure that there was nothing which would suffer from being frozen during the winter. Bob said that cans of drink, for example, would explode and then leak when they thawed. Coming from a warmer climate, I'd never had to think about this before.

On the plane back to Australia, I mused about all that had happened in the last twelve months and decided that although all these vehicle problems were awful at the time, they were all part of the rich kaleidoscope of travel experiences and I should simply treat them as such. Easy to say when everything was going well, of course.

It was on this particular trip home during 1995 that I became involved in Australian radio. Somebody I knew was an announcer at a small station on the outskirts of Melbourne. He had a weekly music show and had invited me as a regular guest presenter. My contribution was playing and talking about the music I had found during my American travels. It was so much fun and gave me a really legitimate reason to meet and interview musicians when I went back to America.

Some time later, in early 1997 I was offered a wonderful six month job back in Australia as Acting Marketing Manager for Open Channel, a film and television training organisation in Melbourne. Of course, I accepted. While I was home I enrolled in a certificated radio production course to learn about interview techniques, presentation, producing radio documentaries, defamation law etc. This led to my own show – *Southern Style* – which I am still presenting all these years later.

After that I decided to apply to the Australian Film Commission for a grant to update their *Guide to Non-Theatrical Distribution in North America*. It was to help Australian filmmakers choose the best distributor for their particular film. I had the right background and already knew most of the appropriate film distributors in the U.S. and Canada, so they gave it to me.

This was wonderful. I based myself for a few weeks in New York. Contacts at the National Film Board of Canada offered the use of an office at their U.S. headquarters in the Rockefeller Center on Manhattan Island, and my friend Mary Jane invited me to stay in her little apartment opposite Central Park. She also worked in the film industry and we had become friends some years before. I had visited her a number of times, and a few years earlier we'd had a wonderful holiday together in Mexico.

I did a lot of the project work by phone and made a few trips – including a memorable train journey up the beautiful east coast to Boston. I was excited to arrive there in the middle of a blizzard, but that excitement soon wore off after I discovered that all my shoes and boots leaked! After appointments I slogged through the snow and slush exploring this historic city, and every night I dried my footwear on the radiator in my room.

Back in New York City I dragged Mary Jane off to a honky-tonk for some dancing, and spent lots of time in galleries and museums. That grant kept me going for many months and my expenses were tax deductible!

Meanwhile my van remained where I had stored it in Detroit. I was looking forward to collecting it and to seeing Bob again. However, another adventure was to come before then ...

With Bob in Detroit

Dancing with Bob

On the Road with Sand Mountain

At one of the Bluegrass festivals I'd met some members of a band called Sand Mountain. I had been introduced to them by their recording company, which had supplied me with their CDs for my fledgling radio show. Sand Mountain was an award-winning traditional Bluegrass band. Every year they spent approximately four months on the road performing at festivals and other events all over the country. They invited me to travel with them on one of these tours. It would be a great chance to see how a band manages on the road and I thought perhaps I could write an article about them and try to have it published somewhere, so I made arrangements to join them. They were travelling through Denver from their base in Florida to performances in Wyoming and Montana. As I had an old friend, Ken, in Denver, who I wanted to visit, this was the ideal place to meet. I flew there after my New York episode.

They collected me from Ken's home in a posh new suburb just outside the city. I must admit that I vaguely wondered what the neighbours thought when this rather battered 1956 ex-Greyhound bus pulled into the quiet street. I was also a little apprehensive. How would the band members feel about having a stranger on board for nearly two weeks? And would we all get on OK? I'd only met two of the five. Cigarette smoke gives me hay fever, so what would I do if they smoked on the bus? I needn't have worried as nobody smoked, and in fact they'd been concerned about any unsavory habits I might have! As it turned out, we got on really well and had a lot of fun. Our biggest problem was trying to understand each other's accents.

Sand Mountain was a family band and on board were band leader and mandolinist Wayne Crain, his eldest son James who played guitar, younger son and upright bass player Jerry, banjo player Kenny Townsel and the youngest member of the band, 18 year old four-times Florida fiddle champion Jason Barie. Also on this trip was Jerry's wife Debbie who, much to their delight, had just discovered she was pregnant with their first child. I think the main reason she came along was to keep me company, otherwise I'd be the only female living in very confined quarters with five men. They all obviously got on well together and each of them loved to travel almost as much as they loved to play music.

We drove north from Denver and over the border into Wyoming, where some roadside repairs were done to get the headlights working, and then west towards the band's first performance in Kemmerer, Wyoming. This was to be a relatively easy trip with time to enjoy the scenery between performances. It was great sitting on one of the two original passenger seats at the front of the bus, listening to some of the band practising while we rolled through the beautiful Wyoming plains into the sunset. Plus I didn't have to drive, navigate, worry about vehicle breakdowns or where I was going to stay each night.

I was assigned a top bunk right at the rear. It was quite high and there was no ladder, so I found it difficult to get into, especially when the bus was moving. It was surprising how much it bumped and swayed at the back, even when the road seemed fairly smooth. Debbie and Jerry were in the bunk immediately below me so I had to be careful not to step on them. The engine and generator were noisy, but at least drowned out any snores. That first night I slept much better than I expected, and dreamed I was on a boat.

The interior of the bus was all home-built, mainly by Jerry, and although not luxurious by any standards it was comfortable – a lounge area with a couch and table, seven bunks in the middle and rear of the bus, plus lots of hanging and storage space, and a very small bathroom with a toilet but no shower. It could become very cramped, especially when the band members were getting ready for a performance. I tried to keep right out of the way then. Even though each person was fairly careful about tidying up, it could easily become cluttered and I managed to lose a pair of shoes on board, which weren't found until the bus had been cleaned out at the end of the trip!

We stopped most days for showers at the large truck stops and, when hungry, either made sandwiches, heated something in the microwave or went to a restaurant. I was a little dismayed at the amount of greasy takeaways and other junk food they all ate. In turn they were amused when I tried to find wholemeal bread and salads. They were also surprised at my efforts at conservation. When I wrote my name on my polystyrene cup so I could re-use it they assured me they had plenty and I could get a fresh one each time I had a drink.

Three of the band were the drivers and had become adept at changing over on the road without even losing speed! It was a relief to discover that they were in fact excellent and responsible, and nobody drank alcohol. When we stopped to refuel, each member had his job and went quietly about it without fuss. Jason usually filled the water bottles; Kenny cleaned the windshield and washed the bus; James, who was the tidiest, looked after the inside and various people filled the petrol and diesel tanks. (The motor ran on diesel, the generator on petrol). Both Kenny and Jerry did repairs. Kenny was a truck driver and quite used to roadside repairs, and Jerry did most of the vehicle maintenance – partly because the bus was garaged at his home. They estimated the bus had done well over ten million miles, and although we did have a few problems along the way, I was impressed that, unlike my own van, it was still going so well.

Most of Sand Mountain's serious rehearsal was done when they arrived at the venues. Their homes were in different states, so it was difficult to get together when not on the road. They also had day jobs.

Everyone except Jerry practised when the bus was on the road. His double bass was too large for that, so he was generally driving and making suggestions while the other four worked on their material. The most popular instrument to play on the bus was the mandolin, mainly because it's so small and not as loud as the banjo.

After driving most of the night we arrived at Kemmerer, a small town in western Wyoming, in time for breakfast, which was traditional fare of eggs, bacon, hash browns and pancakes at a good homely restaurant in town. The concert was not until the next evening, but we had come early so we could spend the day at a lovely lake nearby, where all the men fished and Debbie and I walked through masses of wildflowers. It would have been really peaceful, except that they left the noisy bus generator going so the interior would remain cool. You could hear it for miles. The fishing was a huge success and a scrumptious dinner of grilled trout was prepared by James, who was the chief cook.

The concert was held in an old church now part of the Kemmerer historical museum. It was a small but highly appreciative audience and Sand Mountain gave a talented and professional performance, with Jerry providing plenty of humour, spinning his big double bass around as he played. They always dressed up for concerts to enhance their professional image, and looked very smart in their matching green jackets, black western ties, white shirts and black trousers. Wayne said, *'I think if people come to see a show, they want you to be dressed differently to the average person on the street.'*

They used only one central microphone instead of a separate one for each musician. It allowed them to hear each other naturally rather than through the stage sound monitors, leading to tighter playing and better vocal harmonies. Jason said, *'I love it. I believe it's one of the best systems you can use because you gather around each other and it's almost like jamming.'* It's easier for the sound engineer, too, but does require some interesting choreography by the musicians, as they step forward to play a solo into the microphone or backwards to get out of the way.

After the show everybody showered at a local motel and stocked up at the supermarket. We left at midnight so we could have all next day at Yellowstone National Park. Most of us went straight to bed and slept through the drive. Usually at times like this, one person stayed chatting to the driver to make sure he didn't get too sleepy.

I got up early and was treated to a wonderful moonset over the high, snowy mountains of the Grand Tetons. Standing in the front of the bus, peering out of the huge windscreen, was a favourite place for animal spotting as we drove through the park. We saw elk, moose, buffalo, and James even spotted a grey wolf slinking through the forest.

Early next morning after we'd left Yellowstone Wayne discovered a leak in the air brakes. Apparently we were lucky to have had brakes at all on those Yellowstone Mountains, and we wouldn't be able to continue until they were repaired. Kenny managed to hunt down the parts needed and he and Wayne fixed them while the rest of us slept, oblivious to the drama going on outside. I obviously needed a bunch of handy mechanics travelling with me in Horace.

Next stop was Hamilton in western Montana for the Bitterroot Bluegrass Festival. A rodeo was taking place next to the festival and cowboys on horses often paused to listen to the music. The setting was gorgeous – an open stage in a valley surrounded by mountains, under a beautiful sky with ever shifting clouds and an occasional threat of rain. There was no electricity available for the van and, although it was a bit stuffy inside, I was glad that no generators were allowed. Much more peaceful without them, and the air was cleaner, too.

It was good to see a lot of young people and Sand Mountain was wildly applauded and danced to. I asked Jerry if audience response affected the way the band played, and he explained that, *'if a crowd really gets into it you move up to a different level. You try to put a little more intensity into your music.'* Noticing a certain tension prior to performances, I wondered if this was nerves, but Jerry said that it was actually concentration as each band member *'just wants to get their part right and do the best they can.'*

I felt slightly embarrassed when they introduced me from the stage as an Australian journalist writing a story about them. I wasn't actually a journalist at all but had always enjoyed writing, and decided I would definitely have a go at writing something about them as a kind of thank you for this trip. I had been busily interviewing them and hoped I would be able to live up to their expectations.

It was such a thrill when my article was subsequently accepted by the popular American magazine *Bluegrass Unlimited*. It wasn't commissioned. The editor wasn't even expecting it, but they used it as the cover article, together with a number of my photographs, including one I took of the band's bus with a backdrop of the Grand Teton Mountains. Apparently it was the first time anyone had submitted an article about musician life on the road and, apart from the little piece about myself in the *Fort*

Worth Gazette, it was the first time I'd had anything published. I've been busily sending them articles on festivals, musicians and instrument makers ever since – which I'm happy to say they have always published!

Now we had a lot of travelling to do to get to the next festival at Xenia, Ohio. It was 1,800 miles away. We left Hamilton after a much needed morning at a laundromat, and with a cooler full of elk and cougar (mountain lion) meat, a gift from one of the locals. It was legal to hunt mountain lions in Idaho. This was grilled by James beside the highway. I thought the elk hamburgers were tolerable, but the cougar meat was *very* dark and gamey, strong smelling and strong tasting. In fact, whenever the packet of cooked meat was opened and the odour started wafting out, poor Debbie, who was starting to suffer morning sickness, had to immediately exit the bus. I followed soon afterwards.

After another supermarket visit we drove right across South Dakota and through the attractive rich farming country of Iowa, where the generator broke down several times. It was a relief when Jerry and Kenny finally managed to repair it as it was very hot and humid, especially in the bus sleeping quarters. The rear windows were all covered up, so there was no airflow. To make up for lost time Jerry drove through much of the night, while the others practiced or slept.

Various members of the band talked to me about the importance of getting on well together, especially when they spend three or four months each year on the road. Jerry said, *'Personality is really important. You must weigh up between musicianship, personality and professionalism.'* They all felt that a sense of humour helped enormously and we certainly had lots of laughs, especially at *my* expense when they discovered I had a hang-up about brushing my teeth in front of anybody. The only sink was in the living room area, and although I tried to sneak out my toothbrush when the others were preoccupied, somebody almost always noticed and they made a point of gathering around me!

No friction was evident to me at any time, although I noticed that after two weeks people were a little less communicative, and inclined to sleep more or lie on their bunks reading. Some of the men were missing their loved ones, and life on the road was hard work and tiring. The big names in the music industry all have professional drivers and other people employed to do the work when travelling. Sand Mountain travelled up to 125,000 miles a year and had put a million miles on this old bus.

The last festival on this trip was the Vince Combs' 10th Annual Bluegrass Festival, held at the show grounds in Xenia, Ohio. Vince Combs was a musician himself. He started playing at the age of 16 when his father bought him a $32 mandolin from a catalogue, and his band was one of the festival highlights.

By now I was practically considering myself part of the Sand Mountain family, and was delighted when they received three standing ovations after each of their evening performances.

Then it was time for me to leave. I was going up to Detroit to see Bob, collect Horace from storage and do more travelling. The band members were heading back to their homes, families and day jobs in Alabama and Florida until the next tour.

It was a wonderful experience for me. I had travelled nearly 4,000 miles with them. I learnt a lot about the music, the band and the rigours of life on the road, saw some beautiful countryside, had a lot of fun and made some wonderful friends. We kept in touch for years, and recently I had an unexpected message from one of them when they had tuned into my radio show!

Sand Mountain bus. Tetons, Wyoming

Sand Mountain and bus. Bitterroot Bluegrass festival. Hamilton, WY.

Getting into the band's fast food!

Jerry Crain and Jason Barie, Western Wyoming

Travelling in the North-east

Before collecting Horace from Detroit, I spent some time in Columbus, Ohio, with my elderly friend Charley, and arranged to join him again in several weeks at a house he had rented at Cape Cod on the east coast. We had met a few years earlier at the Columbus Documentary Film Awards. I was there to accept an award on behalf of some Australian filmmakers. Charley was one of the judges and we happened to be sitting next to each other at the dinner. An interesting man, he had been Dean of a large women's university, and had published a number of books – one on the history of Columbus. He also had a weekly television interview programme. We kept in touch and I visited whenever I was in the area. I especially enjoyed watching films with him in his home cinema.

Flowers had arrived from Bob, who also called to say all was well with the van and that he was looking forward to seeing me. The feeling was mutual. So after a few very happy days with Charley, I hired a car for the four-hour trip to Detroit. It was wonderful to be driving something comfortable and modern which wasn't likely to break down at any moment. Even if it did, it wouldn't be my responsibility and presumably another would be supplied with a minimum of fuss. It was much lighter on petrol, too, but would be expensive to keep for any length of time – and I couldn't sleep or cook in it!

When Bob and I arrived at the vehicle storage yard in Detroit it was completely deserted, the gate was open, there was no sign of the guard dog, and mine was the only vehicle there. Weeds were growing up through the front bumper bar. So much for the safe storage assured, but fortunately all was OK and I'd saved some money because I'd paid them a deposit with the balance due on collection of the vehicle. (There's always a silver lining!) I'd been unable to contact them on the phone to let them know I was coming, as there hadn't been any answer. They'd obviously gone out of business and neglected to let me know.

Bob had been there the day before and charged up the battery, so I was able to drive straight out and on to the Detroit Edison Boat Club, where he was living on his boat. The Commodore had given me permission to camp there for a few days. The boat club was right on the water, of course, and just a little north of the city. I had access to their modern bathroom facilities (no spiders!).

Bob liked to cook, so some evenings I was invited to dinner on his boat. One night we took his small speedboat over the river to Canada for dinner at the Windsor Yacht Club. It seemed to be just a matter of making a phone call to Immigration to let them know we were there. I remember trying to whisper my birth date into the phone because I didn't want to let Bob know how old I was! People always assumed I was younger, and I wasn't keen to go out of my way to correct them. Rather vain of me!

A few days later Bob and his friend Ron arranged to meet me at a small Bluegrass festival in Missouri. They'd planned a fishing trip in the area. Although it was in the opposite direction to Cape Cod on the east coast where I was meeting Charley, it wouldn't take too long to get there on the freeway. I thought it would be fun and I needed another music fix.

I arrived first and discovered it was a much more staid affair than the other festivals I'd attended. Nearly everybody was elderly and alcohol was strictly forbidden anywhere on site. As usual, they were surprised to see a woman alone, especially an Australian, and taken aback when two men drove up after dark calling out, *'Hi gorgeous, want a lift?'* and I jumped straight in. I'm sure my reputation was further tarnished (or perhaps enhanced?) when I appeared each day with one or the other on my arm – sometimes one on each arm. They slept in the back of Bob's truck which had a metal cover, making it into something resembling a coffin. Bob solved the alcohol ban by decanting beer into soft drink cans!

The people were really very nice and the music excellent, so we ended up having lots of fun. Ron was a good dancer and Bob cooked wonderful dinners. What more could a woman ask for?

Once at about 2 am – well after the music had finished and everyone else had gone to bed – Bob and I lay in the grass watching a sky full of shooting stars. I really loved the night sky and had often surprised people by lying on picnic tables in campgrounds in the middle of the night to watch it.

Rather sadly, I said goodbye to Bob and set off for Cape Cod. Travelling through a little piece of Canada seemed to be the quickest way to get there. It also meant that I could visit Niagara Falls. I was surprised to discover that crossing in and out of Canada by road posed no immigration or customs problems at all. It's probably different now. My first night was spent sleeping at an unattractive services area on the edge of a busy freeway, but generally I found Western Ontario uncrowded with lots of beautiful farms. A supermarket not far from Toronto had a much more interesting selection than those I was used to in America, so I stocked up.

Next day I missed a vital turn, got horribly lost, frustrated and ended up driving two hours out of my way. I was relieved to eventually reach my goal – Niagara – which is really spectacular. The 'Maid of the Mist' boat trip to the base of Horseshoe Falls is especially exciting. These falls are 167 feet high and 2,200 feet wide, while the American Falls are 184 feet by 1,075 feet wide. Half to three-quarters of the river is diverted to generate electricity before it reaches the falls, but this is often done at night. An amazing amount of water seemed to be pouring over when I was there. All the boat passengers were issued with blue plastic ponchos as the spray went hundreds of feet into the air and rained down upon us.

After Niagara I travelled south to the large Adirondack Park. Its six million acres covers about two thirds of upstate New York. Some of this is privately owned, but much is wilderness with rugged mountains, many rivers and thousands of lakes and ponds. There are some lovely places to camp.

At a little town called Long Lake I stopped to call Bob, and was horrified to see the back of the van splattered with oil *again*. He offered to come and get me if necessary. The local mechanic diagnosed an oil leak from the right head – exactly the same problem as last time – plus one tyre was in very poor condition, and some brake fluid was leaking, which could be dangerous. It was Friday and he couldn't get parts in until Monday.

All the local campgrounds were full so, at his suggestion, I spent the weekend in the forest beside a creek in a beautiful area with some pretty walking trails. I wasn't *particularly* worried because I felt fairly sure he would be able to sort out the problems, so I had a reasonably relaxing time riding my bike and walking. Despite this, I did feel a bit lost and frustrated. I'd rather have been continuing my journey, but I didn't have an impending deadline and could have been stuck in a much worse place. It was peaceful, with only an occasional car coming past, and once a couple of men fished from the little bridge near me.

Bear prints were all around but I didn't see any other signs of them. They would have been black bears which, as I discovered in Glacier National Park, aren't nearly as dangerous as brown bears (grizzlies). So, although I would have been frightened to come across one, I wasn't overly concerned. On my walks I sometimes struggled over muddy peat bogs, but one bonus was the abundance of wild raspberries.

Back at the garage on Monday I discovered the parts *hadn't* arrived as promised. The mechanic had no idea when they would, so he changed the tyre, temporarily cleaned up the brake problem and said I'd be OK to continue on as far as Cape Cod. Horace was getting through a lot of oil, so I stocked up at a big Wal-Mart store where it was relatively cheap.

It was a relief to arrive safely a couple of days later, and to be with a friend. Charley had rented a beautiful house at Truro. It was furnished with antiques and in a quiet forested area not too far from the coast. We spent a lot of time swimming, reading, playing Scrabble and going for long walks on the lovely beaches. One day we went on a whale watching trip in a beautiful large yacht, and were lucky enough to see two humpbacks. They were very active, slapping their tails on the water. One quite close to us breached, so we could see it in its entirety. Just amazing.

It was in Truro that I started to write my article on the trip with Sand Mountain. With no computer access I wrote it all by hand, eventually renting computer time at a store. Charley was an excellent proofreader, being a published writer himself. Finally I sent it off to *Bluegrass Unlimited* magazine on a disc with prints of my photos.

Once again I tried to put my engine problems out of my mind, but within a few days I had to be on my way. After a frustrating morning on the telephone trying to get booked into an appropriate garage, I realised I really *did* have to plan my route around the availability of VW specialists – and at this stage, because of the engine warranty, they had to be *registered* VW dealers, too. Just as well there seemed to be one in most major cities.

The next was in Brockton, Massachusetts, about three hours from Cape Cod. I arrived there around midday, booked the van in for the next morning, and headed off to historic Plymouth to see where the Mayflower supposedly landed. There is a wonderful replica, Mayflower II, which had been built in the UK in the 1950s then sailed over. It wasn't a large ship and I pondered on how difficult it must have been for 102 passengers and their provisions (including animals) to exist in such cramped quarters. On arrival in America, the pilgrims apparently stepped from the ship on to a large stone. I had heard that this had been moved several times from its original place and had even been broken. There it was on the edge of the sea under a protective canopy. At the information centre, I asked a young volunteer if the stone was just as it was when they actually landed. She said, *'Oh no. It didn't have a canopy then!'*

"Camping" at Detroit–Edison Boat Club

Dancing with Ron

Charley Cole at Cape Cod Lighthouse

On Maid of the Mist boat, Niagara

Loons and Lobsters

Next day I hung around the garage for six hours for a decision to be made. As suspected, the cylinder head was *again* loose and leaking lots of oil. Apparently it couldn't be fixed and unbelievably *another* engine was the only solution.

I was left with yet another difficult decision to make. After all my bad experiences, I didn't see the point of putting in yet another motor, and even if I wanted to, I didn't have the money. I couldn't bear to have my trip end in such a dismal way. I had grand plans to see some of the Maine coastline and then drive thousands of miles all the way back to Tuscon, Arizona, to a music festival. But if I kept driving, the engine would eventually lose so much compression that it would no longer start.

I felt I had nobody with whom to discuss the situation or who could advise me. I decided to console myself with a bottle of wine and found a place to camp. Some friendly neighbours invited me to sit around their fire and we shared my wine. After a restful night with the added help of a sleeping tablet, I felt much calmer and better able to make a decision. It crossed my mind that if this level of stress continued, I'd be well on my way to becoming a drug addicted alcoholic!

This was my decision. It was now August 1998, six years since I first started this trip. I had driven more than 150,000 miles, coped with all kinds of problems and been stranded many times. This wretched vehicle had really tested me, but I had *never* given up and I wasn't going to now. I would continue north to Maine and perhaps there I would find a good VW mechanic (eternal hope!) who could give me expert advice, and who may even be able to fix the problem at a reasonable price.

I didn't find a VW mechanic in Maine, but the beauty of its rugged coastline certainly fulfilled my expectations. The countless inlets make a 3,478 mile shoreline within a direct distance of 228 miles. There are lots of lakes and islands, too.

From the historic city of Portland I took the delightful Casco Bay Transit mail-boat run. The small boat called at some of the rocky islands (there are 365 in this particular area) to drop off cargo and groceries, pick up passengers and of course the mail. We sailed past historic lighthouses, a couple of old forts and many beautiful houses perched on the rocky shores. There was lots of evidence of WWII activity. In some places, ships had been sunk to keep out submarines and there was also a naval re-fuelling port, staging and anchorage for the North Atlantic Fleet.

Not far from Portland was a lovely campground on a peninsula, where I found one of the best sites I'd ever stayed in. It was secluded and on the water. I could swim right at my doorstep and in the still of the night I heard distant seals barking. I hadn't been out on my bike for a while and discovered it had a flat tyre, but I was able to buy a new inner tube and fit it myself. If only I could fix Horace so easily. It was a delight to be able to ride around the scenic trails, and I spent three days there. At least when I was staying in one spot the vehicle wasn't continuing to deteriorate.

Wanting to try the famous Maine lobster, I decided on a big night out and went to a local restaurant advertising a lobster special for $10. But as is often the case in such restaurants, it wasn't available at that particular time. Instead I ordered fried clams, which arrived cold in a horrible thick greasy batter. They were virtually inedible. I mentioned this to the waitress, who asked if I wanted to take them home in a doggy bag. They were only fit for a dog, but that wasn't what she meant.

Eventually I did have my lobster from a roadside stall called Red's Eats, which had a reputation for the best lobster rolls in Maine. They cost a whopping $11 but were supposed to contain the flesh from more than one lobster (they must have been small creatures), and this time I wasn't disappointed. I thought they had a stronger and sweeter flavour than our Australian equivalent of crayfish. Unfortunately, I developed a taste for them which I could rarely afford to indulge, but later on I found a place where you could select a live lobster from a tank and have it cooked for you on the spot. Mine weighed one and a quarter pounds and only cost $4. They even cracked the claws ready for me to suck out the flesh. After that it was back to the usual boring pasta dinners.

Maine is not always so attractive away from the coastline. There are lots of rather depressing signs of poverty so I drove on to New Hampshire, where I discovered and fell in love with the common loon – a remarkably beautiful and interesting bird, with a not so beautiful name. At the Loon Center and Markus Wildlife Sanctuary near Moultonborough, there is a lovely hiking trail through the forest with a small lake, mossy stones and lots of mosquitoes.

Disappointingly I didn't see any loons and had to make do with watching them on videos at the visitors centre. They are fairly large, strikingly patterned black and white water birds (not ducks), which raise their chicks on inland lakes further north in Greenland, Iceland and the northern parts of Canada. They have the smallest wings per body size of any flying bird, and need a quarter of a mile of water to take off. This means that many lakes support only one pair. It is thought that they mate for life, and they often visit other couples, with the resident pair appearing to show their visitors around their lake. Chicks sometimes sit on their parents' backs or keep warm under a wing; and adults have an unusually haunting call, which I realised I had probably sometimes mistaken for a wolf or coyote. Loons walk clumsily on land because their legs are towards to the rear of their bodies, but that makes them powerful swimmers. As they have heavier bones than other birds, they can swim up to a depth of two hundred feet and usually stay under water for three to five minutes, but have been recorded underwater for up to fifteen minutes. They can also fly up to 75 mph and live for 20-30 years.

At the Loon Center I met a delightful woman who invited me to her home, set in acres of gorgeous forest on a secluded lake. She gave me lunch and we paddled her canoe around the little lake. It's two miles long, but she called it a pond. It was thrilling to finally spot a loon there. We also saw two occupied beaver lodges, but no sign of their shy inhabitants. It was a real paradise, with only a couple of other houses nearby, and these were set back in the forest like hers, and not visible until you were very close.

She was a Quaker and I would have liked to talk to her about this and to spend more time in her company. I hoped she would invite me to stay the night – I could have slept in my van somewhere on her property – but she didn't, and I didn't like to suggest it, of course.

Driving off in the middle of a thunderstorm I had difficulty finding a place to stay overnight, and ended up in a horrible, overcrowded and noisy campground. My meal had to be cooked inside, causing lots of condensation while the rain thundered down on the roof. Next morning it was still cold and damp, but I couldn't be bothered waiting in the long queue for hot showers. I managed, as I often did, with a bucket of cold water.

While in New Hampshire I took an exciting trip on the world's first ever mountain cog railway. It's powered entirely by steam and the engine is at the rear – pushing the passenger cars up the track. During the three and a quarter miles it took to scale 6,300 ft. Mount Washington, it used one metric ton of coal and 4,000 litres of water – hardly an environmentally friendly trip. The most interesting part was the one in three gradient where the passengers in the front were 14 feet higher than those in the back. When we stood up straight we were at a very odd angle in relation to the train, so it looked as though we were actually leaning backwards. This was so funny that we all took photos of each other and of the two brakemen who entertained us with interesting facts when they weren't working.

On the summit of Mount Washington it was 25 degrees colder and *very* windy. A sign stated that the highest winds on earth were recorded here – 231 mph in 1934.

I also spent a happy day wandering around the lovely Canterbury Shaker village in New Hampshire. Founded in the 1780s, the area's population reached its peak around 1850 when 300 people lived and worked there in 100 buildings on 4,000 acres. 24 original buildings remain on 694 acres and it's now a privately run not-for-profit museum.

Shakers – actually The United Society of Believers in Christ's Second Appearing – are another of the religious sects which fascinated me on this trip. They originally broke away from mainstream Quakerism in

UK. Their founder, Ann Lee, sailed to America in 1774 with her husband and seven members. They got their familiar name because they believed in what they called 'shaking off the flesh,' sometimes shaking their whole bodies during dancing. This could continue for hours in their church services and they sometimes went into a kind of trance. They also believed in separating themselves from the rest of the community, spoke in tongues and practised equality of the sexes and races, common ownership of goods, pacifism and celibacy – the latter of course being their undoing. Children only came when parents joined up with them, so with no other way of producing younger generations, they would eventually die out. The last Canterbury Shaker, Sister Ethel Hudson, died in 1992 aged 96.

There is another Shaker community in Maine – Sabbathay Lake – which in 2016 had just three members and was the only remaining active Shaker community in the United States. Originally there were more than 6,000 members in America. Shaker buildings and furniture are beautifully designed and made, even the door handles. Original Shaker rocking chairs and round wooden boxes are much sought after classics. Apparently Oprah Winfrey paid $10,000 for a box!

It is hard to believe that in the late 19th century Vermont had lost 70% of its forest, because so much of it is forested today. The scenery is lovely and hilly with beautiful farms and lots of streams and rivers. I camped right next to a rushing mountain stream in Green Mountain National Forest. It was so relaxing because nobody else was around and the only sound I could hear was the water. I spent an afternoon writing in my diary and catching up on the usual stuff – washing, sorting and tidying, plus some cooking. The previous day I'd bought a BBQ chicken for five dollars. It was a welcome change and I stretched it out to provide the basis for seven meals: chicken sandwiches, chicken salads, some into a pasta sauce and a big batch of soup from the carcass with a few vegetables, herbs and rice. It all felt like a great treat, and the experience reminded me again of how much more I was able to appreciate the things I used to take for granted.

My frugality also reminded me a little of my childhood, when my poor parents had to work really hard to stretch the family budget. Clergymen didn't get paid very much. We always had our own chickens. Dad grew all our fruit and vegetables, baked our bread, made our soap and glue and mended our shoes. Mum carefully saved any water the vegetables were cooked in to use as a base for soup, and made preserves and chutneys and sewed our clothes. At one stage we had a cow and made our own butter. My brother Keith milked her and sometimes squirted the warm milk straight into my mouth! John operated the milk separator and we all had a go at turning the handle of the butter churn. I'm glad I grew up like that, because I think it gave me a sense of appreciation I wouldn't have had otherwise.

Further north I came across Shelburne Museum – a large and wonderful collection of historic buildings, including an old railway station with vintage railway carriages, a sawmill, 18th and 19th century houses, inns and barns (including a rare *round* barn), boats, and even a 19th century lighthouse. All these buildings housed antiques and various collections. According to the Visitor Guide, *'it was founded in 1947 by Electra Havemeyer Webb to celebrate American craftsmanship and ingenuity'* – another fine example of the philanthropy I was to see so often in the United States. Electra was fortunate to have been born into a wealthy family and also married a descendant of the famous Vanderbilts, so she could afford to indulge her passion.

She acquired historic buildings from all around the Adirondack area and had them moved to the museum site. Many would have been demolished or allowed to disintegrate. Some were removed intact, including the SS Ticonderoga, the last remaining side paddlewheel steamer with a vertical beam engine. It was used on Lake Champlain – a very large lake partly in Vermont, New York and over the Canadian border in Quebec. The steamer is 220 feet long and moving it to the museum must have been quite a feat. Some buildings were specially erected to house specific collections. One of my favourites was the enormous horseshoe-shaped barn, which was built in the 1960s to house three wonderfully carved wooden miniature circuses. The curved part of the 500 foot long building contains a complete circus parade, conceived and carved by Roy Arnold on a scale of one inch to one foot. There are hundreds of human figures, plus all the animals of the circus and the ornamental wagons.

The hall is curved because Electra felt it was much more exciting if you couldn't see the beginning and end of a circus parade at the same time.

Shelburne Museum is enormous. After spending the best part of two days there, I still didn't see it all. I especially loved the collection of 192 pocket size travelling inkwells. They were shaped according to the owners' businesses and included hats, boots, horses, a watering can, dice, violin case and doctor's bag.

Another discovery for me was the 'courting mirror' and the origin of a well-known expression. A young suitor in the early 18th century usually gave a looking glass to the family of the girl he was proposing to. On his next visit he would anxiously look for it. If it was hanging on the wall his offer was accepted, but if it was laid face down on the table he was *'turned down flat.'* This is sometimes expressed as *'flatly refused.'*

A guard at the museum invited me out one afternoon. Vaguely interested, I asked what we'd do. His suggestion was to ride to the airport to watch the planes. This was hardly an attractive proposition and I declined, thinking if that's the best he can come up with he must be a boring person or it's a boring area. On the other hand, maybe that's where the local blokes took their dates when there were no drive-in movie theatres!

Once again I was starting to feel a bit lost, lonely and worried about Horace, which appeared to be running OK but was using more oil than ever. An evening out on the town to cheer me up seemed a good idea. I dressed up in my best outfit – black shirt, trousers and elegant black Italian hat – and decided to check out a nice-looking small brewery pub in Burlington. I parked and walked through the shops, wandering into a large bookshop where I found the perfect guidebook for my travels. At the pub I sat at the bar, placed my book in its wrapper on the counter and considered the drinks menu. A couple of helpful fellows recommended that I try the beer sampler – a very small glass of each of the six beers that were brewed on the premises.

We chatted for some time and eventually one of them asked which book I had bought. I bet them a million dollars if they guessed correctly. After about half an hour and several hints from me, the closest they got was that it was a guidebook for my personal use, so they gave up. They could hardly believe their eyes when I revealed a trucker's guide to truck stops in the U.S. and Canada. It only cost $12 and showed the location of every truck stop, opening hours and their facilities, including whether recreation vehicles were welcome and what shops were in the immediate vicinity. It could be used in conjunction with my camping guidebook, save me heaps of money *and* I wouldn't have to drive all over the place looking for suitable sleeping spots. My companions simply couldn't imagine an apparently educated, sophisticated looking woman driving herself around the country spending her nights sleeping in truck stops ... alone!

I was soon back in the Adirondacks area, and decided to spend a day or two in the attractive place I'd found when I was waiting for vehicle parts to arrive. It had been so peaceful last time that I guess I became a bit lax. Instead of being ready to drive off in an emergency, I had parked my van facing *away* from the road so I could sit outside the sliding door, out of view of the road and next to the little stream. Again I watched out for any vehicles, and made sure I was hidden when they passed. None stopped, and I had retreated into the back of the van to escape the biting insects.

It was beginning to get dark when I was surprised to see a young man walking past on the edge of the forest, staring in my direction. I didn't have the light on inside and knew he couldn't possibly see who was in the van, so I wasn't too alarmed but wondered what he was doing, because I knew the little track didn't lead anywhere. I also wondered where he'd come from, because I was positive I hadn't heard a vehicle.

He walked past several more times and I began to feel afraid. As this was America, I thought he might be carrying a gun. He was wearing tight jeans and I couldn't see anything in his pockets, but guns are sometimes tucked into boots. He then stood in the trees some distance away, still facing me and in full view. I could clearly see that he had unzipped his jeans and was exposing himself.

I had to get out of there quickly, but I'd left lots of things on the ground outside. Should I try to retrieve them? He was far enough away, so I threw the stuff in, jumped into the driver's seat, started the engine and, while shining the headlights on him and sounding the horn, reversed out as quickly as I could. He immediately ran away, and when I reached the road I could just see the tail end of a bicycle disappearing around the corner. I had to drive in that direction, but he must have hidden in the forest, because I didn't see him again.

I was so spooked that I continued for miles until I came to a town where I stopped in a well-lit area to check that all was in order in the back. A saucepan full of pasta sauce was teetering on the edge of the bench. Other things had already fallen on the floor.

I finally found a busy, safe campground to spend the rest of the night. I was really annoyed that I hadn't been more careful – this young man must have been watching for some time to know that I was a woman, alone, before I even knew he was there! Although he hadn't threatened me in any *direct* way and most probably wouldn't have come near me, the incident had given me a terrible fright, and it took a long time to feel safe again.

Mt. Washingston Cog Railway, in New Hampshire's White Mountains

South Through Virginia

Horace made it back to Kentucky via New York State, New Jersey, Delaware and Maryland. I spent a few days in Washington DC, visiting many of its magnificent museums. Then it was on to the beautiful Shenandoah Valley and Shenandoah National Park. Lots of songs written about this area. One is the lovely 'Shenandoah Waltz' by Bluegrass musicians Clyde Moody and Chubby Wise, and recorded by many others, including country singers Ernest Tubb and Hank Thompson.

The spectacular Blue Ridge Parkway runs through this national park, in the eastern section of the Appalachian Mountains. I really loved the Parkway with its magnificent views over misty ridges of mountains, acres of rhododendrons, wildflower meadows, beautiful hiking trails and plenty of camping areas close by.

As well as wonderful scenery, this area (Virginia, West Virginia, Kentucky, North Carolina etc.) has almost more music history than anywhere else in the United States. There are many performance venues and instrument makers, and generations of musicians have lived in this area. The music has been handed down over hundreds of years. A 300 mile music heritage trail has now been set up. It's called 'The Crooked Road,' and using guidebooks and apps you can now explore the musical history of Southwest Virginia. Included is the little town of Floyd which I visited, and which has a famous country store hosting a Friday night dance with local musicians and plenty of dancers – mainly clogging.

The legendary Carter Family – A. P. Carter, his wife Sara and her cousin Maybelle – came from just near Hiltons also in Virginia. They first recorded in 1927, and they're some of the most influential voices of early country music. I was not too far from there so, even though I was a bit concerned about Horace's performance, I decided to go in case I never had the chance again. A.P. Carter and Sara's daughter Janette had founded the Carter Family Fold there – a concert venue to help keep the music alive – and her brother Joe, a skilled carpenter, had built most of it. I was able to meet them both, and enjoyed a wonderful concert with a Bluegrass band and plenty of locals dancing on the wooden floor in front of the stage. The building was fairly rough at that time – open at the back and sides, with makeshift seating, which included old car seats.

It was quite a long drive for me to the nearest town, down tiny country roads which I wasn't keen to tackle after dark. I asked Janette's son Dale Jett if it would be OK for me to sleep in my van in their car park. He immediately offered me the couch in the venue's green room. I explained I would probably be more comfortable locked in my van, but he insisted on leaving the building open so I could use the bathroom and the phone if needed. When I thanked him profusely, he said, *'Oh, it's not a problem. We sometimes have a dozen overseas visitors staying overnight in their sleeping bags.'* Such generosity and trust – the stage was full of Carter Family memorabilia and old photos etc., and there was no security system.

Although they are world famous, they are genuinely decent, humble people. I *did* use their phone to make a reverse charge call to Australia, describing to Barb the nostalgia I felt sitting on this famous stage all alone at midnight. It was slightly eerie and I could feel the presence of all the musicians who had played there over the years. A few years later, after I had interviewed Dale Jett for my radio show, he and his wife Teresa invited me to stay with them for a few days during a festival. Their home was Joe Carter's original old log house.

Now I was about to tackle the drive all the way back to Tucson, Arizona, where I wanted to attend the International Western Music Association Festival. I was very much looking forward to this festival, but Tucson was more than 2,000 miles away. Nobody could tell whether the motor would hold out, and I was strongly advised against driving so far. I decided to ignore this and take the risk. With luck I would make it, and have an interesting journey. At worst, I could abandon poor Horace somewhere along the way, hire a car for a few days and buy a tent.

I stocked up with oil and set off early one morning, taking the most direct route on freeways via Tennessee, spending another memorable evening in Memphis listening to the blues on Beale Street, and a night sleeping at the truck stop I'd discovered on my last visit.

Next day in Arkansas I stopped for fuel and Horace refused to re-start. Oh, no! Is this as far as I was going to get? Fortunately, a truck driver who was also stranded suggested the air filter might be clogged. We temporarily removed it and I was on the road again, but feeling even *more* apprehensive.

I spent the next two days driving right across Texas, noting again how the countryside changed from hilly and timbered in the east, to vast flat plains decorated with oil rigs and old rusty drilling equipment. The towns in the southwest seemed more rundown and very dusty. Not much traffic on the freeways here.

On the fourth morning I again had difficulty starting the motor, but I managed and it was fine once it got going. I drove the whole day without turning it off, becoming blasé about leaving it running while I shopped or ate (I had a spare set of keys of course), but I didn't want to take the risk of leaving it running unattended in the middle of a town. Unfortunately this meant missing out on exploring El Paso, which had always intrigued me because it is a border town, with Mexico just across the Rio Grande River.

Of course I couldn't drive all night or keep the motor going all night, so I stayed in Franklin Mountains State Park on a slope to increase the chances of being able to start next morning. As the ranger locked the park gates behind me, he told me I would be the only person there. I found this exciting, but did a double-take when I nearly stepped on a very large tarantula out for its evening walk. (Another Horace?) I just hoped it wouldn't get into my van, because if it did I knew I would be too terrified to get in there with it.

Franklin Mountains State Park is huge, encompassing several mountains. It was a clear evening, with a wonderful full moon bright enough for me to follow a trail to the top of a hill after dark without even needing my torch. From there I could see the twinkling lights of El Paso, the Rio Grande River and the inky black mountains.

Next morning, despite the precaution of parking on a hill, I had to walk several miles for help. Fortunately I found a group of park volunteers who were only too happy to give me a push. People often seemed to enjoy this kind of distraction, and they all waved me goodbye and good luck. I was wondering if this *really* was the beginning of the end of my travels, but thought there was still a chance I could make it to Tucson.

That night I found another beautiful State Park. I had phoned in advance to see if it met my needs – a sloping campground with other campers who could help when I was ready to leave. Rockhound State Park had this, plus a great setting in the desert at the bottom of a mountain, which I climbed next morning for a view right into Mexico thirty miles away.

This was such an attractive place, and I had three days before the festival started, so I decided to stay and make a dash for Tucson on the last day. It was early November and the weather was clear and warm during the day and chilly at night. My camping site had its own picnic table in a little shelter. I rigged up lines and did all my washing, sorting and tidying. I felt that I was saying goodbye to this van which, despite its refusal to run smoothly for any length of time, had been my cosy home for several years.

One night, feeling a bit lonely, I dreamt my sister came to join me in my travels, arriving with an enormously heavy bag full of tools. She told me somewhat sheepishly that her husband thought we really should have these in case the van broke down again. I indignantly replied, '*I've travelled all over the U.S. with only a pair of pliers and a screwdriver,*' which actually was true!

So – the final dash. More oil to get first. I was now buying it by the *case*. Greedy Horace was using a quart for every 50 miles – most of it splattering over the engine and back door. Happily we made it to Tucson and drove straight out into the desert to Old Tucson Studios, where the festival was to be held. They told me of the Gilbert Ray Campground nearby, which had some gentle hills and hopefully some helpful people. After settling in there I finally turned the motor off, wondering if it would ever start again and what I would do when the festival finished.

L-R Dale Jett (Janettes' Son), Janette & Joe Carter

With A.P Carter's guitar, purchased by him in Texas, 1930s.

With Janette Carter (A.P. Carter's daughter) at Carterfold, Virginia.

Rockhound State Park, New Mexico

Western Music in Western Setting

I'd been looking forward to the experience of the International Western Music Association Festival for a long time, hoping to learn more about the history of this music, the American cowboy, and all the associated myths.

As soon as I arrived at the campground in Tucson Mountain Park – a ten minute walk from Old Tucson – I knew this must be the perfect setting for a Western festival. It's in a beautiful valley, surrounded by mountains and dotted with large Saguaro cacti – the kind which we always associate with Hollywood Westerns – with their arms reaching towards the vivid blue sky. They seemed especially exotic in the pink sunsets with distant coyotes calling, or silhouetted against the starry sky at midnight.

The walking trail to Old Tucson wound through other exotic plants like the Prickly Hedgehog cactus and the Teddy-bear Cholla, which I'd encountered earlier in my travels. I didn't want to brush against one as I knew that getting its prickles in my skin would be very painful. The full moon was bright enough for me to walk this trail after dark, but in addition to the prickly cacti, I had to keep a careful watch for rattle snakes. Driving around wasn't an option for me of course. If I did manage to get the van started, it would mean taking the chance of being stranded at the venue or on a lonely road.

At Old Tucson Studios I was greeted by members of the International Western Music Association in cowboy dress. I thought this was just for the occasion, but realised later that many of them are actual cowboys or own ranches, and this is probably their normal attire. In fact most people attending this festival dressed in the western style, so I dug out the boots, jeans and the colourful shirts I'd bought to wear dancing. The studios were built by Columbia Pictures in 1939 as a replica of Tucson in the 1860s for the filming of *Arizona*. Over 300 productions have now been made there. How intriguing to be walking in the place where *Tombstone*, *Lighting Jack* and television series such as *High Chaparral*, *Gunsmoke* and *How The West Was Won* were filmed. Of course, the mountain backdrop and many of the buildings looked familiar.

There was a lot of entertainment there, even when there was no special festival. A music hall show in the old saloon featured Diamond Lil and there were stagecoach rides, museums, Native American story-telling, rodeos, gunfights, stunts, and trick riding. Restaurants served food from the American south west, including 'Chuck Wagon Suppers' of barbecue beef, beans, coleslaw, canned corn and biscuits, which are what we call scones in Australia. The Chuck Wagon was the horse-drawn kitchen, accompanying the early wagon trains or used by cowboys droving cattle.

I soon got to know some of the other campers there for the festival, so lifts home were fairly easy to arrange. There were no showers in the campground, but some of the wonderful musicians drove me into Tucson to shower in their hotel rooms and listen to their nightly jam sessions.

One evening I was invited to a kind of swap meet, which a group of women musicians organised each year. They brought and exchanged clothes. I didn't have anything to contribute, but I just loved the experience of being included. One of the participants in this fun evening was singer/ songwriter/ yodeller Jean Prescott. She gave me a copy of her CD, which I immediately added to my favourite van playlist. On it was a song she and her husband Gary wrote called 'Cowgirl Blues.' I played it over and over while driving, eventually learning to yodel a little bit, copying her style!

The International Western Music Association was celebrating its 10th anniversary, and that year was dedicated to 'King of the Cowboys' Roy Rogers and 'America's favourite singing Cowboy' Gene Autry. Gene Autry's cowboy code was quoted in the programme:

1. *The cowboy must never shoot first, hit a smaller man, or take unfair advantage.*

2. *He must never go back on his word, or a trust confided in him.*

3. *He must always tell the truth.*

4. *He must be gentle with children, the elderly and animals.*

5. *He must not advocate or possess racially or religiously intolerant ideas.*

6. *He must help people in distress.*

7. *He must be a good worker.*

8. *He must keep himself clean in thought, speech, action, and personal habits.*

9. *He must respect women, parents, and his nation's laws.*

10. *The cowboy is a patriot.*

I was surprised at the diversity of music. I had expected yodelling and old cowboy songs extolling the virtues of life on the range. While there was certainly plenty of that, there were also a lot of young singer-songwriters, some western swing, and bands with wonderful names like Daughters of the Purple Sage, Hoot & Annie, Riders in the Sky, Prickly Pair (a husband and wife duo) and The Texas Trailhands. There was also a Mexican Mariachi band – International Mariachi America – which had recently won an award at the Edinburgh Festival, as well as top honour at the International Mariachi Festival, at which 1200 bands compete in Tucson each year. One Mariachi band was great, but I thought 1200 in one place might be a bit much for me! This lively music originated in western Mexico and a traditional band comprises of mainly stringed instruments, such as various guitars including a large bass guitar called a guitarron, a folk harp with up to 40 strings, violins, and sometimes bass or snare drums. Trumpets were added in the 1930s.

One of the festival's more colourful characters was 'Washtub' Jerry from Texas. He had converted a Mexican galvanised iron washtub into a very effective bass, using a clutch cable from a Porsche car and a wooden lumberjack pole called a PV pole, normally used to turn logs in the water or at the sawmill. The sound he could produce with it was very distinctive and an octave lower than other basses. He'd stand right on top of his washtub to play it, and as he was a very tall man wearing a very tall cowboy hat, he certainly dominated the stage.

In case anyone thinks that playing the washtub bass is a hick thing to do, it's actually quite difficult. To change notes, he'd alter the tension of the cable. The tighter the cable, the higher the note; the looser the cable, the lower the note. In his other life, he worked at a space centre and had a degree in electronic engineering!

A special feature of the International Western Music Association festival that year, 1998, was called 'From Whence Came the Cowboy,' paying tribute to the Spanish Vaqueros, who influenced much of the dress, language, equipment and values of the American cowboy. When we talk of American cowboys, we tend to think only of the Anglo-Americans, but of the 35,000 cowboys who rode the trails from Texas during the cattle drive years, historians estimate that 5,000 were Mexican and more than 5,000 black.

In addition to the music performance venues dotted around The Old Tucson Studios, there were seminars and films on topics such as the history of the music, portrayal of cowboys and use of music in films, and how to improve your act. The International Yodelling Championships were held, plus the annual Awards Ceremony and Hall of Fame Induction and evening all-star concerts. As an overseas visitor and a radio presenter I was given a VIP pass and always had a seat in the front row! One night I sat next to Beverly Losey, daughter of the legendary Patsy Montana. She was keen to tell me about her son Michael, who was carrying on Patsy's tradition of singing and songwriting. I never did have a chance to hear Michael perform, but assume he has picked up some of his grandmother's musical talents.

When I wasn't at the festival, I explored the network of trails in Tucson Mountain Park and enjoyed the beauty and peace of the campground with its many birds.

Camped next to me for a few days was a man from Austria who was sleeping in the back of his station wagon. As he seemed to be existing on an even *lower* budget than me, I invited him to a pasta dinner. He said it was the first hot meal he'd had for weeks. In return, he drove me through the desert to explore a particularly scenic walking trail.

On the way, in the middle of nowhere, we were surprised to see a lone man bashing away on a full set of drums in a deserted carpark. Had his wife thrown him out? Maybe the neighbours complained and this was the only place he could practice.

Camping in Tucson Mountain Park

With The Desert Sons, Western Music Association Festival, Old Tucson.

'Washtub' Jerry

Daughters of
the Purple Sage.

The Final Dash

I'd spent a marvellous week listening to music and meeting interesting people from various parts of USA and Canada. I'd even forgotten about my vehicle problems for a while. But the day finally came when I had to decide how I was going to leave.

First I contacted various Volkswagen garages in the hope of selling the van. As I'd previously discovered, nobody wants to buy a vehicle which is barely running. The best offer I had was $300 and the stereo alone cost more than that.

I ended up consulting with Ken in Denver. He suggested that if I could get it there, he and a mate would do some work on it and sell it for me. Ken raced a Porsche and was quite adept at repairs. Since Ferdinand Porsche had also designed the original Volkswagen Beetle motor, I thought my more modern, but still air cooled engine might have some similarities with Ken's Porsche. His wonderful offer seemed the best option and led to yet another adventure.

The distance between Tucson and Denver is about 1,000 miles. I felt fairly certain that Horace would not want to travel this far, especially as the route is quite mountainous. I was also thoroughly sick of worrying about being stranded. My best option was to tow it.

I hired the smallest vehicle capable of towing it – a 24 foot furniture removal van with a towing dolly attached. With a push start I was able to get myself from the campground to the rental company, but they wouldn't put my van on to the tow dolly. I had to drive it on myself, and it was nerve wracking. If I drove too quickly the wheels would go right over it and be stuck on the other side, but too slowly and it would stall and not re-start! I edged forward nervously and fortunately managed it first go. I even had to secure it with the chains and straps myself, but refused to leave until one of the staff checked that I'd done that correctly. They advised me not to drive over 40 mph and not to even *think* about trying to reverse.

The whole rig was about 44 feet long. I was mildly terrified. I hadn't driven anything larger than a VW van and had never towed anything in my life. The truck was so wide that I couldn't even *see* my vehicle from the cabin, and stopped frequently to make sure it was still attached. Sometimes if the sun was in the right direction I could see its shadow, which was reassuring.

Fortunately the hire place was quite close to the freeway, which I was relieved to reach because driving on small streets was challenging. But then I noticed that the petrol gauge showed almost empty and I worried that it would be difficult to find a garage with enough space in which to manoeuvre. I needn't have been concerned, as most garages along American freeways are set up for large trucks, so I just looked out for places catering to them. After all, I was used to truck stops and already had my guidebook.

The other problem was where and how to camp. The trip would take three or four days, because I intended to make the most of it and enjoy the scenery. I didn't want to spend every night in a noisy truck stop. The first night I found a campground with plenty of wide, open space in the desert close to the freeway. No facilities, but there was a toilet in a petrol station about a mile away – a quick ride on my bike. At only three dollars for the night, the price was certainly right.

With its two front wheels stuck up on the tow dolly, my van was on a steep angle so I decided to make up a bed in the back of the truck. I couldn't close its rear roller door as there was no way to open it from the inside. I'd be trapped because it wasn't possible to get from the back into the driving cabin. These furniture removal vans just aren't set up for people to sleep in them! When I tried to close it part of the way it just kept rolling back up, so I used a couple of bungee straps to secure it in place, leaving a gap of about three feet.

The Final Dash

It was well below freezing and a nearby camper, noticing my plight, lent me a very long extension lead so I could plug my little heater into the electricity at his site. Despite this I still felt cold and a bit unsafe, so the next night I tried sleeping inside the VW, which was much more comfortable than I'd expected. I hardly noticed the slope. I cooked inside my van, too, and thought it must have looked a bit strange to see me living inside a vehicle in such a situation!

On the second night I camped in a private campground on the edge of Albuquerque in New Mexico. I'd phoned to make sure they had enough space for me to manoeuvre, as there was no way I was going to attempt to reverse. Instead of asking if there was a hill in the campground, I was now having to ask if there were drive-through sites for a 44 foot rig! They assured me all was OK, but you can imagine how shocked I was on arrival when the manager rushed out and said, *'You shouldn't have driven that in here. There's not enough room to turn it round and get it out again.'* It certainly was a tight squeeze, but somehow I managed with his directions and lots of manoeuvring. I think I was always surprised when Horace on his tow dolly actually *followed* the truck.

By the third day, I was getting used to driving the rig and began to really enjoy it. I felt like a trucker or someone in an American road movie, and contrary to instructions I was zipping along at *well* over 40 mph.

My last night was in Lathrop State Park in southern Colorado. It was now mid-November and cold and windy. I was the only person there, and had a most wonderful view of a range of snow-covered mountains called Spanish Peaks. The highest of these, West Spanish Peak, is over 13,000 feet. There was electricity available, so I was able to sit comfortably inside my van with the little heater. This would be the very last time I was to sleep in it, and despite all the difficulties it had caused I felt quite nostalgic.

Both vehicles and I arrived safely in Denver, but the saga was still not over. Ken had moved since my last visit and I got lost twice trying to find his street – and ended up driving *miles* on a narrow winding road through hills, because I couldn't find anywhere big enough in which to turn around. It was also getting dark and I felt a bit panicky. Finally I managed to locate his house and parked outside, exhausted after the long trip. He lived on the side of an extremely steep hill, and I parked on the opposite side of the road facing up hill.

Ken gave me a glass of wine to settle me down, and after that suggested we detach my van straight away, rather than waiting until tomorrow's daylight. I thought better of it, but for some strange reason did what I was told. (Could that be because I'm a woman? I'm not usually particularly obedient.) Horace, however, *was* obedient, and came off the tow dolly without any problems. It simply involved removing the chains, taking off the hand brake and rolling back.

Ken then suggested I should try to start the motor going *backwards* down the hill in the dark, and then get it back up and into his driveway! I haven't the faintest idea why I agreed to this part. It's terribly hard to jump-start a vehicle when you are careering backwards down a very steep hill. Every time the motor started, I had to brake because of the speed the van had built up, and this of course caused it to stall. I ended up on the edge of somebody's front lawn with the back wheels firmly wedged against a little wall. Nobody was home, so we just left them a note and decided to deal with the situation next day.

Ken said, *'Don't worry, when I get home from work we'll get my truck and pull your van up with a tow rope.'* I'd had enough of his suggestions, and as soon as he left next morning, I did what I should have done in the first place.

After returning the furniture van to the rental company, I called the American Automobile Association. An efficient-looking fellow arrived with a tow truck. I needed him to tow my van back up the hill and then reverse it into Ken's driveway.

He hooked it up and started pulling out from the kerb, but he hadn't done it properly and my van *detached.* I have never seen anyone move more quickly, as he leapt out of his truck and chased the van down the hill! It seemed that Horace was absolutely determined to get away at any cost! Amazingly, it lodged itself against a tree without doing any visible damage, and was finally hauled safely into the driveway.

I'd been watching all this from the balcony and was a bit disappointed at the rescue. I was hoping it would crash into something with more force (preferably not another vehicle and certainly not a person), so I could claim on the tow truck company's insurance and not have to worry about repairing or selling it!

For the very last time I removed all my stuff, repacking some of it in my suitcases to take home, and storing some in Ken's spare room. I couldn't believe I'd accumulated so much and found it quite difficult to deal with! The only thing I was really sad to leave behind was my little pink bike, and I hoped I would be able to collect it again on a future trip. I've never been back to Denver, and as far as I know it's still there in the old garden shed.

I left with very mixed feelings. It was the end of my trip and I was mightily relieved that I wouldn't have to continue coping with all the wretched vehicle problems, but also sad that a wonderful era had come to an end. It had been a real love-hate relationship with Horace, which really did seem to have a mind of its own – determined to test me to my limits.

Travelling and living in a small vehicle for such long periods was hard work, and very occasionally became tedious, but this was more than compensated for by the variety of places I'd visited, the music I'd discovered, the people I met and the adventures I'd had. I especially loved being completely free to do whatever I felt like. It was a real journey of self-discovery. I learnt a lot about self-reliance, resilience and making do. I was stronger than I'd realised, coped reasonably well with all kinds of problems and situations, and made some difficult decisions, which somehow usually turned out to be the right ones.

Now I was looking forward to going home to family and friends, and to my fledging radio show, *Southern Style*. I felt that both I and the show had been greatly enriched by the knowledge and experience gleaned from my adventures. It had been more than six years since I'd lived in my house in Melbourne and, although it was just a one bedroom cottage, it felt too large after the van.

I have since returned to America regularly to immerse myself even more in the music I love, and to travel thousands more miles, but with reliable rented or loaned vehicles and a tent and even an occasional motel room.

Oh, and Ken did manage to sell Horace for $1,500 – without even having to make any repairs!

Leaving Tucson for Denver.

Spanish Mountains from Campground, Lathrop State Park, Colorado, (camping in my VW)

Acknowledgements

Thank you to Phillip Adams (Broadcaster, Journalist, Filmmaker & Writer) for his very encouraging comments after kindly reading through an early draft – and to the anonymous manuscript assessor secured through Writers Victoria.

To all those wonderful people I met on my travels, and my dear friends and family who supported me and believed all my angst was worth the effort! Especially my sister Alison and her husband Bill, Glenn Nelson, Lin Pape, Norm Paterson, Jenny Clark, John and Susan Boothroyd and Ian Benjamin.

Also thanks to Busybird Publishing and my invaluable editor Meg Hellyer.

Outline of

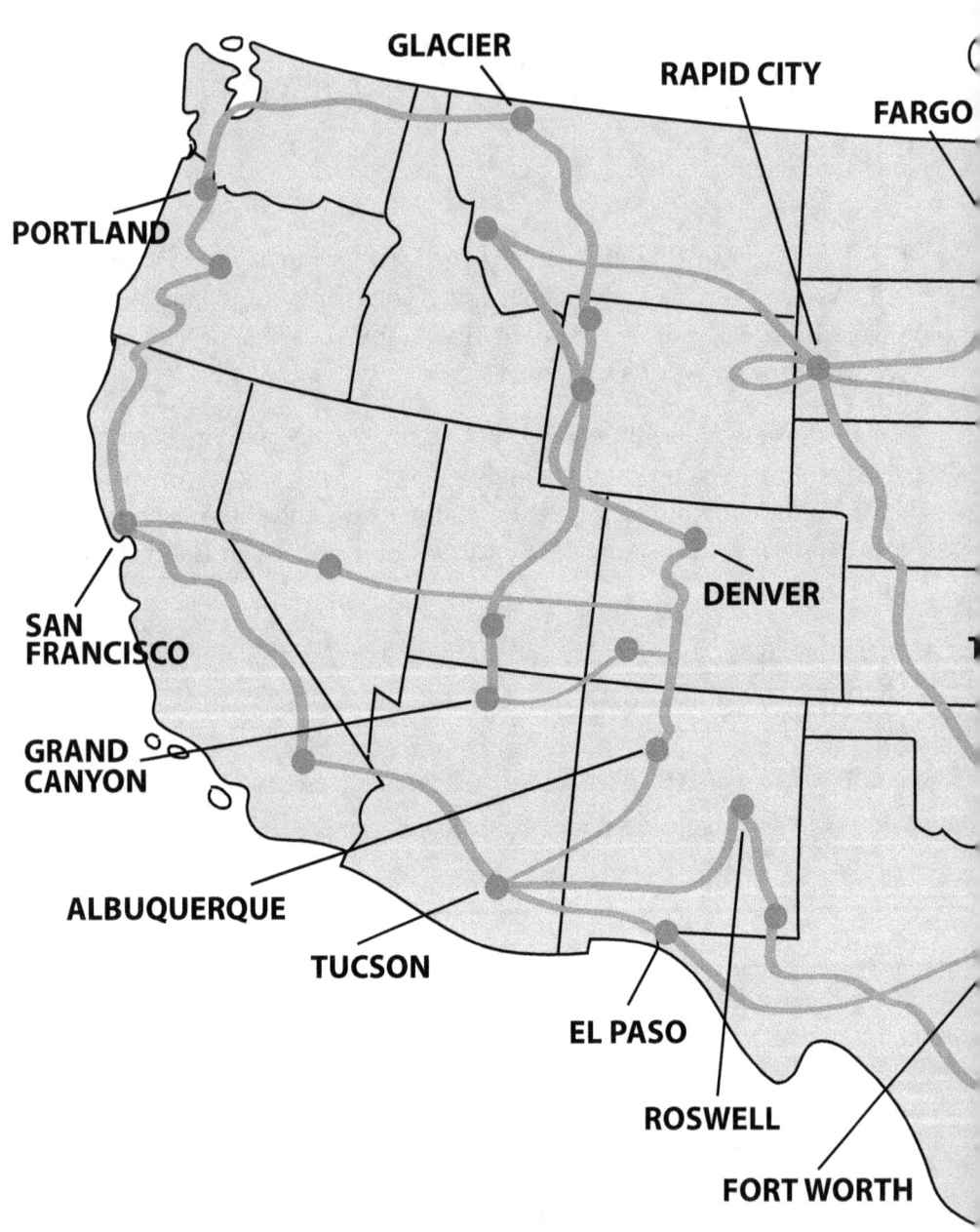

My Journey

www.ingramcontent.com/pod-product-compliance
Lightning Source LLC
Chambersburg PA
CBHW071604080526
44588CB00010B/1012